FIRST KILLS

FIRST KILLS

The Illustrated Biography of Fighter Pilot
Władysław Gnyś

STEFAN W. C. GNYŚ

Illustrated by
John D. Bindon

CASEMATE
Philadelphia & Oxford

Published in the United States of America and Great Britain in 2017 by
CASEMATE PUBLISHERS
1950 Lawrence Road, Havertown, PA 19083, USA
and
The Old Music Hall, 106–108 Cowley Road, Oxford OX4 1JE, UK

Photographic credits: most photos are from the collection of Władysław Gnyś and therefore do
not show a source credit; however, for others, the source is given. Photos of World War II public
figures and shots of aircraft are from the public domain unless otherwise indicated.

Hardcover Edition: ISBN 978-1-61200-556-0
Digital Edition: ISBN 978-1-61200-557-7

A CIP record for this book is available from the Library of Congress and the British Library

Printed and bound in India by Replika Press

For a complete list of Casemate titles, please contact:

CASEMATE PUBLISHERS (US)
Telephone (610) 853-9131
Fax (610) 853-9146
Email: casemate@casematepublishers.com
www.casematepublishers.com

CASEMATE PUBLISHERS (UK)
Telephone (01865) 241249
Fax (01865) 794449
Email: casemate-uk@casematepublishers.co.uk
www.casematepublishers.co.uk

To Barbara Mary Simmons-Gnyś (1921–1995)

Her will and determination to become a competent writer was achieved
with *First Kill, Pierwsze Spotkanie (First Encounter), One Lovely Yesterday*
and two poetry booklets that gave me the inspiration to follow
in her very large footsteps.

Contents

Author's Note

What follows is a true account of our father, former Squadron Leader Władysław (Vwa-dis-wav) Gnyś (G'nish). Władek (Vwa-deck) for short, was credited with shooting down the first two German aircraft of World War II, on September 1st, 1939 when Poland was invaded by Nazi Germany. As a Polish fighter pilot, he flew and fought for Poland, France and Britain. He participated in the Battle for France and the Battle of Britain with the Royal Air Force.

During the latter part of the Normandy invasion, Władek was shot down over France, wounded, taken prisoner and then escaped. Ironically, his life was spared by the enemy on more than one occasion. He carried a bullet in his liver for 56 years, from 1944 to 2000 when he passed away.

Fifty years after the invasion of Poland in 1939, he was reunited with German Stuka pilot Frank Neubert who attacked Władek's squadron, killing his captain as they were taking off to intercept the invaders who had just bombed Kraków. Władek, who barely survived himself, evaded the section of Stuka Ju 87s on his tail. The two former enemies shook hands in the summer of 1989, reconciled their differences and became friends until their deaths.

Many personal wartime photos and powerful illustrations provide visual support for this photo-illustrative profile. The intent is to provide a pictorially documented journey of a brave and distinguished World War II fighter pilot from his childhood.

First and foremost, I would like to apologize for any mistakes, omissions or inaccuracies made in this book. I have taken the upmost care in their avoidance. One of the most challenging things has been working with the Polish language as it was not spoken at home growing up in Canada with an English-speaking mother. Probably half of my research dealt with Polish documentation. However, I had expert Polish-to-English translation from family in Poland who took the greatest care in getting it right.

The question arises as to why our father was historically unique, because there were many other Polish fighter pilots who saw more action and had more victories than he did. The obvious answer is that he was credited with shooting down the first two German aircraft of the war and half a century later making peace with the Stuka pilot who killed his captain and almost himself. This is special indeed but he also fought in three campaigns and survived. Having a charismatic personality also added a little extra to his persona.

Over a period of five years, I have done my best to create a book that highlights his life with the use of not just facts and figures, but with original photos and expressive artwork by renowned artist, John D. Bindon. I hope you enjoy it.

Stefan W. C. Gnyś

Illustrator's Note

Stefan Gnyś and I go back to 1975. He was one of my grade 10 high-school teachers. I ended up also taking grade 11 and 12 classes from him as he had become a favorite instructor, thus cementing a strong student/teacher bond which led to a commissioned artwork in the fall of 1978.

We kept in touch a little bit over the years, but an unexpected phone call came through in late November 2012 from "a former geography teacher" regarding the desire for me to contribute art to a photo-biographical sequel to *First Kill*.

Well, knowing the historical significance of Władek Gnyś, I was immediately on board and excited to delve into this project. Stefan and I got together and discussed the book further. I had some war art samples that kindled the possible look and content direction.

Comprehensive layouts with most, if not all of the content, was necessary as each image was developed. The terrific amount of research trying to get things accurate proved to be a most challenging endeavor. Fortunately, we were blessed with some very detailed and accurate dates and information which allowed W. Gnyś's specific aircraft and markings to be adhered to. Stefan, as the writer/art director, imagined much of the scenes through his father's accounts over many years, and was able to convey to me, for the most part, the scene and contents with good clarity.

All of the elements were first rendered in pencil, scanned and refined digitally as they were "dropped" into the scene allowing tremendous flexibility in composing each scene with grey tones added after.

It was a challenging "back and forth," as we inspired each other to enhance the reality and authenticity of each illustration, and I would not have arrived at some of it without his tremendous input.

John D. Bindon

Acknowledgements

This book would not have been possible without the unique contributions of the following people to whom I am eternally grateful: John Bindon for his many artistic talents and creative genius, Jerzy B. Cynk for his inspiration and many books on the PAF and in-depth research on W. Gnyś, Michael Dobrzelecki for bringing together two former enemies, plus his research and text contributions, Agnieszka Gnyś for her enthusiasm and countless hours of Polish document translation, Ashley Gnyś for his brotherly support and thought-provoking epilogue, Laurie Johnson for being my intuitive mentor and role model throughout this process, Herbert Kretzmer for being an outstanding wordsmith and an example of excellence, Waldemar Serocki for his endless organizational skills and devotion to his uncle Władek, Peter Sikora for his wealth of knowledge about the PAF and keeping me accurate and historically correct on an ongoing basis and Janet Taylor for her daily support, ideas, suggestions, encouragement and patience.

My enduring thanks go out to contributors Bartek Belcarz, Pierre Ben, Maria Brzeska, Warren Carroll, Jeff Chan, Doug Cockell, Sharyn Thomas-Counce, Pierre Delpart, Wojtek Deluga (PISM), Eric Dessouroux, Witek Duklas, Michał Erdmański, Tom Ferjak, Ania Gnyś, Lodzia Gnyś, Reginka Gnyś, Władysław Gnyś (cousin to Col Gnyś), Zbyszek Gnyś, Robert Gretzyngier, Archiwum Fotografii Ośrodka (KARTA), John Kaye (né Kurowski), Dominik Kościelny, Ewa Kowalska, Joanna Kowalska, Danusia Komuńska, Jacek Komunski, Jagoda Kniaś, Zdzisław Kowalski, Chris Kropiński, Piotr Kuryłłowicz, Francesik Kornicki, Jan Łaguna, James Lansdale, Władysław Macherzyński, Wojtek Matusiak, Kamila Mazur, Kate O'Mara, Doug Patterson, Renata Pogodzik, Dave Randle, Ray Ravoi, Dan Stirland, Cherrie Taylor, Katarzyna Terech, Laurent Viton, Chris Vogel, Gudrun Vogel, Adam Weresch, Dr. Krzysztof Wielgus, S/Ldr Richard Willis, John Woodley and Antoni Zawadzki.

Equally supportive have been Apple Corporation, Natalie Chan (née Gnyś), EunKyung Choi-Gnyś, Mike Covey, Mike Hyde, Stefan Gabszewicz, Anton Gabszewicz, Danusia Gnyś, Valerie Gnyś, Wesley Gnyś, Sybil Kretzmer, Joanna Lumley, Jim McMaster, D'Arcy Richardson, Sanci Richardson, Dr. Harpal Singh, Dr. Paul Singleton, Irwin Stanley, Dylan Taylor, Jessica Taylor, Clare Toothill, Neil Toothill, Richard Whelan, Sarah Whelan, Greg Wiener and Stefanie Wiener (née Gnyś).

Abbreviations & Glossary

Abbreviations

AA	anti-aircraft (gun): ack-ack
a/c	aircraft
CBC	Canadian Broadcasting Corporation
coll.	collection
C.-in-C.	Commander-in-Chief
C.O.	Commanding Officer
c/n	construction number
DFC	Distinguished Flying Cross
FAF	French Air Force
GC	Groupe de Chasse (French Fighter Wing)
HQ	Headquarters
KIA	killed in action
kill	the act of destroying or disabling an enemy aircraft
LW	Lotnictwo Wojskowe (Military Aviation, or "Aviation Force of the Polish Army")
MFH	Military Field Hospital
NAC	Narodowe Archiwum Cyfrowe (National Digital Archives, Warsaw)
NCO	Non-commissioned officer
nn	name unknown
PAF	Polish Air Force
PD	Public Domain
PISM	Polish Institute & Sikorski Museum
pil.	pilot
PoW	prisoner of war
PZL	Polish Aerospace Manufacturer

RAF	Royal Air Force
R&R	Rest & Recreation
RCAF	Royal Canadian Air Force
recce	reconnaissance
reg	regiment
sqn	squadron
TAF	Tactical Air Force
USAAF	United States Army Air Force
WAAF	Women's Auxiliary Air Force
W. G.	Władysław Gnyś
VIC	formation of 3 (or more) aircraft in close formation resembling the letter V

Glossary of code names for operational sorties

Circus: daylight attacks by small bomber formations escorted by large fighter formations against short-range or "fringe" targets, intended to bring German fighters to battle (came into effect in early 1941)

Ramrod: similar to a Circus, but with destruction of the target as the primary objective

Rhubarb: low level, small-scale fighter or fighter-bomber attacks on ground targets of opportunity

Rodeo: sweeps over enemy territory by fighter aircraft only, to draw enemy fighters into the battle of attrition

(Source: J. Cynk, *The Polish Air Force at War, Vol. 1.* p. 23)

Air Force Rank Structure

Polish Rank (abbr./Eng. abbr.)	RAF Rank Equivalent (abbr.)
OTHER RANKS	
szeregowy (szer/AC 2)	Aircraftman No. 2 (AC 2)
starszy szeregowy (st szer/AC 1)	Aircraftman No. 1 (AC 1)
kapral (kpr/LAC)	Leading Aircraftman (LAC)
plutonowy (plut/Cpl)	Corporal (Cpl)
sierżant (sierż/Sgt)	Sergeant (Sgt)
starszy sierżant (st sierż/Sgt Mjr)	Flight Sergeant (F/Sgt)
chorąży (chor/W/O)	Warrant Officer (W/O)
podchorąży (pchor/C-Off)	(no equivalent)
OFFICERS	
podporucznik (ppor/S-Lt)	(Sub-Lt/2nd Lt) Pilot Officer (P/O)
porucznik (por/Lt)	(Lieutenant) Flying Officer (F/O)
kapitan (kpt/Cpt)	Flight Lieutenant (F/Lt)

major (mjr/Mjr)   Squadron Leader (S/Ldr)
podpułkownik (ppłk/S-Col)   (Sub-Col/Lt Col) Wing Commander
                                          (W/Cdr)

pułkownik (płk/Col)   Group Captain (G/Cpt)
generał brygady (gen bryg/Brig Gen)   Air Vice-Marshal (AVM)
generał dywizji (gen dyw/none)   Air Marshal (AM)
generał broni (gen br/none)   Air Chief Marshal (ACM)

(Source: J. Cynk, *The Polish Air Force at War, Vol. 1*, pp. 21–22)

Forewords

Władek Gnyś is one of Churchill's famous "few" whose selfless bravery bought enough time for a nation to survive. Although his modesty and reluctance to seek the limelight was typical of the man, his extraordinary war memoirs are the justification for this book. It exists for future generations to read and learn, with gratitude, that such men existed.

Laurie Johnson MBE
(author, conductor, movie producer, music composer for stage, TV, and film)
Laurie was 14 when he first met Władek in 1941. A mutual bond of respect and admiration ensued.

The life of Władek Gnyś was, to an unusual degree, a series of encounters which tested to the full both his moral courage and his military daring. This is no longer a world that seems to breed, or need, heroes—a word that would have been rejected outright by Władek himself. It is salutary to be reminded, that not long ago our civilization was saved from an all-engulfing slavery, by men of such spirit and strength.

Herbert Kretzmer OBE
(author, critic, journalist, lyricist: Tony, Grammy, Oscar-winning for *Les Misérables*)
Herbert was Barbara's coach and mentor in the writing of First Kill*, in 1979.*

CHAPTER I

Rural Poland and the Old Mill

It wasn't easy for families living and working the land in rural Poland. There were always dangers lurking around every corner. At the turn of the twentieth century, Eastern Europe was ever changing politically, but not always for the good of the common people. Conflict and survival were most often the order of the day.

The family unit however, was very strong and very much alive, but each member had to work hard to put food on the table. Couples tended to have many children in order to work the farm and look after them in old age. The days were long and there were many hardships, but they did their best to survive life's challenges. They were courageous people who looked out for one another and would die if necessary to protect their fragile existence. Love of family, their animals and country would always prevail in the face of adversity. They knew when to run and when to fight.

Sarnów (Sarnuf) was, and still is, a small rural village consisting of farms which grow various types of grains and raise livestock. Carp ponds can still be found as well as the occasional apple orchard. The houses are small, but neatly kept with abundant flowers growing in the front. Vegetable gardens are popular and do well in the dark soil. In Poland there are at least nine centers with the same name.

This one in particular is in the administrative district of Gmina Gniewoszów within the Masovian Voivodeship, in east–central Poland. It is located about three miles southwest of Gniewoszów and 63 miles southeast of Warsaw, the capital. It is within reach of Puławy and Dęblin Air Force Base where Władek spent time training before the war. The city of Radom is at least an hour by car to the west.

Sarnów is where the Gnyś family originated in the 1840s. This is where Władek was born, where his life revolved around the old grist mill that was jointly owned by his father Jan and his uncle Antoni (Toni). In the early 2000s, the old mill was totally renovated and today stands a lavish house sitting on picturesque property occupied by Gnyś' descendants.

Places in Poland in reference to text.

Stanisław Gnyś came to Sarnów around 1840. He was married to Marjanna (Maria) née Rutkowska, and the couple had three boys—Jan, Piotr and Szczepan—and it is thought three girls.

Szczepan Gnyś (1849–1922) married Matylda Urbanów (1856–1918) and they had seven boys and a girl: Jan, Józef, Władysław (drowned age two), Stanisław, Antoni (Toni) (1895–1969), Wincenty, another (first name repetition was common) Władysław (a PAF pilot killed in a crash in 1938), and Bronisława (Bronka).

Jan Gnyś (1887–1962) was married to Marjanna (Maria) (1881–1931) and they had six girls and two boys. Previously married as Marjanna Gogacz, Maria's husband had been killed in an accident when she was twenty. A daughter Anna (Ania) by that marriage became Jan's step-daughter. The other children were Maria (Marysia), Bronisława (Bronka), Stanisława, Helena (Hela), Jadwiga (Jadzia), Antoni (Toni) and Władysław. Jan was the debonair extrovert while Maria was quite the opposite: her maiden name Burza means "storm." However, she was anything but. Maria was a gentle, quiet, petite woman with soft brown hair and large sad eyes. She was not afraid of hard work and

The effects of the Great War (1914–18) on Europe were devastating. In 1915, aged five, Władek, with his father Jan, saw his very first aircraft crash nearby after being shot down.

rarely had time for rest. Maria was brave and firm when she had to be, responsible, compassionate, wise and honest with a gentle understanding of life. Her care and love for her eight children was paramount in her life. She maintained her loyalty to Jan even though he was often abusive to her. She died of a stroke at age fifty.

Jan was in the carp and milling business in Sarnów with his brother Toni, but his passion was his horses. Władek learned to share this passion with his father. Even though Jan loved his wife and children, he did not always behave like a responsible husband and father. He was an alcoholic, had an eye for the ladies and would physically knock Maria around. One day after a drinking binge, he came home late in a foul mood and was going to take it out on Maria. Władek bravely picked up a big stick and protected his mother. After that Jan never abused his wife again. Overall, he was not a good role model for his children.

As a child, Władek was nicknamed "Kalalocek" because of his diminutive stature; the word has no English equivalent. He attended the local primary school where the sign above the door read "Szkoła Podstawowa w Sarnowie"—Sarnów Primary School. It was literally two minutes from home. He started school in 1915, aged five, and remembered a teacher by the name of Mrs Michalec.

In 1919 his parents sent him to the elementary school in Gniewoszów, about three miles from Sarnów. Here, he spent the next three years soaking up knowledge: he loved school and was an excellent student. Władek liked all his teachers and the feeling was mutual.

Later, his parents enrolled him in a *gimnazjum* or junior secondary school located in Radom called Jan Kochanowski School which was all male. The building was first converted into a private school in 1912. From Sarnów, young Władek had to take the train to get there. His parents boarded him with a family in Radom. As expected, he became very homesick.

A letter written in 1996 by Mr. Macherzyński, a former teacher at this high school, stated that Władek was a graduate of Kochanowski, but since he moved to Kawęczyn at age 16, he hadn't quite finished his four years there. So while in the army in Toruń in 1932, he got permission to take part-time classes and completed his high school studies. Writing the Matura exam was and still is the basic educational goal of every Polish person. Without this, one's secondary school education is incomplete.

During the war, secret classes were undertaken, called *tajne komplety* (clandestine classes) which allowed people to continue their education and secretly sit their Matura exam. Educators who were caught were executed by the Nazis: Polish children did not warrant education. In the same vein, teachers were a threat to Nazi control. In fact, any educated person was a threat. In Władek's school in Radom, a number of teachers were caught and put to death: the Math and Physics teacher January Krzymowski died at Auschwitz, the History teacher Michał Małuja died at Auschwitz (he had been holding clandestine classes) and the French teacher Kazimierz Rogosz died at Auschwitz. The ultimate irony was that the headmaster Stanisław Egiejman was murdered in 1947 by the UB, the communist secret police (Urząd Bezpieczeństwa).[1]

Jasik, Władek's favorite cousin taught him many fun things to do like collecting tasty eggs from crows' nests. However, the trick was to see how far out on the branch one could go without breaking the branch and falling. Jasik always urged him to go out to the edge of the branch. Most often they were successful, but sometimes they would end up with "egg on their face"—and clothing, not to mention the bruises and scratches.

Władek and Jasik liked to fool about and push each other around when the teacher wasn't looking. One day, however, Władek's elbow smashed through a classroom window. As punishment, they were kept after school and made to kneel on dried peas.

The temptation of taking delicious red apples from a farmer's trees on the way home from school was too great for the boys. Jasik had had his eye on the biggest and best apple, but had to climb the tree to pick it. Of course the branch broke and he came crashing down resulting in a very loud "Ahhhh." The farmer chased them down the road, yelling and violently shaking his fist.

Władek's mother was constantly bothered by an extremely persistent Jewish peddler who sold many things. He never took no for an answer and became so annoying that Maria eventually refused to open the door to him.

One afternoon while the peddler was bending over a carp pond mesmerized by the fish, Władek snuck up behind and pushed him in. The peddler never did find out who was responsible for his unplanned bath. It was sweet revenge.

Two weeks later, however, he was back bothering Mother again. So Władek waited for another chance to get him. After lunch, the peddler took a nap under one of their trees. Young Gnyś had a brilliant idea. He got some of his father's honey and poured it all over the man's shoes. In no time, hundreds of bees from their hives came to collect the sweet liquid. When he woke up, he swatted at them with his hat making them angry and the more he swatted the more he got stung. The last Władek saw of him, he was running down the road like a lunatic, never to bother Maria again.

One July day while staying with his sister Anna and her husband Thomas, Władek met Hiram, a gypsy boy. At the time, Władek was trying to fish but was not having any luck; however, Hiram was having the best of luck. So he enthusiastically showed Władek the secret of using worms that were kept in a urine moss environment. They worked like a charm. The two boys bonded instantly.

Hiram's family had parked their three caravans in a nearby clearing with permission from Władek's sister and husband who owned the land, in the village of Siekierka. Hiram had a very attractive younger sister by the name of Chaya who was 14 or 15, and Władek, now 16, developed an instant crush. Soon, he got to meet the parents who were very kind and welcoming.

They invited everyone on several occasions to join them for dinner, dance and music. It was such fun dancing around a large bonfire under star-studded skies. There was magic in the air. When the day came for the gypsies to depart, the three young people were quite sad as they had become such good friends.

★

One day, several influences would combine to produce a man of high moral character who was not afraid to stand up to tyranny and was willing to risk his life fighting for the rights and freedoms of his beloved Poland. Other than his belief in God, they are:

Władek's grandfather, Szczepan Gnyś

At the age of 18, Szczepan worked in a small mill grinding grain into flour for locals and feed for their livestock. Eventually, he would own this mill and build another and hire villagers to work for him. He established the mill in Sarnów. He was very wise, generous and kind and everyone loved and respected him. As time passed, he became a village elder who would offer advice and help to those in need.

"All my young life, 'Władziu Serce' had been my closest friend, playmate and protector. He taught me many things—he loved me as if I had been his own son."

Sometimes the local Jews would lend money and if families couldn't pay off these high-interest loans, the lenders would try to foreclose. The villagers would come to Szczepan with their problems. He would sometimes pay off their debts, admonish the money lenders and allow the villagers to repay him by working in the mill. In some cases he would provide food for widows and their children when winters were harsh and supplies were scarce; many would have starved without his help. In return, they would work for him the following season.

Władek was 12 when Szczepan died in 1922. Great mourning followed even from the Jewish community, a most unheard of occurrence. He was a model citizen who instilled moral values in young Gnyś who missed his larger-than-life grandfather very much.

Farmhand Władysław Molenda

One of the most positively influential adults in young Władek's life was Władysław Molenda who worked for Jan and Uncle Toni. He did everything from caring for the horses, working the fields, tending to the carp and ensuring the smooth operation of the grist mill. He was a tall, strong, good-looking man with a large mustache. He lived in Sarnów with his second wife. (They didn't have any children of their own, perhaps why he was so fatherly towards young Władek.)

Since Władysław is a common Polish name, the people close to him called him "Serce" ("The Heart") or Władziu Serce, no doubt from his good heart and gentle demeanor. He was more of a father to the boy than Władek's own father Jan. For example, he

Heroic Asik gets shot by bandits as he tries to protect Władek's sisters Anna and Bronka. The robbers then jumped onto their horses and escaped, injured, but no richer.

selected Asik (Ashik) from a litter of puppies, who became a "life-changing" pet; he helped evacuate the Gnyś family at the beginning of the Great War in 1914; he stayed behind to protect the farm and livestock from invaders; he introduced Władek to the newborn colt, Kasztanka; he took Władek, Asik and the two horses for a daily swim in the river; he taught the boy how and where to fish; he twice saved Władek's life from drowning; he always met him at the station after leaving boarding school in Radom; he was affectionate and reassuring; he genuinely quizzed him about progress at school and stressed the importance of education; he buried Asik under Władek's favorite willow tree and told him, "Never be afraid to cry" and gently explained why Jan had to sell Kasztanka and Sheba; he helped save livestock and work horses from the burning barn and taught him about understanding, forgiveness and compassion.

Asik, farm boy's best friend

Born around 1910, this mixed breed dog grew into a large, powerful, intelligent and loyal companion to young Władek. Despite his size, he was incredibly gentle with the

Hiding Kasztanka after the chase Władek said, "No matter how exhausted, she must not lie down because we may have to run again."

Gnyś children and would not only play, but watch over them. He would chase stray dogs away from the farm and bring back cows that had broken through the fence and gotten into a neighbor's field.

During one evacuation from Sarnów during World War I, Władek got separated from the convoy of wagons. His parents went crazy trying to find him. Asik was untied and sent out to search for the seven-year-old and, soon enough, found him. He stayed with the boy, barking until help arrived.

When Władek's horse Kasztanka was a foal, Asik was always nearby watching in a "fatherly" way. Eventually, these two animals developed a tight bond of friendship. Asik loved going down to the river with the horses for their daily swim. One day while swimming with older sister Anna, Władek got cramps and started yelling for help. In an instant, Asik broke his rope and plunged into the water. The boy quickly grabbed onto his collar and was towed back to safety.

During the Russian Revolution of 1917, chaos reigned. Bandits roamed the countryside, looting villages and beating or killing those who resisted them. One night, two thieves surprised sisters Anna and Bronka on their way to the outhouse and forcefully tried to prevent them from warning their father. Asik who slept inside the stable heard the sisters screaming. Coming to the rescue, he attacked the bandits and was doing considerable damage with his powerful jaws until one of them took out his gun and shot Asik in the side before they fled. Asik died early next morning in Władek's arms. Everyone wept, heartbroken. Władek, Kasztanka and Asik were a team and until then, they were inseparable. Life would never be quite the same without this much loved dog. Władek said, "He was my constant companion and played a large role in my growing-up years ... this dog, with his loving, loyal heart, was a hero. Sometimes, when he would place his head on my knees and look into my eyes, it seemed to me that I could see into the depths of his soul, for if ever a dog had a soul, our Asik had."

Kasztanka

Sheba (previously owned by the Russian Cavalry) gave birth to a filly fathered by an Arabian stallion. She thrived and grew into a beautiful chestnut with a distinctive blond

The revolution of 1917 and World War I created havoc and unrest in Poland due to its geographic proximity to these events. Good riding horses were always in demand to replenish dwindling numbers: the Polish cavalry was no exception.

mane and tail (*kasztanka* means chestnut). Young Władek always rode her bareback using only a bridle. In the summer, Władziu Serce would take the horses down to the river for their daily swim. Asik would join them in the water with Władek on Kasztanka's back and sometimes his cousin Jasik on Sheba's back. Serce would be standing watch, enjoying the antics.

Sleigh rides in the winter were of equal fun with the two horses pulling the Gnyś family in and around Sarnów. A deep bonding of boy and horse developed. It was painful for Władek when he had to go away to boarding school in Radom as he couldn't be with his beloved Kasztanka. He longed for the summers so that he could be re-united with his close friend.

During the Bolshevik Revolution and World War I, there was a great shortage of horses for army cavalry units. Horse thieves were everywhere and the confiscation of village horses by government officials was common.

Many times the village boys would ride their prized horses deep into the local pastures and woods to hide out from approaching cavalry seeking new animals. Cousin Jasik and Władek with the other boys would stay away from Sarnów until the danger had passed. If enough warning was given, mothers would provide them with blankets and food. It wasn't uncommon for them to stay hidden for several days and nights, which were always long, cold and damp. Often they were pursued by the cavalry which resulted in many close calls.

After nine months at school, Władek returned to Sarnów and was most anxious to see Kasztanka. Running into the barn with excitement and calling her name, he could not find her or Sheba. With fear in his voice and tears in his eyes, he asked Father about his missing horse.

Jan said, "Son … forgive me. I have sold both Kasztanka and Sheba."

Władek stood there rooted to the ground, shocked rigid. His world came tumbling down around him. All he could say over and over again was, "No! No! No!"

Władziu Serce gently explained that due to the constant pressure from thieves and cavalry scouts, Father had no choice but to sell them, to an officer buying mares of good breeding for the stables of the King of Greece. Also, the money offered was exorbitant. Władek's heart was broken again.

Żwirko and Wigura

Franciszek Żwirko (1895–1932) became a prominent Polish sport and military aviator. Born near Wilno, then part of the Russian Empire, he fought in the Russian Army against the Germans in World War I. In 1918, he fought against the Bolsheviks in the Russian Civil War and after the Bolshevik victory in 1921, he fought his way to Poland. He became a fighter pilot and was also active in sports aviation, distinguishing himself as a calm, skilled pilot.

Stanisław Wigura (1903–1932) was a Polish aircraft designer and aviator. Born in Warsaw, he developed a great interest in mechanics and aviation. In 1920, during the Polish-Soviet War, he joined the 8th Field Artillery Regiment. In 1921, he studied at Warsaw Tech and began building aircraft. By 1929, he had graduated as an engineer and had also completed a pilot course.

Both men often flew together in sporting events and won many international contests in Europe using Wigura-designed aircraft. By August 28th, 1932, both pilots had become national heroes in Poland. Unfortunately, on September 11th, 1932 while flying to a meet in Prague, their plane crashed killing them both. Żwirko was 36, Wigura 29. The nation was stunned. They were buried together and have a common grave in Powązki Military Cemetery in Warsaw. Despite this tragedy, Władek became increasingly motivated to become a pilot.

Józef Piłsudski (1867–1935)

Poland's first Marshal, Józef Piłsudski, became a national hero who served Poland tirelessly from 1914–35 in various capacities. He held many senior positions from Chief of State, Minister of Military Affairs to Prime Minister. Imprisoned three times, Józef developed a deep distrust of the Germans and a hatred of the controlling Russian Empire. In 1920, he brilliantly defeated the Red Army, regaining Polish territory. He was a pro-active Polish nationalist, revolutionary and statesman who devoted his life to the realization of a free and independent Polish nation which it became in 1918.

Today, he is perceived as the "father of the nation" and his infectious desire for freedom will live on forever.

Uncle Władziu

Władziu (Vwad-zoo)—Władysław—was Władek's father's youngest brother. When his parents died young Władziu lived with Władek's family and was more like an older brother than an uncle, with only eight years difference. Władziu was an achiever and had high moral standards. Władek was named after him.

When his uncle left for school, Władek really missed him. When he returned home they spent many enjoyable days together. In the summer they would go for horseback rides to their river and swim. One day Władek dove down and got his head caught in some plant roots while Władziu was laying on the bank. Fortunately, his uncle sensed that something was wrong, dove in and rescued his nephew from drowning.

In 1918, aged 16, Uncle left school to join the Polish army to help fight the Bolshevik insurgency that was spreading into Poland and other neighboring countries. After being wounded in the leg, he returned to finish his education. Later, he would become an officer and an instructor at the PAF Academy in Dęblin. He had it all: looks, charisma, rank and beautiful girlfriends.

As Władek grew up, Władziu became his mentor and contributed to the positive development of his nephew's character. He instilled in him the love of flying and hoped that Władek would one day follow in his footsteps.

In the summer of 1938, he and a pilot friend, Captain Waliszewski, had planned a holiday in Greece, but on Friday, July 22nd, at 5.38 p.m., nearing Bucharest, the Polish Airlines Lockheed twin-engine passenger aircraft suddenly went down and crashed into a wooded hill during a storm—lightning may have been the cause. Władek and family went into denial. Sarnów had lost a son. The PAF had lost a shining star destined for great things in the impending war. His death was a staggering loss and it affected Władek deeply. His idol, mentor and friend was dead, at 36. Captain pilot Władziu Gnyś is buried at the cemetery in Oleksów not far from where he was born in the village of Sarnów.

All fifteen on board perished in the crash, including the crew of three: Pilot Captain Władysław Kotarba (a most experienced pilot decorated with the Bronze and Silver Cross of Merit and the Greek Order of the Phoenix), Radio Operator Zygmunt Zarzycki (army platoon leader) and Flight Engineer Franciszek Panek (Bronze Cross of Merit). Other passengers included Captain Olimpiusz Nartowski, a decorated pilot and instructor; P.L.L. Lockheed pilot Edward Gozdowski (or Grazdowski), an employee of the Polish embassy in Athens; Colonel Masakatsu Waka on his way to Bucharest to take up the post of Military Attaché at the Japanese embassy; Bulgarian diplomat Radi Radew; American physician, journalist and passionate aviator Dr. Lemuel Caro; Captain Gheorghe Ionescu,

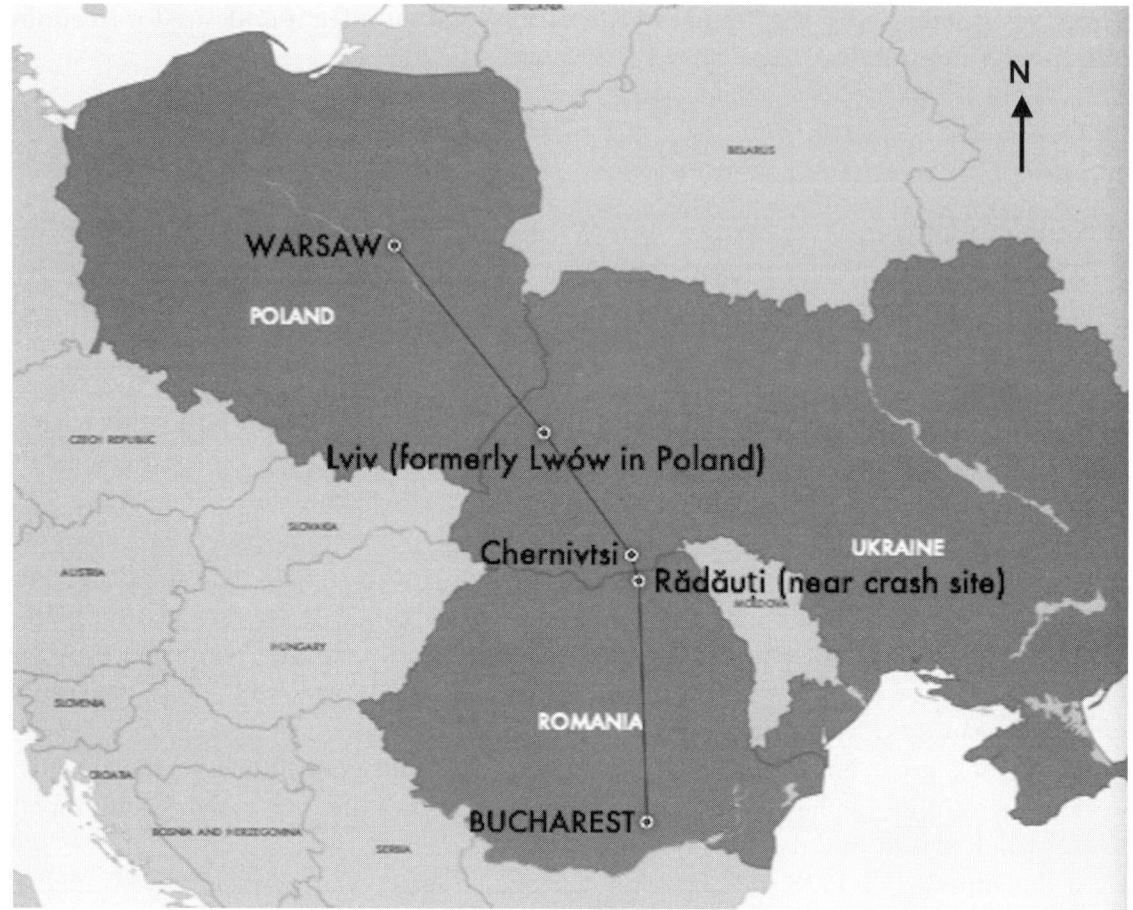

The crash of Lockheed L-14.

Romanian citizen and commander of Chernivtsi airport; Dr. Isidor Bodea, director of the children's hospital in Chernivtsi; Dr. Karl Nussenbaum; Ionel Fernic, famous Romanian composer, writer, aviator and parachutist and Mr. Ternir, an engineer.[2]

★

In 1926, Władek's father Jan decided he wanted to sell his half of the mill and the house in Sarnów and invest in a collective/co-operative enterprise purchasing big tracts of land with good soil in a place called Kujawy in central Poland about 200 miles west of Sarnów. Uncle Toni and Władek's mother Maria thought the scheme was too risky plus she and Jan still had seven children to provide for. But Jan was determined that it was a good idea especially in light of the declining economy. The organizer of the collective made Jan the spokesman. Unfortunately, due to legal problems, the deal went sour and the many families became destitute. Jan was blamed for not looking into the situation more carefully.

The Gnyś family had to rent a run-down leaky shack from a farmer. It was damp and had only two rooms with a clay floor. The farmer agreed to let Władek and sisters Bronka and Marysia work in his fields harvesting sugar beets in return for the rent. Father Jan was unable to work as he had gone into a deep depression and Maria was ill and run down trying to care for the other children. The situation was bleak.

When the sugar beets had all been harvested, 16-year-old Władek managed to get a job on a nearby estate loading wagons and doing odd jobs. He was working with two boys who were older, bigger and far more muscular. One of them was average height, stocky with close-cropped hair and protruding yellow teeth. The other was overweight and not very bright. When they learned that Władek had gone to school, they ridiculed him and pushed him around.

One day, the stocky boy kept goading and poking Gnyś and would not leave him alone. Władek had had enough. He took his pitchfork and, like a baseball bat, swung it and hit the bully square in the face, knocking him out cold. He had to be taken to a doctor. The estate manager didn't fire Władek but instead took pity on him and his family by providing food and a job in his office.

Finally, the courts took over and the local government divided the land up between the stranded families. The Gnyś family received 24 acres in a place called Kawęczyn. The new settlers felled trees and helped each other build houses just before winter. With financial support from uncles Toni in Sarnów and Władziu in Warsaw, Władek bought a horse, wagon and food for the family. Mother was still not well, but Jan was now able to work. Eventually they built a granary, a barn for livestock and dug a well.

Building a new home with his father, then later adding a new addition to it and to the barn plus all the daily chores in running a farm, was very demanding on everyone. However, as a team, they managed to eke out a living from the soil.

It seemed that Maria was always in a state of pregnancy which physically took its toll on her over the years. Looking after eight children and an unruly husband was more than most women could bear. But underneath all these demands was a mother who loved each of her children passionately. For some reason, her relationship with Władek was different from the rest. Perhaps it was his maturity and love of family that made him stand out. They developed a special bond. Moving from their established roots in Sarnów to Kawęczyn turned out to be a terrible mistake. This move and the further stress of living in near poverty was too much for Maria. Her health deteriorated even further and one day she just collapsed. Her family rallied round, but to no avail: she died of a stroke aged fifty. They all took it very hard. Władek could not bear the pain—prayers were not enough—so he headed out into the fields for a day without food or water and just walked and walked; he could not stop crying. At 21, he realized that he now had to make something of himself, on his own, without his mother's guidance and support.

In that five-year period, from 1926 to 1931, Władek developed great stamina and physical strength. He was able to carry heavy sacks of grain or coal or whatever needed

There was no time to waste: two men had succumbed to a pocket of methane gas during the construction of a well not far from where Władek lived in Kawęczyn. Risking his own life and holding his breath, he went down and saved the first rescuer, but the other man died from asphyxiation.

moving without showing excessive fatigue. This daily "workout" would prove to be a blessing when he joined the Polish military in 1931 and had to endure intensive army training.

Unknown to him at the time, his quick thinking and muscular physique would save a man's life. While still living on the farm in Kawęczyn, he volunteered to help a neighbor a couple of farms down the road, repair his fence. About half way there, he was distracted by a commotion in front of an old farmhouse. People were in a frenzy yelling and screaming and pointing to something on the ground. As he got closer, Władek realized that there had been an incident around the digging of a well. Apparently, a laborer at the bottom had hit a pocket of methane gas that had rendered him unconscious. Another man had been lowered down to pull him out, but he also succumbed to the effects of the gas. Without thinking of his own safety, Władek jumped forward and told the men to lower him down. Realizing what had happened to both men, he knew he had to hold his breath otherwise he would lose consciousness and probably die.

After holding onto the rope and standing in the bucket, he filled his lungs to capacity and gave the thumbs-up for the men to lower him down. The dry well was at least 12 feet deep and both men were slumped at the bottom. A spotter at the top directed the operation and kept constant visual contact. When Władek reached the bottom, he grabbed hold of the rescuer who had fallen on top of the laborer. Holding him under his arms, and keeping one foot in the bucket, he looked up as the spotter yelled, "Pull! Pull! Pull!" The 21-year-old's lungs were bursting with the exertion and screaming for air, his face contorted with the strain. Then, just before reaching the surface, he exhaled explosively and took a deep breath. The people at the top dragged both men over the lip and into the fresh air.

As Władek regained his composure, the others started to work on the man's chest trying to get him to breathe. In a few minutes, they saw signs of life then success as he started to take in air on his own. If he had been down any longer he would not have survived. However, by the time the methane had cleared and they got the well digger out, he was dead. The man Władek had saved was now sitting up so he talked to him quietly and made sure he was alright. After an exchange of smiles and a few pats on the back by the man's relatives, he was off again down the dusty road to help the neighbor mend his fence.

Władek spent the winter of 1930, and spring and summer of 1931, finishing off the many jobs that needed doing around the new homestead in Kawęczyn. He and his father completed the addition to the barn and added another bedroom to their house.

He had put in his application to join the Polish military, but knew that his dad (still a healthy 44-year-old) would miss his help. Fortunately, his older sisters were very capable young women. They were all still depressed about losing their mother. With tears in his eyes, and suitcase in hand, he said goodbye to his family. A new life lay ahead.

CHAPTER 2

Joining the Polish Air Force

After passing a vigorous physical examination, Władek was accepted into the Polish Armed Forces on October 29th, 1931 and joined the 4th Air Regiment in Toruń. His rank was szeregowy (Aircraftman No. 2 in the RAF, the lowest rank).

For the first two years, the young recruit trained as a regular soldier. The highly disciplined training was extremely intensive and demanding. They would drop onto their beds at night from long maneuvers with full army packs on their backs. The drill each day was of the highest precision and their muscles would ache from the strain of the everlasting exercises.

Władek had a need to finish his interrupted high-school education. In his second year of training he got permission to take courses part time. It was a challenge studying and training at the same time, but he was successful and passed the final Matura exam and got his *gimnazjum* diploma. This rite of passage along with further studies and exams would allow him in the future to enter the hallowed halls of Dęblin—the School of Eaglets—in 1936, to take the pilot instructor course and later into their Officer School.

Finally with army training and three months of mechanics' training (January 2nd–April 1st, 1932) behind him, Władek was now ready for his true calling: flying. On May 2nd, 1933, he commenced Flying Training School (4th Air Regiment) as a non-commissioned officer (NCO) at Grudziądz in north-central Poland, just north of Toruń. Here, he learned how to fly. The students also learned about various aircraft including those flown in World War I. One aircraft that they would eventually fly was a French-made metal biplane called the Breguet, a light bomber.

Władek did well and was posted to the 42nd Light Bomber Squadron in Toruń. Their emblem, an elephant, was painted on their aircraft fuselage.

The French Breguet XIX was produced from 1924 as a light bomber and reconnaissance aircraft. (This was probably the same aircraft that his uncle Władziu had trained on years before. He had taken his 12-year-old nephew to see one and allowed him to get into it

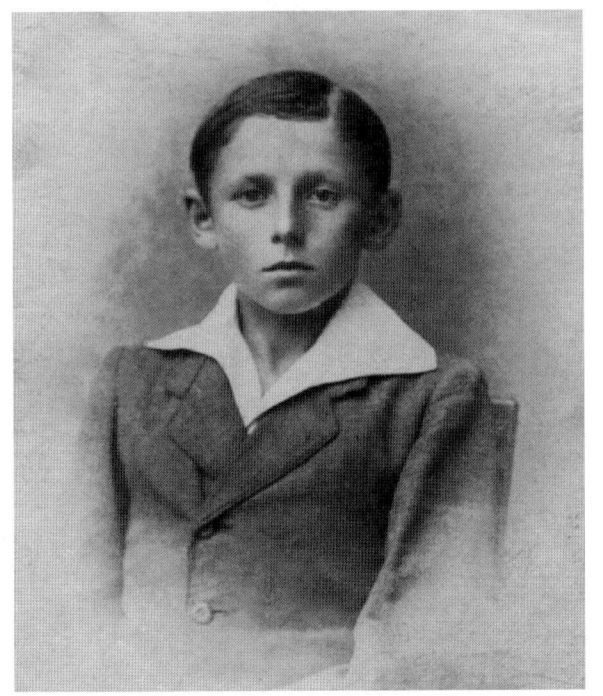

Szczepan's grain mill was the heart of Gnyś family life. After his death it was co-owned by Władek's father and his uncle Toni. The waterwheel on the left was under permanent shelter. (*Gnyś/Sarnów coll.*)

"Kalalocek" (Władek's nickname) is 14 in this 1924 photo. He attended secondary school (*gimnazjum*) Jan Kochanowski in Radom.

Szczepan Gnyś, Władek's grandfather, 1849–1922. (*Sarnów coll.*)

Poland's first Marshal, Józef Piłsudski (1867–1935) became a national hero who served Poland tirelessly from 1914 to 1935 in various capacities. He held many senior positions from Chief of State and Minister of Military Affairs to Prime Minister. Imprisoned three times, Józef developed a deep distrust of the Germans and hatred for the controlling Russian Empire. In 1920, he brilliantly defeated the Red Army and recovered Polish territory. He was a pro-active Polish nationalist, revolutionary and statesman who devoted his life to the realization of a free and independent Polish nation which it became in 1918. Today, he is perceived as '"the father of the nation."

Józef Piłsudski died in 1935. He wanted his heart buried in his mother's grave (above), in Rasos cemetery, Vilnius, Lithuania. Władek is facing the wreath, reaching down to it.

Władek's uncle was on his way from Poland to Greece in July 1938, but over northern Romania ran into a storm and was likely struck by lightning, after which the plane crashed into a forested area, killing all on board *(NAC 1-G-4226)*

Cpt Władysław Gnyś (1902–38)—"Uncle Władziu." Promoted to cpt, January 1st, 1936. *(T. Kopański via P. Sikora)*

Władek in the winter of 1930, just before he joined the Polish Air Force (PAF).

Above: Polish cavalry.

Far left: Army training: rifle and bayonet drills, Władek (front left) at the age of twenty-one.

Left: Military training continued throughout the winter of 1931/32 at Toruń. These young men in their late teens or early 20s were put through rigorous marches and drills. Władek (21) is at center.

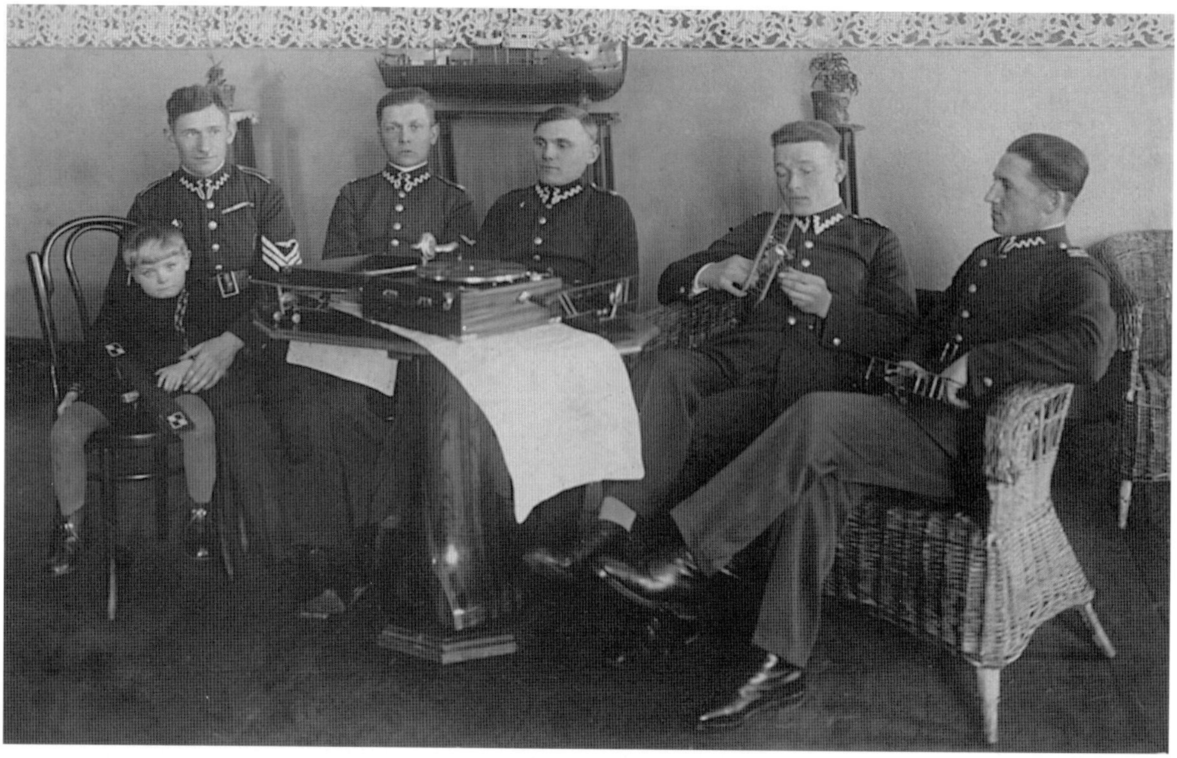

The boy is the son of the sergeant in charge of training at Toruń, early 1933 (Władek is far right). Note the gramophone as an instructional aid. It could have been used in conjunction with the model aircraft they are holding which appear to be replicas of a biplane trainer aircraft.

Władek's first parachute jump while at flying school, Grudziądz, 1933.

Leading Aircraftman (Kapral) Pilot Gnyś successfully completed the flying course at Grudziądz at the age of 23 in 1933. He proudly wears the aviator badge of the Polish Air Force. In use since the 1920s, the badge is called a *gapa* and is a symbolic silver eagle in flight with a laurel wreath in its beak. With a chain, it is located on the upper left side below the collar. It was worn by the PAF pilots in the French Air Force and the Royal Air Force during the Second World War.

Gnyś with a fellow pilot at Fighter School in Grudziądz, 1934. This two-seater biplane is probably a PWS-14 trainer.

Squadron on summer maneuvers in Poland, 1934.

Grudziądz 1934: ready to board a Farman Goliath F.68 BN4 for a jump at the end of fighter course. Stanisław Kłosowski (left) later flew with an RAF bomber squadron. Gnyś is second from left.

which made a huge impression on the boy, an experience he would never forget.) Gnyś
and other pilots nicknamed it the "Flying Coffin." If you didn't have enough speed on
a turn for example, the aircraft could go into a spinning nose-dive. It was very difficult
for the pilot at that point to level out the plane. A few unlucky pilots-in-training crashed
because of this complication. Władek himself ran into trouble one day while flying the
Brequet when it went into a spin without any warning. He tried everything possible
to steady the aircraft. Finally, with only several hundred feet before hitting the ground,
he managed to pull it out of the spiral and escape certain death. Officials watching on
the ground later praised him for his skill and ingenuity. Later in fact, he showed others
his technique which then became part of the course.

On May 2nd, 1934, he was sent to the Advanced Flying School at Grudziądz to take
the fighter pilot course. (The cities of Grudziądz, Toruń and Bydgoszcz are less than an
hour apart.) As of October 2nd, 1934, he served with 142 Squadron (*eskadra*).

Just prior to this move, however, there was the matter of the unauthorized maneuver.
Probably the only time Władek ever acted irresponsibly as a pilot was in Toruń, 1934.
However, it wasn't a last minute bit of recklessness: it was a calculated bit of daring
and fun.

There was a very nice resort on the Vistula River in the suburbs of Toruń. During off-
duty times, he and friends would go there to swim and to tan. Nearby was a fairly wide
bridge and Władek fantasized about flying underneath it. Initially, it was a challenge,
but after a while it became an obsession. Fighter school training was very thorough and
sometimes pilots became overconfident when performing aerobatics.

One beautiful summer day, the 24-year-old Gnyś had been practicing various
maneuvers and found himself alone near the banks of the Vistula. In the distance the
bridge came into full view. He could no longer resist the temptation. Władek descended
and flew low over the water as the bridge loomed ahead. Thoughts of insubordination
and disciplinary action went through his head as well as the possibility of crashing and
killing himself or injuring innocent people crossing the bridge. At the same time his
mind drifted back to his mentor uncle Władziu who always taught him to follow the
rules, know right from wrong and use common sense at all times. It was now too late
to turn back. His plane swooped under the bridge just above the surface of the water,
the roar of the engine echoing under the steel structure. In an instance he was through.
Władek heaved a sigh of relief.

Satisfied, he then returned to base and taxied towards the hangar to be met by the
duty officer who bluntly ordered him to report to the station commander at 0900 sharp
the next morning … someone had seen his prank. He immediately reported to his
squadron leader who said that this action could cost him his wings. The next morning
Gnyś and his squadron leader reported to Group Captain Heller who was Commanding
Officer of the 4th Air Regiment in Tórun. As it turned out, Heller had been on the
beach with his family at the time and had witnessed the stunt.

Alley-oop! It was probably a Potez XXV trainer that Władek flew under a bridge at Toruń in 1934.

Surprisingly he said, "It was quite well done!" He then turned to the squadron leader, "How is he doing otherwise?"

"Very well, sir," was the reply.

The wise C.O. said only "Don't do it again!"

Władek was surprised, but happy with such a mild reprimand.

As part of the fighter course, the pilots were taken to the northwestern industrial port city of Gdynia on the Baltic Sea. They were given a tour of the harbor and its many facilities. In the 1920s, Gdynia was the only transit and special seaport designed for coal exports. By 1939, it became a universal seaport and was the largest and most modern on the Baltic.

While Władek was at Grudziądz in 1934, taking the advanced flying course to become a fighter pilot, coincidence had it that Władziu, his young uncle was stationed there as an instructor. It gave Władek great pleasure to be able to see him almost every day. After all, it was mainly because of his uncle that he had become a pilot.

They had more in common now than ever before. Not only in class, but privately Władziu gave him much advice about flying and how to become a better pilot. Władek finished the program and received a new American Colt revolver for taking first place. The graduation ceremony was a significant achievement for the young pilot especially under the watchful eye and tutelage of his uncle.

Mid-air collision

Now as a fighter pilot, he was transferred to Toruń in 1935 for a period of six months and attached to the 142nd Fighter Squadron, 4th Air Regiment as an NCO pilot. His rank at the time was a Leading Aircraftman (kapral). Here, he would be able to apply his fighter pilot skills in an established squadron.

Major Leopold Pamuła was their squadron leader who was in charge of flying exercises and related activities. Mock dogfights and aerobatics were part of their training and became routine. Władek affectionately referred to the group as, "Pamuła's Fighter Squadron." They took their work seriously, worked hard as a fighting unit, but they always made time to have some fun.

On May 11th, 1935 Gnyś and S-Lt Dionizy Durko were scheduled for a mock battle and aerobatics. Such maneuvers required a great deal of concentration and precise timing. Their last exercise was to make loops, turn together in a half roll, dive and straighten out. But all of a sudden, after completing the half roll, Durko came dangerously close … too close.

"He's going to hit me!" yelled Gnyś.

Durko's cockpit struck the right wheel of Władek's PZL P.7 (aircraft no. 6.78). Both the wheel and undercarriage were torn off and a hole was gouged in his wing. Dionizy Durko was killed instantly and his PZL P.7 slowly spiraled to the ground and crashed on the edge of the field. Gnyś was slightly injured as a result of the sudden jolt, but was more startled than anything else.

Sadly, this miscalculation by Durko cost him his life. Pilots, mechanics and other personnel below were shocked. A flare from below signaled Władek to parachute from his plane, but instead he skillfully landed on one wheel and saved his aircraft. Everyone came running out to help and then congratulated him for his spectacular landing. Under any circumstance, it is not an easy thing to land on one wheel because the pilot has to struggle to keep the aircraft level and not destroy the tipped wing when the plane makes contact with the ground.

Observers on the ground reported that S-Lt Durko tried to save his aircraft, but this author was told by his father that right after the crash, he looked down and saw a permanent reflection from Durko's goggles as if he was looking back up during his downward spiral. The implication here is that the lieutenant's neck had been broken by the force of the impact.

During an aerobatic maneuver, S-Lt Dionizy Durko accidently collided with Gnyś and was killed.

For his bravery for saving the plane, Władek received a written praise from the C.O. of the 4th Air Regiment (order no. 127/35 dated June 6th, 1935). An archived document (LOT.A.V.97/15/9) in the Polish Institute and Sikorski Museum in London states:

> On the orders of the Head of the Aeronautics Department dated June 1935 commended [Władysław Gnyś] for keeping presence of mind, composure and prudence and skillful landing despite having the right half of [his] undercarriage with the wheel cut off while performing aerobatic maneuvers and collision. Awarded the Bronze Cross of Merit on June 18th, 1935 for the first time for service in the air force.

However, despite the accolades, Władek felt very sad for the senseless loss of Dionizy. It was a terrible tragedy. The moment of impact and the death of his friend stayed with him for years.

Then on August 1st of the same year, Gnyś accidentally collided on the ground with PZL P.7 (aircraft no. 6.130). This time it was his fault. He was taxiing his PZL P.7 (aircraft no. 6.87) and did not see the other plane on the runway until it was too late. Fortunately, there were no injuries: just aircraft damage to both PZLs. Accidents on the ground like this were not uncommon.

School of Eaglets, Dęblin, 1936

Dęblin is a military school located in eastern Poland. Its current name is Wyższa Szkoła Oficerska sił Powietrznych, the Polish Air Force Academy. It is known as the "School of Eaglets" and is carrying on the traditions of the Air Force Officer School which was started in 1918. It was then established in Grudziądz in 1925 before being transferred to Dęblin in 1927. From 1928, under the name of Air Force Officer Cadet School, it began training pilots and observers who were to become Polish Air Force officers. In 1968, it was re-organized and given the status of a university-level school under the name of Air Force Officer Training College. In 1994, the School was re-organized again and given its current name of the Polish Air Force Academy. Today, cadets undergo training in one of the following: Pilot, Navigator, Air Traffic Controller or Aircraft Maintenance.

From March 2nd to May 1st, 1936, with the rank of kapral (Leading Aircraftman), Władek took the pilot instructor course at C.W.O.L. (Aviation Officers' Training Center) in Dęblin. Then from May 2nd to September 29th, 1936 he became a pilot instructor at S.P.L. (Aviation Cadet-Officer School) in the Dęblin Aviation Officers' Training Center.

Most trainees were just out of high school and most had only completed glider training but Władek had joined the school as an experienced NCO pilot.

He spent five months teaching cadets to fly using a trainer aircraft that had two open cockpits that were in tandem to each other with dual controls. Twelve hours' flying time with trainees was the normal time spent before their solo flights. However, Gnyś developed his own unique teaching style which involved a combination of stick and foot pedal controls. Using his method, he was able to train each of them in six hours: a 50 percent reduction in time. At this point they were now qualified to fly by themselves.

Several group members later flew in the Battle of Britain with Władek in 1940. (One pilot was Wacław (Wacek) Król who in Poland flew PZL P.11c # 2, the only surviving fighter of its kind in the world. It is on display at the Aviation Museum in Kraków.)

In October 1936, Władek transferred to the facility at Bydgoszcz that was designed for candidates for any officers' school in Poland to advance their education to eventually become an officer in their respective fields such as army, air force, cavalry and artillery. As a pilot, his continued post-secondary education took place at Cadet School for NCOs here in Bydgoszcz. It began on October 1st, 1936 and was completed by August 15th, 1938 during which time he passed all required exams with honors. Thus, he spent the better part of two years preparing to become a fully-fledged commissioned officer which he would accomplish back at Dęblin shortly after.

His NCO rank during these years was Platoon Officer Cadet. Władek left Cadet School for NCOs in Bydgoszcz on August 15th, 1938 and was transferred to the Cadet Officer Pilot School in Dęblin for his final year before becoming a commissioned officer. Not all NCOs wanted to go to the Cadet Officer School and become officers: it was a personal decision.

Bear in mind that in 1936 Władek took the pilot instructor course at Dęblin from the beginning of March to the end of April, then became a qualified pilot instructor May to September inclusive, a period of seven months of learning and teaching. He was therefore very familiar with the facilities and functions of the Dęblin base.

Thus, on August 16th, 1938, he enrolled in the revered Officer Cadet School (12th entry class), his second time at Dęblin, but this time in a different capacity. His objective was to become a commissioned officer in the PAF, something he had been working towards for many years. He stayed here until June 1st, 1939.

At Dęblin, as a qualified flying instructor, Gnyś had the unusual honor of being a student and an instructor at the school at the same time, just like in 1936.

Franciszek Kornicki (20) reported as a cadet in the 12th entry class at the PAF Academy in Dęblin in January 1937. At that time it was called The Air Force Training Center Dęblin (CWL Dęblin).[1]

He gave insight to this author during an interview in terms of his perception of Władek as a man and as an experienced instructor back then. Born in 1916, 96-year-old Franciszek vividly remembered W. Gnyś as "a nice fellow, a gentleman, charming, modest, unassuming, very open, had a shy smile, very much liked, friendly, was respected and treated the new learners with respect, was taller and older."

Upon arrival at the base as a young cadet, Kornicki's recollection of pilot Stanisław Chałupa was also clear and he remembered how Chałupa on the very first day, took him up spontaneously in a trainer aircraft for a spin around the base. Stan made him feel very welcome and special that day, and Franciszek never forgot his kindness.

Later, Kornicki was posted to 162 Squadron just before war. He flew for France then Britain where he served with Nos. 303 and 315. At 26 he became C.O. of No. 308— youngest in the PAF, then C.O. of 317 Polish Fighter Squadron.

With the new rank of Sergeant (sierżant) and seven months into his own personal officer training, Władek again assumed the role of instructor to the Dęblin cadets. He really enjoyed teaching.

CHAPTER 3

September 1939: Blitzkrieg

"Poland was the first to stand up and fight!"

W. G.

For months there had been great unrest in Europe and everyone felt that an invasion of Poland by Nazi Germany was inevitable. Hitler's troops had already occupied the Rhineland, Austria and Czechoslovakia and on August 23rd, 1939, unknown to Poland (the Second Polish Republic), the Soviets signed a non-aggression pact with Germany.

While at Dęblin Air Force Base on June 2nd, 1939, Władek Gnyś was assigned to 121 Eskadra (Squadron) located at Rakowice airbase in Kraków. The 2nd Air Regiment in Kraków consisted of three fighter units: 121, 122 and 123. As a precaution, all fighter units of the Polish Air Force were moved away from their home airfields which would be logical Luftwaffe targets. In all, by September 1939, 15 Polish fighter units were on standby in various secret locations throughout Poland.

On September 1st, 1939, 121 Squadron of III/2 Fighter Wing, 2nd Air Regiment, Kraków, had ten PZL P.11 fighter aircraft. In charge were C.O. kpt pilot Tadeusz Sędzielowski and his deputy ppor pilot Wacław Król. The eleven other pilots were ppor Tadeusz Kowalewski, ppor Tadeusz Nowak, ppor Władysław Gnyś (from the 12th entry class at Dęblin, 1938), ppor Władysław Chciuk (from the same class as Gnyś), ppor Ryszard Koczor (from the same class as Gnyś), ppor Franciszek Surma (from the same class as Gnyś), sierż Leopold Flanek, kpr Jan Kremski, kpr Piotr Zaniewski, st szer Tadeusz Arabski and st szer Marian Futro.

As war was expected at any moment, four aircraft on August 20th from 121 squadron in Rakowice, left for Aleksandrowice (west of Balice), from where they operated as an ambush unit. Tensions were high … timing was everything.

Ground crew were moved to Balice (about 6 miles to the west of Kraków and east of the German border) during the night of August 26th/27th to set up emergency base defenses.

On August 31st, under the command of Cpt M. Medwecki, 16 aircraft from 121 and 122 Squadrons and 10 aircraft from 123 Squadron flew to Balice from Rakowice to wait. But on the same day at 4 p.m., 123 left for Warsaw after being attached to the Pursuit Brigade to help protect Warsaw.

The Luftwaffe would likely attack the PAF bases in the larger centers so the relocation of the fighter units was an insightful and calculated move by the Polish high command. In Balice, HQ had located a very large field with numerous trees around the edge that provided excellent camouflage for Cpt Medwecki's squadrons. For accommodation, pilots in Balice were housed in a large private

This map shows how Poland, prior to the 1939 invasion, was surrounded by Germany in the north (East Prussia), west and south and on the eastern flank by Soviet Russia.

home that was close to the makeshift airfield. Ground crew were in tents near the aircraft. Balice consisted of large grassy fields; today it is John Paul II International Airport.

Władek settled in for the night thinking about what the future would hold. He knew Hitler's forces were well equipped with superior aircraft, weapons and ordnance. Many Poles would die in defense of their country. What would become of his precious family? How long would the war last? Would he himself survive the invasion? All these questions went through his head before falling asleep in the quiet of his room.

Then in the early hours of September 1st, he was abruptly awakened by the sound of terrifying explosions and the roar of planes overhead. He sprang out of bed and rushed to the window ... the sky above Kraków in the distance was crimson red. The 29-year-old veteran flyer pulled on his flying overalls and aggressively opened his bedroom door to see his comrades scrambling about, stunned by what they had just witnessed.

At that moment, his C.O. Cpt Mieczysław Medwecki came yelling down the corridor: "It is war! It is war! Get to your aircraft immediately!" He caught sight of Władek and shouted, "Władek, you will take off with me!"

Władek followed Medwecki tearing down the outside stairs two at time, almost falling, then down to the nearby field. The mechanics already had the propellers turning. Władek jumped onto the footstep of his gull-winged fighter aircraft and dropped into the cockpit. The mechanic attached the parachute, snapped the safety harness shut and jumped to the ground as the plane taxied down the field with the throttle fully open, about 60 feet to the right of Medwecki. Their wheels left the ground and the planes rose above the trees. It was still fairly dark. They climbed to around 1,000 feet when Władek noticed tracer bullets in front of him and three dark silhouettes overhead. Instinctively, he threw his still accelerating plane to the left and down. He was at takeoff speed with nothing to spare. He felt the plane dropping and his foremost thought was to prevent himself from crashing while skillfully trying to outmaneuver the attacking German fighters.

Letting the plane slide to gain speed and with the throttle still wide open, he managed to pull up just above the treetops, evading the attacking Stukas. Now under control, he climbed again; it was a close shave. Gnyś saw Medwecki's aircraft swaying from side to side out of control.

Still dark, pilots scramble to their waiting planes to intercept Luftwaffe aircraft that had just bombed the Kraków airfield. Cpt Medwecki is center, pilots Gnyś at left heads for No. 5 and Arabski runs to far left.

"He's been hit!" Władek thought as he passed above him.

These Stukas—returning after they had dropped their bombs on Rakowice aerodrome—had surprised Władek and his captain who were just beginning to take off from Balice. It was Unteroffizier Frank Neubert flying one of these Stuka dive-bombers who shot down and killed Cpt M. Medwecki, the C.O. of III/2 Fighter Wing. Because of Neubert's actions, this was the Luftwaffe's first aerial combat victory, the first kill of the war.[1]

Still climbing, S-Lt Gnyś managed two bursts of his guns into the engine of another Stuka which turned away and disappeared into the clouds. He continued to climb rapidly toward the German border hoping to meet other enemy bombers on their way back to base after bombing Kraków. He spotted two Dornier bombers flying on his left side approximately 3,300 feet below. Even though it was still quite early, visibility was much better above the clouds and he had the advantage of height. The Dorniers were flying in a tight formation which would contribute to their demise.

Putting his small fighter into a near-vertical dive, Władek banked steeply toward the Dornier on his right which was closest and slightly ahead of the other. Its rear gunner

Very early on September 1st, 1939, after the Luftwaffe had bombed the Kraków airfield, Stuka pilot Frank Neubert attacked Polish pilots Gnyś and Medwecki as they were taking off to intercept the returning bombers. Cpt Medwecki was killed. Instinctively, Gnyś quickly pulled to the left and down.

started to fire as he swooped down upon it. Gnyś returned fire with his four machine guns silencing the gunner and hitting the port engine. He then climbed sharply and banked to the left, away from the smoking bomber to avoid collision. Again he pursued the same Dornier and at relatively close range he aimed and fired at its port side getting hits on the cockpit. Władek quickly dove beneath it, again closely escaping collision. Both bombers were dangerously close to each other and the possibility of a collision was very real … the thought flashed through his head.

He found himself close to the ground. When he climbed again, he had lost sight of the Dorniers. Unknown to S–Lt Gnyś at the time, he had achieved the first two victories over the Luftwaffe in World War II.

The victorious pilot did not see the two crashed bombers burning below in the village of Żurada[2] near Olkusz in southwest Poland. All six crew members from the bombers where killed; one of them had unsuccessfully attempted to parachute from one of the Dorniers.

As he pulled up, he noticed a Heinkel (He 111) in the far distance and fired a short burst at it, but his guns stopped short: he was out of ammunition. He then turned and headed back to base to make his report to Cpt T. Sędzielowski.

Just minutes before, Cpt Medwecki had been killed by Stuka pilot Frank Neubert. Władek managed to elude the pursuing Ju 87s just above the treetops.

But before landing at the off-site airbase at Balice to give his report, Władek decided to fly over burning Rakowice. The destruction was overwhelming. The better weather over southern Poland allowed Luftflotte 4, one of the primary divisions of the German air force, to operate more easily at first light, with the main attack on Kraków's Rakowice airbase. It was fortunate that Władek and company had vacated Rakowice aerodrome just days before.

Rakowice was first bombed by 60 Heinkels (He 111s) of KG 4, then by Stukas (Ju 87s) of I/St.G 2 and finally by the Do 17s of KG 77: in total over 150 warplanes.[3]

When Gnyś returned to Balice, he saw a plane burning on the edge of the field: it was Cpt Medwecki's. A half-hour earlier he had run across the field shouting, "Władek, you will take off with me!" Now he was gone.

Combat report by Władysław Gnyś for September 1st, 1939[4]

It is important to note that discovering the following document written during the war by the pilot himself is significant and it was a rare find. The fact remains that Władek was there and he did indeed witness his Captain's death and then make the first two Allied kills of the air war. Thus, regarding the early morning events of September 1st, 1939, here is W. Gnyś's own statement prepared for the Historical Commission of the Polish Air Force:

On September 1st, 1939 around seven in the morning,[5] I took off from a landing field in Balice near Kraków along with Cpt Medwecki, the commander of the squadron. Having joined Cpt Medwecki at a height of about 1,000 feet, we were suddenly shot at from behind by German aircraft flying by. I managed to escape the line of fire by taking an abrupt turn to the left. Flying at relatively low speed, my aircraft dove and I was able to pull it up just before reaching the ground.

Having pulled the aircraft up, I noticed that Cpt Medwecki's aircraft was swinging from one side to another and failing to maintain even flight.

Suddenly, I noticed two German airplanes flying on my left side about 3,300 feet below. They were flying on the Kraków–Olkusz route. I attacked the one flying at the back. At first I noticed that the gunner was firing at me; however, after a couple of bursts, he ceased fire and the left engine started to smoke slightly. I rapidly pulled the plane up.

The German aircraft started to descend. Once again, I went after the plane which I previously attacked as it was moving to my right side.[6] A gunner was firing at me. I fired a couple of bursts, long and well-aimed as I reckoned, and then I descended abruptly. I found myself to be quite low above the ground.

Having pulled the plane up, I did not see any aircraft and I concluded that they may have hidden behind a hill. Even though I analyzed the probable direction in which they could have been flying, I was not able to spot any aircraft. I found it quite strange though.

I did see something smoking on the ground, but I did not look at it closely and I set course back for the airport. The aircraft that I had been attacking had twin tail fins and at that time, I recognized them as Dorniers.

On my way back I fired a short burst towards an He 111 flying by at quite a large distance at about 90° angle, but due to lack of ammunition, I flew back to base. Bursts of fire rendered ineffective. On my way back I noticed Cpt Medwecki's plane burning on the ground.

Combat Scores of 121 Fighter Squadron: the first three days[7]

September 1st, 1939

- ppor Wacław Król/kpr Paweł Kowala HS 126 damaged at Bzie Zameckie, near Pszczyna: the A/C crash landed
- ppor Władysław Gnyś 2 × Do 17 over Żurada
- kpr Jan Kremski Do 17 over Brenna Leśnica, near Skoczów

September 2nd, 1939

- plut Antoni Markiewicz, plut Władysław Majchrzyk, pchor Bolesław Własnowolski, pchor Franciszek Kozłowski of 122 Eskadra and ppor Tadeusz Nowak, ppor Franciszek Surma and ppor Ryszard Koczor of 121 Eskadra. A Ju 87 over Dwory, near Oświęcim (officially and erroneously two Ju 87 were given: one only to Własnowolski and Majchrzyk; second to Kozłowski and Markiewicz).

September 3rd, 1939

- st szer Tadeusz Arabski—1/2 Heinkel He 111 damaged, over Gołuchowice, near Siewierz
- sierż Leopold Flanek—1/2 Heinkel He 111 damaged, over Gołuchowice, near Siewierz
- kpr Jan Kremski—1/2 Heinkel He 111 shot down, over Gołuchowice, near Siewierz

Notes on the first victory[8]

by PAF historian Jerzy B. Cynk

The explanation of what happened to Gnyś's prey can be found in a detailed report by Lt Zdzislaw Pirszel, prepared for the Historical Commission of the PAF in France in April 1940 and supported by several photographs of remnants of two Dornier Do 17E bombers. On the fuselage of one of them the Luftwaffe code 3Z+FR (3Z indicating aircraft of the KG77, which bombed Kraków in the morning of September 1st) is clearly visible.

On September 1st, 1939 he (Pirszel) was traveling in a car with another officer, 2nd Lt Jerzy Rejnowicz on the Trzebina–Olkusz road, when some three miles south of Olkusz they were stopped by local villagers who informed them that two German aircraft had crashed to the ground in the nearby village of Żurada. When the officers arrived on the spot they found debris of two Dornier Do 17E bombers scattered over a distance of some 100 meters, still smoldering and ammunition still exploding. Five charred bodies were inside the remnants of the cockpits and the sixth—NCO Klose in a half-developed parachute entangled in the wreckage—was lying beside one of the fuselages. A number of maps and documents including the Luftwaffe's signal and communication codes and flight orders identifying Kraków as the prime target and Olkusz as the secondary one, were retrieved from the wreckage. Lt Pirszel continued:

> We wrote down statements of eyewitnesses, indicating that three vics [tight V-shaped sections of three] of Dorniers flew from east to west at about 2,000 m. The last three, trailing some distance behind, were attacked by a solitary Polish fighter and then two of the Dorniers, flying in close formation, departed from the rest and came down very low being persistently chased and fired at by the fighter. At a certain moment both Dorniers fell to the ground. The Polish aircraft flew away in a southeasterly direction.
>
> After securing the wreckage, we drove to Kraków, where we surrendered the found documents to the Chief of the II Department [Intelligence] of the Army Kraków who directed us to take some to the papers to the Army's Aviation Command. Its Chief, Col Sznuk asked us to return to Żurada and bring back some specific Dornier parts.
>
> On September 2nd we transported to Kraków—to the army's Aviation Command the following items: one B.M.W. engine; one T/R wireless set; three machine guns with ammunition; photo cameras and several other small items.

Ironically enough, when documents, statements and claims relating to Polish kills in the September campaign of 1939 were scrutinized during the war, Gnyś was at first officially credited with the destruction of one Ju 87 on the morning of September 1st and later, on the final credit list, this was amended to one He 111. This misunderstanding can only be explained by 'war fever'.

However, in view of the above solid evidence from various, completely independent sources, corroborated by photographs, there can be no doubt that Gnyś's lonely attack resulted in the destruction of two Do 17E bombers from the KG 77 which were returning from bombardment of Kraków on September 1st, 1939 at about 7 a.m. No other Polish fighter operated at the time in the Olkusz area and even if the disabled Dorniers collided in mid-air, this was the direct outcome of Gnyś's action. These were the first two Luftwaffe warplanes to fall to the guns of an Allied fighter in World War II.

★

The Luftwaffe continued doing reconnaissance on the morning's damage. Then, more strafing and bombing by waves of bombers and fighters. Hitler's first strikes were from the north and south of Germany's eastern border and from Slovakia. East Prussia on Poland's northern boundary contained many Luftwaffe airfields.

Many Polish peacetime and military airfields were hit along with aircraft factories resulting in a loss of about 180 planes. The majority of these were older aircraft, trainers, private and nonmilitary types, many of which were left in the open as "decoy" aircraft. Only several dozen were military reserve planes of which nine were Łoś bombers. However, the 15 Polish combat units that were moved from their home bases to well-camouflaged airfields were not really affected by these attacks.

Extensive German reconnaissance did not locate the hidden Polish combat airfields nor did they see any large formations of warplanes. Their conclusion was that the L.W. (Lotnictwo Wojskowe or Military Aviation, the air arm of the Polish Army) had been totally wiped out by the first strikes on their known bases. This belief was of course, false: the L.W. would indeed fight another day.

Many cities, towns and villages were indiscriminately bombed, civilian casualties were high. Warsaw was protected by the Pursuit Brigade (the large fighter unit formed in haste in late August) which downed over a dozen of the enemy, but generally speaking Polish air space was largely unprotected as most of the Polish fighter units were spread thinly across the country. Also, since "ambush" was really their only defensive strategy, the air arm was really ineffective.

In the afternoon, S-Lt Gnyś with the other pilots of 121 and 122 squadrons were moved to Igołomia 16 miles east of Kraków. 123 Squadron was ordered to leave Balice and join the Pursuit Brigade at the Okęcie airfield near Warsaw, then to move to Poniatów airfield in a suburb of Warsaw.

By the end of the first day, Luftflotte 1 (which concentrated on the northern half of Poland) and Luftlotte 4 (southern half of Poland) flew some 2,700 sorties (combat missions which included fighters, bombers and reconnaissance aircraft) against Polish home base airfields, army units and naval facilities and achieved nine air victories with a total loss of 37 of their aircraft. Polish fighters claimed the majority of these while Polish army anti-aircraft fire (AA) most likely was responsible for the rest. However, Poland's 280 sorties do not compare to the Luftwaffe's 2,700. The loss to Poland was 29 aircraft, 19 of which were fighters. This was just the first day.

The next morning, September 2nd, at Igołomia, 121 and 122 Fighter Units strapped themselves into the cockpits of their already warmed-up aircraft. They waited to scramble without delay if the enemy showed his face, but the weather was poor with a low ceiling and the Germans did not appear. Władek obtained permission to take off to have a look above the clouds and kapral John Kremski asked to join him: none was found. But elsewhere, the Luftwaffe continued to pound the Polish air arm, industrial sites, anti-aircraft emplacements and radio stations. For example, CWL Dęblin (Centrum Wyszkolenia Lotnictwa or Aviation Training Center) and its various airfields were savagely attacked and practically destroyed. Not too long before Władek had spent many happy seasons there as a trainee and as an instructor.

On September 3rd Eskadra 121 and 122 were moved to Podlodów near Dęblin. They were to protect what was left of Dęblin and the Puławy region for several days although Dęblin's school had been abandoned early as a safety precaution. They were there not only to protect the Polish Air Force Training Center, but to protect the general area.

The following quote by S-Lt Gnyś, taken from a document from the Polish Institute and Sikorski Museum, describes the events of his third day of the invasion:[9]

On September 3rd the squadron took off to go after a formation flying towards Kraków.

Due to some difficulties with starting the engine, my plane was one of the last ones to take off. While gaining height I noticed the squadron's aircraft attacking a German flight formation flying towards Kraków, as well as Wacław Król parachuting. As my aircraft's height was insufficient, I was not able to take part in the attack.

Soon afterwards I noticed a solitary German He 111-type aircraft flying from Kraków. I attacked it just above the Igołomia airport. The aircraft started escaping towards a rather small cumulus that was in its way. I carried out the attack at three-quarters from behind on the left with slight advantage in height.

After the initial bursts of fire the aircraft abruptly turned right, but then it turned into a cumulus which was at a relatively close distance. I fired the last burst at the clouds in which the enemy's aircraft soon disappeared. I finished the attack at about 650 feet. Hoping to meet the aircraft I had been attacking, I flew around the cumulus which turned out to be relatively small. Unfortunately, I did not see the enemy's airplane.

After I had landed, Sgt Bartecki claimed that he had seen the attack from the airport. In my opinion, the aircraft must have been at least damaged.

My propeller blades were shot through. According to the mechanics, while carrying out the attack, I myself was being attacked by five He 111s flying above me, of which I had not been aware!

Geographically, Dęblin is about eight miles from Sarnów where Władek was born. He asked his C.O. for permission to visit his family and assured him that he would return before sunrise ready for duty. He was given a motorcycle with a sidecar and drove to Sarnów and to the old mill. Władek's visit completely surprised Uncle Toni and family who lived in the mill. The mood that evening was somber for they all knew that Poland had little chance of stopping Hitler's advance. They were all saddened by the possibility that they might never see each other again. At four o'clock in the morning, they said goodbye and he set off in the direction of his squadron.

Not far from the old mill just on the outskirts of Sarnów was an old wooden cross that stood on the side of the road. Władek stopped, looked up at its silhouette and said, "Jesus, if you will allow me to survive the war, I will come back here one day, bow down and kiss your feet." This story and his promise over time became something of a legend in parts of Poland. In fact, he did survive and 26 years later, he came back to the cross, bowed down, gave thanks to God for his survival and kissed the cross. On subsequent trips, he would always return to this landmark and give thanks. (This writer was so inspired by his father's story that he wrote a song entitled "Jesus I Will Kiss Your Feet." When Mother passed away in August 1995, this song was performed at her eulogy by a full church choir and orchestra. She loved the song so much that it was only fitting it be performed in such a way. It was an emotional moment (lyrics appear in the appendices).

Meanwhile, from September 3rd onwards, the Luftwaffe was confident that it now dominated the air space so it began to concentrate on supporting its forces on the ground. Their plan was to trap the Polish army west of the Vistula. However, air and naval bases continued to be heavily bombed. Warsaw was the target for many strikes. The Pursuit

Brigade with its 40 fighter aircraft had little success in trying to stop the ever persistent Luftwaffe. Bombing continued day and night and many munition sites were destroyed.

It was on the 3rd that the Polish Bomber Brigade under the command of Col Władysław Heller successfully maximized the use of Karaś light bombers attacking German panzer units which had broken through the Polish defenses in the southwest. Bombing by theses Karaś squadrons inflicted significant damage on German armor. Along with the fighter units, the LW was still a contender.

From the 4th to the 6th, the Germans broke through the Polish defenses in the north and south. However, this was also the day that the Polish Bomber Brigade with its Łoś bombers did significant damage to the XVI Panzer Corps. Despite this victory, the Luftwaffe, flying more than 2,000 sorties per day, pounded airfields, road and rail networks, virtually paralyzing military command. On September 5th, Władek with 121 Squadron, along with 122, were deployed to the village of Kraczewice, just west of Lublin and southeast of Dęblin.

It was on September 6th that the Polish government decided to leave Warsaw as German spearheads were advancing rapidly onto the capital. The Pursuit Brigade tried their best to keep the Luftwaffe at bay, but to no avail.

The first six days of combat were brutally intense. The Polish fighter pilots who flew obsolete aircraft were outnumbered, outgunned and overwhelmed. The Luftwaffe at this time was the most powerful air force in the world. Even though they experienced higher losses than they had expected, they were still unstoppable and were not seriously challenged. In these first few days the aviation arm of the Polish Army lost around 40 percent of its total strength.

On September 9th, while still in Kraczewice, Władek took off to pursue some German bombers that had just completed a raid in the Dęblin area and were heading back to Germany. He started chasing an He 111 bomber that at the same time was trying to "uncover" him so that the rear gunner could get him in his sights. S-Lt Gnyś had only seconds to maneuver his PZL P.11c out of the line of fire, take aim and shoot. As he sprayed the rear of the Heinkel with his four machine guns, the gunner became quiet. However, Gnyś's plane was hit and damaged in the exchange. He was so angry that he flew right under the bomber's fuselage, took out his large service revolver and fired upward hoping to hit some vital spot, but it kept on flying towards Germany unimpeded.

This action of using his revolver was not officially reported to his C.O. because he was probably not proud of his rather reckless and unorthodox attempt in trying to bring down a German aircraft in this fashion, so he kept it to himself. It was only much later that he shared it with his family. It was an act of frustration fueled by adrenaline. He hated the fact that his beautiful country was being invaded and there was very little the Poles could do to prevent it. This was typical of the man as even later in the war he didn't report every incident if he didn't feel right about it. He was not egocentric or boastful.

Out of sheer frustration fueled by adrenalin, Władek flew dangerously close under the He 111 bomber and with his service revolver fired at its belly, hoping to hit a vulnerable spot.

Later on the 9th, S-Lt Gnyś and the remaining planes of the two squadrons were on the move again endeavoring to stay ahead of the fast-moving panzer columns and hard-pressing Luftwaffe. This time they readied themselves in Strzelce near the town of Hrubieszów in southeastern Poland.

From September 7th–17th, the Luftwaffe's main objective was to prevent the trapped Polish army from retreating eastward over the Vistula and to neutralize them. Warsaw was heavily shelled by German armor and massively attacked by the Luftwaffe, but resisted collapse for almost three more weeks. The Pursuit Brigade moved around in the Lublin area and other fighter units joined them. There was an extreme shortage of fuel, ground crew, supplies and the breakdown of communication with operational command. This condition also applied to other aviation units which resulted in uncoordinated sorties.

In addition, these constant changes of airfields in order to stay one step ahead of the enemy became a nightmare as the ground personnel and transport supply columns were unable to keep up with the moving squadrons. Without these supplies, including parts for damaged aircraft, their battle-worthiness was drastically reduced.

Meanwhile, orders were received to find the panzer spearheads on the western side of the Vistula River, west of Dęblin. Only one plane was required and Gnyś knew the area well. Sarnów was part of it, so he volunteered for the assignment. Flying low, he could clearly make out the long lines of evacuees. It reminded him of the evacuations he took part in as a child in 1915. He could see the destructive work of German bombers on the landscape with large bomb craters everywhere. Chimneys stood here and there amongst the smoldering rubble of once quaint and happy family homes. Villages and towns were reduced to dust. The smell of smoke from the charred remains rose into the air, assailing his nostrils as he looked down with horror at the devastation. The civilian death toll had to be huge. He started to weep, shaking uncontrollably in the cockpit. All he could think of now was revenge.

After regaining his composure, Władek continued with his mission objective. He reached the edge of Dęblin and crossed the Vistula. As he passed close to the old aerodrome, home of the officer school, he saw that almost every building had been destroyed. Passing Sarnów on the right side he flew over the pasture between the two rivers and the woods where as a boy he had ridden beautiful Kasztanka.

About 50 miles west of the Vistula he noticed German units moving east. He made a mental note of the size and location of the advancing forces. Farther west, he flew over more large woods and was shocked as he almost flew right over a panzer division. It appears that they were equally surprised to see him. The Germans started shooting at him. Władek zigzagged and made a speedy exit back over the large woods.

He thought, "I will get you!"

He turned his PZL aircraft around so that he would come at them from behind, avoiding a frontal confrontation. Staying low, just above the trees, Gnyś pounced on the column. Starting at the end of the panzer line and with all his machine guns blazing, he ripped a deadly path following the curvature of the road. Soldiers on foot and in troop carriers collapsed like falling leaves. Combat vehicles exploded as he rained fire upon them. Not pushing his luck, as he was now starting to take reciprocal fire, he pulled away sharply leaving many dead and wounded German invaders behind.

His mission now over, it was time to turn back. On the way he decided to see Sarnów just once more from the air. On his approach, flying low over the mill, he recognized his Uncle Toni, his wife and three children as they ran out of the mill. They knew it had to be Władek! He turned, circled around, and threw out a weighted oil cloth "envelope"—inside were his letters to them. With a big smile and a wave, he set course for the base. He asked God to keep them safe from the Nazi invaders and allow him to see them again one day.

On September 12th, S-Lt Gnyś and squadrons 121 with 122 were ordered to join the Pursuit Brigade as their numbers were depleted and needed reinforcement. On the 13th, they moved to Werba near Włodzimierz Wołyński and two hours later to Petikowice near Buczacz, all in southeastern Poland. At that time, aircraft from other fighter units

were detached from the III/2 Fighter Wing. They patrolled Rawa-Ruska, Sokal, Lwów and Czortków—again, centers in the southeast.

September 14th saw the destruction of over a dozen of the Bomber Brigade's Karaś aircraft on an active Polish airfield. Orders were received for the balance of the Brigade to cross into neutral Romania to the southeast, but they delayed actioning the command to carry out more combat sorties against the enemy. But defeat was only a matter of time now. Poland would still have to bleed some more … alone.

Early in the morning on the 17th, the Red Army crossed Poland's eastern border supported by several thousand Soviet aircraft. As coincidence would have it, Gnyś was performing a reconnaissance flight over Czortków when he spotted a tremendous number of aircraft flying from east to west and recognized them as Russian.

"Are they coming to help us or fight us?" he wondered.

Little did anyone know about the secret German-Soviet Non-Aggression Pact that had been signed just prior to the invasion. The Russians were there to claim the spoils

While stationed at nearby Dęblin Training Center, Władek would occasionally fly over the Sarnów mill and drop a pouch containing his letters to the delight of his uncle, aunt and family. From left: Aunt Franciszka (Frania), older son Czesław, Uncle Toni (with fork), other son Władysław (Władzio) and daughter Genowefa (Gienia).

of war, disregarding previous "friendly" ties with the Polish government. Now Poland stood no chance.

The main thrust of the Soviet invasion was focused on the very south of the country to block the retreating Polish military from crossing into King Carol's neutral Romania. Later, he would be coerced into joining Hitler's side.

Official evacuation of all usable aircraft commenced on the evening of the 17th. Władek and III/2 DM along with other Polish fighter units were part of the painful exodus. However, while in flight, he almost collapsed in the cockpit due to extreme stomach pain that had started several days prior. Due to the lack of clean water and properly prepared food, Władek had developed a severe case of dysentery. He was too ill to fly into Romania with the others: he would have to go by land, but could not do it alone.

CHAPTER 4

On the Run: Romania to the French Air Force

Władek was given an army car and driver. He lay on the back seat, angry at his weakened condition. After several hours of driving on a bumpy road, he felt the car come to a screeching stop. He then heard the deafening sound of explosions.

Jan the driver (51) turned his head: "Sir, someone is shooting at us."

Władek pulled himself up and looked out the front windscreen. The shelling was coming from Russian tanks on the road up ahead.

"We'd better get out of here now!" Jan yelled.

Extreme urgency did not allow him to turn around on the narrow country road. Without hesitation, Jan Kociołek threw the car into reverse and at full speed drove backwards in a cloud of dust for almost a mile until he found a roadway onto which he could turn around. Fortunately, the Russian tanks were not in sight, but both knew they were somewhere close.

The intestinal infection had really knocked the life out of Władek. He lay utterly helpless in the back seat. Jan was wonderful as he carried him to a nearby river and washed him like a child and found clean dry clothes for him from a local farmer. They drove all night and early in the morning on the 18th they arrived at the Polish border town of Kuty situated on the Czeremosz River.

However, the town was congested with cars, trucks and horse-drawn carts winding their way down towards the river crossing. Thousands of fleeing Polish soldiers, airmen, government officials, diplomats, wealthy Poles and civilian refugees crossed the two-lane bridge escaping from their beloved country that was rapidly collapsing behind them. Overhead, low-flying Polish aircraft made their way across the river on their way to internment at the Romanian airfield at Cernauti. That afternoon the Polish government held its last meeting on Polish soil and that evening, the president, his officials and army commander entered Romania, the prelude to forming a government in exile.

September 17th, 1939. Delirious in the back seat, Władek could not believe that they were being shot at by Soviet tanks. No time to turn around, the driver threw the car in reverse and floored it until he found a safe place to turn. The Red Army was on their tail all the way to Kuty.

Prior to crossing however, all military personnel were ordered to dispose of their weapons, uniforms and anything that would identify them as Polish servicemen. Rather than surrendering their rifles and pistols to the Romanians, the retreating soldiers flung them off the bridge: thousands of weapons eventually choked up the shallow river.

Władek had his American Colt .22 calibre revolver and ceremonial dagger (*kord*) with him, awards received during the Fighter Training course. With a heavy heart, he bound them together and dropped them from the bridge into the Czeremosz River below. He and Jan entered Romania at 10 a.m. on September 18th; not a moment too soon: the Red Army was now in Kuty.

September 18th to 30th was the last phase of the campaign. The Luftwaffe and the Wehrmacht concentrated on eliminating pockets of resistance such as on the northern Hel Peninsula, the Bzura River west of Warsaw, the Modlin Fortress north of Warsaw and Warsaw itself. On the 25th for example, the Luftwaffe carried out probably the largest air assault of the war on the capital with non-stop bombardment. Almost half the city was

After the invasion of Poland on September 1st, 1939 by the superior German forces, it was not long before Poland's military infrastructure started to crumble. They were simply no match for the Luftwaffe and the Wehrmacht. Adding fuel to the fire and without formal warning, the Soviet Union invaded Poland from the east early on September 17th. Seeing that the end was in sight, the Polish military was ordered to evacuate. The bulk of the evacuees made their way to southern Poland to the small town of Kuty and crossed into neutral Romania

using the bridge over the River Czeremosz. During the 17th and 18th, thousands of Polish troops, pilots (some in planes), government officials and civilians left Poland. Władek and his driver crossed on the 18th with the Red Army closing in. Not wanting to surrender their weapons to the Romanians, soldiers flung them into the shallow river, choking it. With regret, he threw his prized pistol and sword into the water. Next stop was the Black Sea and France.

either reduced to rubble or damaged beyond repair. All basic needs such as electricity and water were no longer available. Warsaw was on fire. The defenders were tough and they fought with incredible courage, but to no avail. Warsaw surrendered on the 28th.

October 6th marked the end of the Polish campaign with the surrender of troops after the Battle of Kock near the town of Kock in eastern Poland. This was the final battle and a sad day for Poland. At this point in the war, total Nazi losses amounted to over 16,000 killed, Polish losses were over 70,000 killed with almost 600,000 taken prisoner.[1]

If England and France had acted quickly in early September against Germany as promised, Hitler could have been defeated, but they did nothing. Alone, Polish troops, sailors and airmen stood up to the aggressors and bled for freedom. Their heroic action lasted 35 days. Poland lost the battle, but did not surrender. Władek said, "Although the war was lost in Poland, the fight went on."

In Paris, towards the end of September, 1939, Władysław Raczkiewicz became the new Polish president and was sworn into office on September 30th. The first two things he did were to formally dissolve the pre-war government and to appoint General Władysław Sikorski to the position of Prime Minister and Minister of Military Affairs. In early October, General Sikorski formed the Polish government-in-exile which consisted of prominent (liberal) politicians from all Polish parties. Political stability had now been established even though it wasn't on Polish soil. On November 7th, President Raczkiewicz empowered Sikorski once more, but this time to the lofty position of Commander-in-Chief of the Polish Armed Forces.

Thanks to General Sikorski and the Polish government-in-exile, underground networks with assembly/transit points were set up throughout Europe to assist the escaping military to get to points west … to England, but mainly to France. These men were not just refugees, but men on a mission determined to make another stand against tyranny. S-Lt W. Gnyś summed up their courageous first efforts when he said, "My friends, fighter pilots, bomber pilots and our army fought shoulder to shoulder despite the odds. I pay the highest respect to all of them for their total sacrifice in their fight for freedom."

Mass evacuation of military personnel created major headaches for the Polish leaders and put a strain on Poland's transitional treasury. Romania particularly was a major transshipment point for the PAF. Providing safe shelter, transportation, food, civilian clothing, for example, required huge amounts of money. Bribing certain officials along the way was also a necessity. Private vehicles, aircraft and personal effects had to be sold to help supplement the evacuation fund. Bucharest was the main destination for the fliers.

Themselves now threatened, England and France finally got serious and realized that extra manpower could be very useful against Hitler. Thus, they ordered their embassies in Bucharest to help with the secret evacuation of Polish military personnel, with priority given to pilots and air crew.

Each was given money, a forged passport with a new identity and new profession such as clergyman or monk or any other "creative" calling. Władek became a student. They were told to stay low and travel in small groups.

Other escape avenues to the west were through Hungary, Lithuania, Latvia, Sweden, the Netherlands, Lebanon, Egypt, Italy, and even from Soviet ports and Germany itself. These risky journeys could last up to months.

So, for the next five days, September 18th–22nd, with Jan at the wheel and Gnyś laying flat out on the back seat, they journeyed southward through the Romanian centers of Suceava, Roman, Focşani to Tulcea. They were like many thousands of other military escapees heading for Bucharest then to the Black Sea ports of Constanţa and Balchik to board hired ships that would take them to France where they hoped they would soon be fighting the Germans again and liberating their homeland. Greek ships like the SS *Patris* and the SS *St. Nicholas* along with many other vessels from other nations took part in this massive exodus. On board, conditions were usually poor due to overcrowding.

Jan and Władek stayed in Tulcea for a total of 13 days, September 23rd–October 5th. However, by the beginning of October, Romanian authorities began moving Polish airmen from their initial gathering points around Tulcea to internment camps in Babadag (located on a small marshy lake) near the coast. Because their car had military markings that Jan had been unable to erase completely, they were escorted by Romanian soldiers

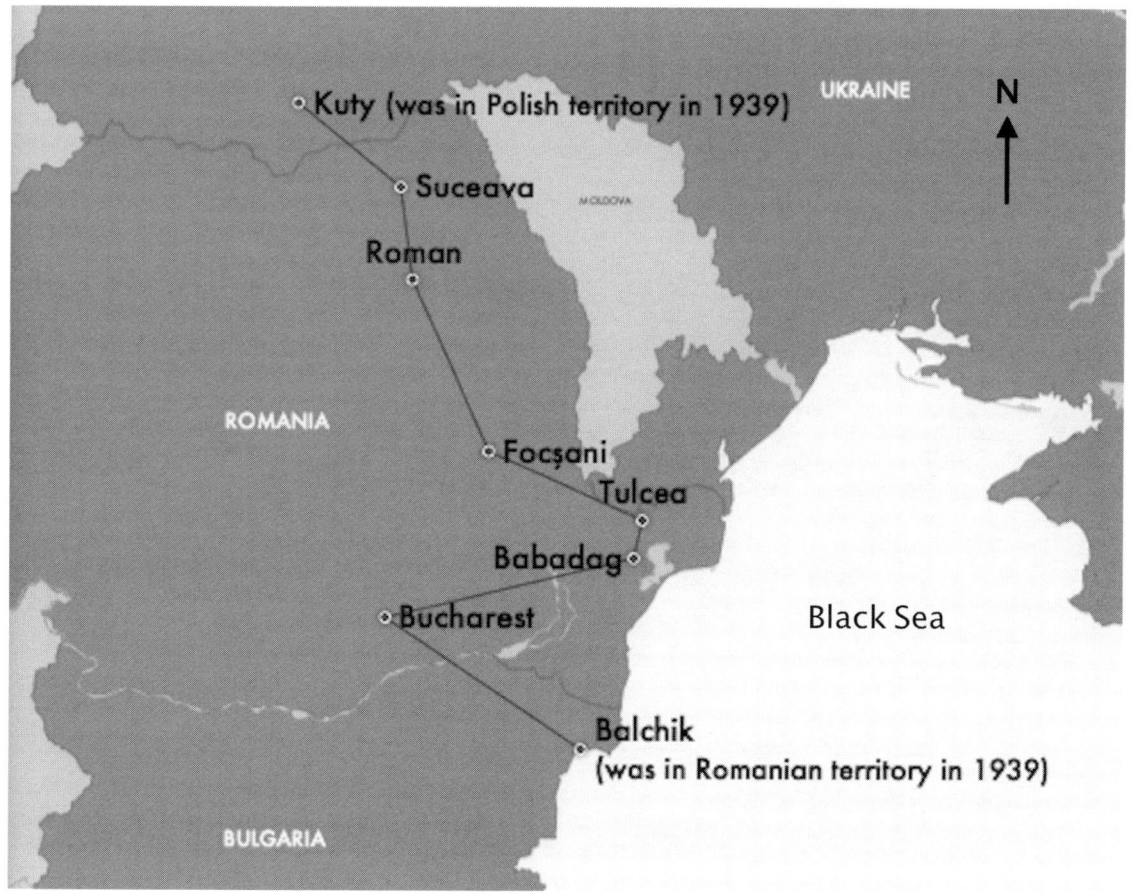

Władek's journey to the Black Sea, September 18th–November 5th, 1939.

to Babadag where their Polish military vehicle was confiscated. The air buzzed with malaria-carrying mosquitoes. Władek was now on the mend and was the last person who needed to come down with another illness: Jan knew they had to escape.

During the night, as Władek slept, Jan slipped out of the barrack to siphon gasoline from the other confiscated vehicles to fill their car's tank plus extra containers for later.

"Sir, wake up, we have to leave now," he whispered.

Silently they made their way to the car and crawled inside. The plan was to drive quickly out of the holding yard but Władek asked about the guards.

Jan replied, "It's alright, they're asleep."

Without switching on the headlights, they drove at full speed and crashed through the barrier where a sleeping sentry was on duty. He leaped up with great surprise and fumbled for his rifle. By the time he got it up to his shoulder to shoot, the car was well out of sight, it had vanished into the darkness.

Jan drove almost non-stop until they reached Bucharest where they stayed for several days (October 6th–8th). Thanks to generous Romanians along the way who provided them with lodging and food such as homemade bread or hot soup, Władek was now feeling his old self again.

Jan floors the car past the sleeping guard and crashes out of the internment compound at Babadag, Romania.

Positively speaking, almost all those military personnel who were interned in transit camps in Hungary and Romania escaped between the autumn of 1939 and the summer months of 1940. Often, guards were bribed to look the other way as detainees escaped. Under extreme pressure from Hitler, Romanian and Hungarian government leaders espoused anti-Polish sentiments while the people fortunately remained mainly supportive and assisted the refugees in escaping. Camp conditions were very poor to say the least and medical supplies were meager. Quinine for example was in short supply and those in the camps in the Danube basin around Tulcea such as Babadag came down with malaria. It was a good thing that Jan and Władek escaped when they did.

His work done, Jan explained that he must return to Poland to find his wife and children. Władek sold the car and gave him the money to help with his dangerous trip back into Nazi-held Poland.

He embraced Władek warmly, "God bless you sir, I'm sure you will be alright now and good luck."

"I will be forever grateful for what you have done, my friend. I will never forget you," Władek replied as a tear ran down his cheek. It was an emotional moment and then Jan departed. They would never see each other again. Władek owed his life to this brave and selfless man: Jan Kociołek.

Władek and many other airmen arrived in the Romanian port city of Balchik on the Black Sea. Here he stayed for 28 days, October 9th–November 5th, waiting for not one, but, as it turned out, two ships to rendezvous and commence embarkation. In civilian clothes, they were all told to "disappear" until the vessels arrived. Many stayed in private homes opened up to them by local Romanians.

Unfortunately, within a few days, Władek and a fellow flier were arrested and interrogated by the Romanian police. They remembered the orders not to say anything self-incriminating. Władek had a bad scar on his hand from a farming accident so he quickly gave the impression he was not a person fit for military service. He distorted his hand by holding it in a twisted position and told the police he was a student at the Polytechnic. They looked at the "crippled" hand and believed his story. His friend said that he had rectal problems and much to the disgust of the police, he dropped his pants, bent over and opened his buttocks to reveal bleeding hemorrhoids. The shocked look on their faces was priceless as they quickly made for the door. As mentioned, even though Romania was neutral, Hitler was putting tremendous pressure on Romanian leadership not to be sympathetic to Polish evacuees and to detain any military personnel, especially pilots. He did not want able-bodied Polish pilots to fight another battle against his Luftwaffe.

The port town of Balchik is nicely nestled in a sheltered harbor on the Black Sea and is extremely picturesque. It is built on hilly terraces that descend to the sea. During Romania's administration, before 1940, the Balchik Palace was the favorite summer residence of Queen Marie of Romania and her immediate family. Today, it is one of Bulgaria's famous resort cities.

During the day, Władek hid out on a secluded recess of rock partway down a terrace with an amazing view of the Black Sea. As he lay watching the waves, he thought about Kasztanka and Asik and how they loved to splash in the river.

During the inter-war period, Balchik had been a popular spot for Romanian avant-garde painters who came to paint and study at the Balchik School of Painting. Władek noticed a girl who came daily to paint the scenery and that she had noticed him. He had the feeling that she suspected he was a Pole on the run and would somehow be sympathetic with his plight.

One morning she approached him, smiled and asked if she could sit down. He smiled back and nodded. She said that she was a landscape artist and asked his permission to paint him lying there. He agreed and they met daily as she continued her work. Constanta was 21; he was eight years her senior.

She would pack a basket of fruit, cheese, sausage and bread and the occasional bottle of wine to enjoy during the time they were together. There was no question that in a relatively short time, they developed a deep fondness for each other. They made a very handsome couple and when she wasn't painting, they would stroll hand in hand down

Constanta worked on a portrait of Władek overlooking the Black Sea as he waited for his ship to France.

During the winters between 1934 and 1938 Władek (fifth from right in top photo) and fellow pilots enjoyed skiing in the beautiful Tatra mountains of southern Poland. Skiing was not only for pleasure, but was part of their military training as well.

Graduating class of 1934, Grudziądz: Aviation School for Gunnery and Bombing. The proud young man from Sarnów (second from right) is now a qualified fighter pilot.

The Bronze Cross of Merit (Brązowy Krzyż Zasługi) was awarded to W. Gnyś on June 18th, 1935 for landing his aircraft on one wheel after the mid-air crash with S-Lt Durko. If he had jumped from his PZL as instructed, it would have been destroyed. *(Gnyś coll.)*

A gifted PAF pilot, S-Lt Dionizy Durko was killed in a mid-air crash with Gnyś on May 11th, 1935, a tragic and senseless loss. *(P. Sikora)*

Mjr Leopold Pamuła (center) was the respected squadron leader of "Pamuła's Fighter Squadron," a tight-knit group of 19 pilots. On either side of Pamuła are his flight commanders Makowski (left) and Orzechowski (right). Sixth from right is Kazimierz (Kazek) Bursztyn; seventh from left is Toni Beda; Władek is fourth from right. The PZL.7 was their aircraft of choice.

Greater Poland School of Infantry, Bydgoszcz, November 1936. Władek was here from October 1st, 1936 to August 15th, 1938.

Władek stands at attention next to one of the two field gun emplacements and the statue of Józef Piłsudski in front of the School of Infantry, Bydgoszcz. From here he returned to Dęblin on August 16th, 1938 to the Officer Cadet Pilot School, where he became an instructor and eventually an officer.

Top left: Bydgoszcz: Second year of Officer Cadet school, 1937. Having a day out with friends, Władek reminisces with Stasio "Staszek" Przywara (right) and Ryżko (center).

Left: Franciszek Kornicki was posted to 162 Squadron just before war. He flew for France then Britain where he served with Nos 303 and 315. At 26 he became C.O. of No. 308, the youngest C.O. in the PAF, then C.O. of 317 Polish Fighter Squadron. *(P. Sikora)*

Below: 12th Intake Group, Officer School, Dęblin, 1939 just before war. In order to be posted to fighter units, training was cut short so there was no graduation. Center is Brigade General (generał brigade) Ludomił Rayski C.O. PAF. Gnyś is third from left. *(P. Sikora)*

Gnyś's aircraft No. 5 was a PZL P.11c with four machine guns. The emblem of 121 Eskadra on the fuselage is an arrow and wing. Checkerboards with Polish colors are evident on the tail and on both wings. It has an open cockpit with a fixed undercarriage. This image of the first (Allied) kills by Gnyś was painted by Roy Grinnell ASAA. *(R. Grinnell)*

Rakowice airbase at Kraków—home to III/2 Fighter Wing of the Kraków Army Air Arm—was first bombed by Heinkel 111s, then by Stuka Ju 87s and finally by Dornier 17s, "the flying pencils." Collectively they were far superior in every respect to Polish aircraft.

Luftwaffe pilot Frank Neubert who shot down Cpt Medwecki on September 1st, 1939 over Balice, Poland, flew a Junkers (Stuka) Ju 87B T6+GH. It was the first aerial victory of World War II. (*F. Neubert*)

At the age of 35, Mieczysław Adolf Medwecki (1904–39) was the first pilot to die in World War II, on September 1st, 1939. (His middle name was commonly used before the war.) In 1938 he was promoted captain and C.O. of III/2 Dywizjon Mysliwski (Fighter Wing), the youngest commander in Poland. Prior to this, Mieczysław had crashed twice causing severe damage to his body. But flying was his passion and he came back stronger each time. Right to the end he displayed his incredible leadership. The first to fight and the first to die, he was loved by all who knew him.

The rear fuselage of the second Dornier from KG 77 brought down by Władek shortly after Medwecki was killed. It crashed into a farmyard where locals witnessed the event. *(J. B. Cynk)*

PZL.37 Łoś bombers with their pilots and aircrew, 1939. This Polish aircraft was a twin-engine medium bomber built in Warsaw.

Many escaping Polish airmen in civilian clothing walked the streets of Bucharest in the fall of 1939. Hiding out and obtaining phoney passports were their initial objectives.

the terraces to the sea and watch the waves lap against the shore. It had been a long time since Władek had been with a woman. She took his mind off the war. Sometimes in the evening under the setting sun, they would lie together on the warm grass. They both knew that their time together would soon be over which made them both very sad.

One day three men in uniform came walking along the cliff towards them. Dismantling her easel and closing her paint box, she handed them to Władek. "Don't speak," she whispered, "just let me do the talking." She stood up. "Follow me and act casual."

In a nonchalant manner they walked directly toward the oncoming trio. Two of them, Romanian policemen, obviously knew her and greeted her amiably. The third man was a Gestapo agent. Quite composed she told them that Władek was her cousin visiting from the south. They smiled, nodded their heads and continued on their way, totally taken in by her straightforward approach. It was a close call. Władek knew that his days in Romania were numbered.

Then, around October 22nd, a ship arrived. There was great excitement among the escapees who had been anxiously waiting for many weeks. Władek was jubilant, but then remembered Constanta, who was standing beside him, also looking at the huge vessel as it dropped anchor about 1,000 feet offshore.

She had mixed emotions about him leaving, but realized he had to go. Even though they had only known each other for a very short time, she loved him very much and would miss him a great deal. He felt the same about her. Without looking back, he left her side and made his way down to the water's edge.

The shore teemed with Polish servicemen waiting in long lines to embark. Together with two others, Władek decided to ignore the queue and swim for the ship. About half way, he was in trouble. A combination of choppy waves, the soaked clothing bundled behind his head and lack of strength due to the prolonged dysentery … he began to go under. To make matters worse, the ship, already overloaded with men, was pulling out. The two friends quickly untied the bundle and supported him on both sides. They turned and swam back and finally reached the shore, exhausted and gasping on the beach.

Constanta, now almost hysterical, had been helplessly watching from a lower terrace. As soon as she realized that they had turned around to come back to shore, she ran down to the beach to help anyway she could. "Władek, Władek, are you alright?" she cried.

After catching their breath, the two kind friends took him back to Constanta's place not far away. It wasn't long until she had heated them up some homemade soup which she served with slices of thick bread. Grateful for her hospitality, the two left Władek and Constanta alone. He slept well that night. Disappointed that he did not make this departure, he knew that another vessel would be back in about two weeks to pick up more evacuees. In one way, it was a blessing: he and Constanta would be together again.

During the next two weeks, Władek noticed the presence of more Nazi agents in town snooping around and pressuring local leaders to block the evacuation.

Finally, another ship arrived (possibly the SS *Patris*) and dropped anchor. It prepared to set sail on November 5th for Malta then Marseilles. Władek and Constanta spent their last night together trying not to talk about the future. The next morning they said their tearful goodbyes.

This time, Władek did not try to swim for it: he had learned his lesson. Instead, he lined up with the others to board ship. Like the previous one, it filled up to overcapacity. At last, they steamed out of the harbor. It was November 6th, 1939.

The eventual destination for the Polish pilots was the airbase at Lyon-Bron in France. The voyage started out from Balchik on the Black Sea, through the Bosphorus Strait passing Istanbul, into the Sea of Marmara, through the Dardanelles Strait past Çanakkale to the Aegean Sea, into the Mediterranean Sea and then docking at Malta before sailing to Marseilles, France.

Unfortunately, it wasn't always plain sailing. The ship was critically overloaded. A storm in the Aegean would have capsized her if it wasn't for two Poles who had tied

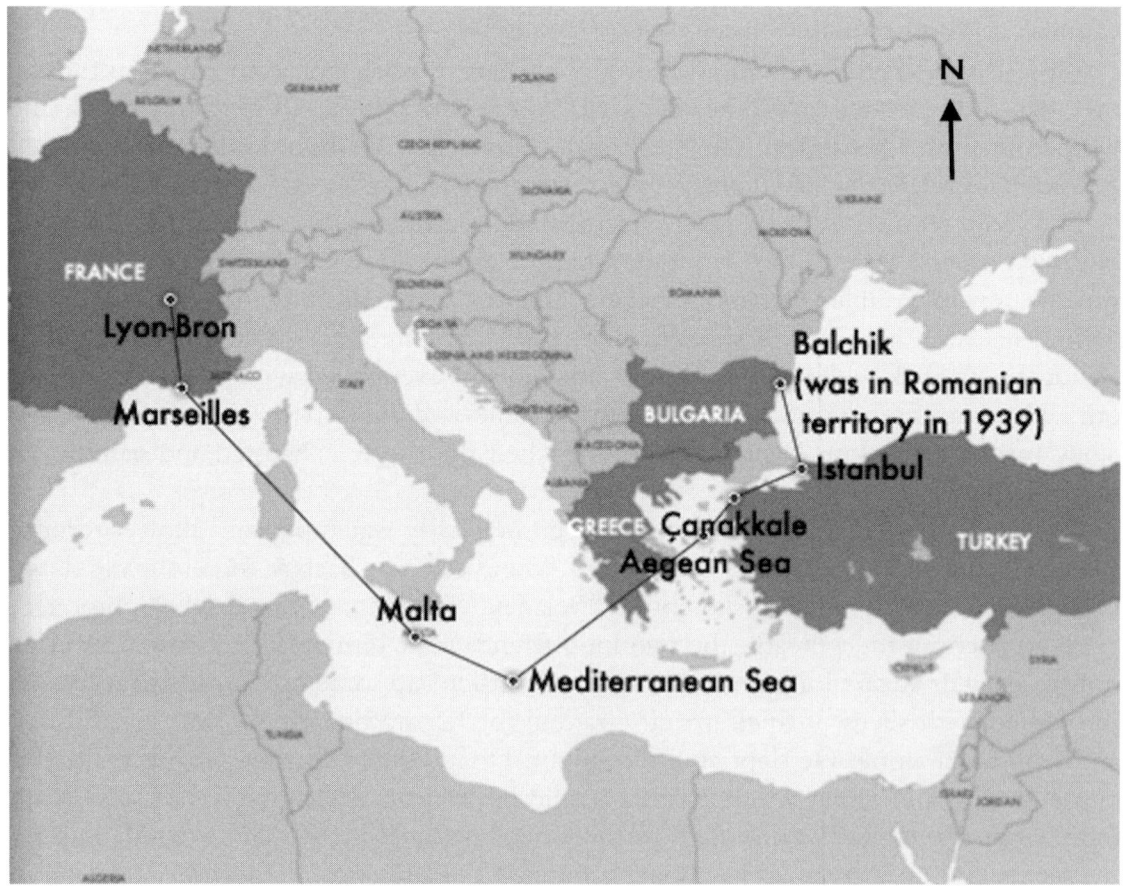

Władek's escape from Balchik to Lyon-Bron, November 6th–20th, 1939.

themselves to the center mast directing the passengers using loud-speakers to move from side to side. This back-and-forth listing lasted 16 exhausting hours.

The island of Malta was a beautiful stopover and a sight for sore eyes. It was a pleasure to stand on firm ground again, even for just a day. In Malta they had their first decent meal in weeks. On November 19th, they sailed for Marseilles, the main gathering point for Poles in France. Here, they rested for several days before heading to Lyon-Bron. Hospitable locals provided for their needs.

Despite the devastating defeat and human losses at the hands of the Nazis, more than 80 percent of Polish airmen and crew escaped from the country. In addition, tens of thousands of Polish soldiers and sailors also managed to evade capture. Once the dust settled in May, 1940, over 10,500 men were under PAF command, approximately 20 percent of these in Great Britain, but the majority in France.

The first major topic on the agenda in late October 1939 in Paris, between the Polish, French and British was the future of the Polish Air Force. This was not a simple matter as everyone had their own ideas. General Sikorski, for example, wanted the rebuilding of the PAF to take place solely in Britain. The French and British however wanted to split the Polish fliers between their two nations and run concurrent training programs, thinking that this would speed things up making the pilots operational and war-ready. Overall, it was difficult to agree on what to do with so many PAF personnel.

The end of October 1939 saw the arrival of the first shiploads of Polish pilots and crew to France. They were posted to such places as Salon and Le Bourget. There were many other locations within France that received them, but the largest was at Bron airfield near Lyon, north of Marseilles. Gnyś landed at Marseilles on November 19th and proceeded to Lyon-Bron on the 20th.

For the majority, the living conditions in Lyon-Bron were bleak to say the least. The facilities lacked beds, blankets and adequate heat in the winter. Clothing was scarce and food was rationed. This greatly affected morale. Officers had it better with some living in hotels and others billeted in private homes.

Finally, on December 29th, progress was achieved: it was decided that the Polish pilots would learn on French aircraft. The first batch would start their training at the Centre d'Instruction d'Aviation de Chasse (French Fighter School) in Montpellier, commencing January, 1940. The training would take place over four months.

Meanwhile, back in November 1939, Władek along with two other officers was fortunate enough to be billeted in a large, private and comfortable French home in Lyon-Bron. By contrast, lower ranking pilots, as mentioned, had miserable accommodation. The home was owned by 37-year-old Madam Nevette and her 16-year-old daughter Sonja. The mother was a class act who would have given French movie stars a run for their money and Sonja was a spitting image of her mother, just a younger version. The husband/father was not around for reasons unknown.

All five of them got along very well despite the language and cultural differences. Since the house had numerous bedrooms, they all managed to adjust to the new living arrangements quite quickly. In return for decent rent, the women provided the airmen with fresh bedding, towels and home-cooked meals. Communication became easier because the Poles were eager to learn French and the two hostesses were eager to teach them.

It did not take long for Władek and Madame Nevette to get acquainted. He was lucky as she was attracted more to him than the other officers. One thing led to another and before he knew it, she came into his room one night—unannounced. He was a little startled, but not too surprised. It was a memorable dalliance. She then left as quietly as she arrived. As he lay there, his mind drifted back to Romania. It wasn't that long ago that he was with the lovely Constanta in the picturesque Black Sea port of Balchik waiting for a ship to take him to Marseilles. Little did he know then what was waiting for him in France.

Meanwhile, their relationship went on undisturbed and undiscovered for about a month until one day Władek got a knock on his door: it was Sonja. Apparently, her mother told her in confidence about their relationship. Władek was quite embarrassed when Sonja said, "My mother loves you too much … I want to love you also."

His mouth dropped, and he replied in broken French, "But you are only sixteen and I am twenty-nine."

Over the next few days Sonja became increasingly persistent, but each time he turned her down. But then, in his own words and with a smile on his face he said, "I finally gave in." It was, after all, a time of war.

Then on January 1st, 1940, he departed Lyon-Bron to begin training with the French in Montpellier in southern France.

Over the next few months, Władek would see Sonja and her mother for brief periods due to training commitments and of course, later, defending France during the German invasion. The women missed him, especially young Sonja who fell deeply in love with this older, debonair Polish pilot.

When France fell in late June, Gnyś with other airmen had to escape France and make their way to England. He was most upset having to leave them behind, but had no choice.

Later, in July, he received a letter via Rome from Sonja in which she wrote, "I love you and I will wait for you to return no matter how long it takes." Władek knew that he had to bring closure to this relationship. For one thing, there was a war going on, and the second was that he met his future wife. Thanks to a friend who spoke fluent French, he dictated a most painful letter explaining why he could not return. The last line read, "I will always keep you in my heart and may God keep you and your mother safe." And so it ended. Władek admitted many years later that he always thought about them fondly and whether they survived the war. In fact, after all those years, he could still remember their address.

★

As far as an official military agreement between France and Poland for the reconstruction of the Polish Armed Forces in France was concerned, one was signed January 4th, 1940. Particular focus was on the air force. Parties to the signing included French Prime Minister Daladier and General Sikorski. The agreement provided details regarding the status and well-being of the fliers, their sovereignty and allegiance; they would be treated like French pilots, and were totally dependent upon the French for supplies/equipment and came under French command.

As a result, General Sikorski came to the fliers' rescue at Lyon-Bron in late January, 1940. After a thorough inspection of the unacceptable living conditions of the airmen, he not only made life pleasant for them, but made sure that they got paid according to their rank and on par with the French pilots. Here was an example of the Franco-Polish Military Agreement being realized. Sikorski was a hit and so was the news that air training, at long last, was in progress.

On February 17th another agreement was endorsed which provided for the establishment of two Polish fighter squadrons, one or two army cooperation flights and several reserve units. It also stipulated that some Polish pilots were to train with the French at Bron. In May, a Polish amendment with regard to the above numbers of its air force units in France, called for six fighter, four reconnaissance and two bomber squadrons. According to Władek's official records he would not be back again to Lyon-Bron until March 25th at the Aviation Training Center.

As alluded to, it was decided on December 29th that the first batch of Polish pilots would start training at the French Fighter School in Montpellier in early January, 1940. They would do conversion training on French aircraft, particularly the Morane-Saulnier (MS 406) fighter over a maximum period of four months. Senior Polish airmen said two months would be more than enough for their already experienced pilots. Future training of similar groups was also tabled.

Col Pawlikowski (C.O. of Aviation Training Center and former commander of the Pursuit Brigade) was informed of the decision and asked to select the first group of 19 pilots to go to Montpellier. The selection from so many eager Poles was not easy. He said the whole group should be made up of pilots from the same wing with the balance forming a second squadron to be trained—plus ground personnel—simultaneously at the Lyon Training Center.

Two contenders were 1st Warsaw Fighter Wing under S-Col Leopold Pamuła (Władek's squadron leader, Toruń, 1935) whose pilots were from the Pursuit Brigade, and the 2nd Poznań Fighter Wing under Mjr Mieczysław Mümler whose pilots were from the former 3rd (Poznań) and 2nd (Kraków) air regiments. Władek was with the

Kraków Regiment. Mümler's wing was chosen because in September's defeat his unit had the most success.

Eventually the 19 pilots, who felt deeply honored to be among the first group of Polish pilots to undergo practical training, were chosen to form Mjr Mümler's "Montpellier Squadron." They were: captains Stefan Łaszkiewicz (in command), Mieczysław Wiórkiewicz, Mieczysław Sulerzycki and Jan Pentz; lieutenants Kazimierz Bursztyn, Stefan Zantara, Józef Brzeziński; sub-lieutenants Erwin Kawnik, Włodzimierz Karwowski, Bolesław Rychlicki, Stanisław Chałupa, Władysław Chciuk, Bohdan Anders, Władysław Gnyś and Wacław Król; NCOs Leopold Flanek, Antoni Beda and Eugeniusz Nowakiewicz. The Liaison and interpreter was Lt Jerzy de Jenko-Sokołowski, a Frenchman with Polish roots.[2]

Now that they were officially a cohesive group of pilots, it was time to trade in their rags for real uniforms. All men received very smart navy-blue French uniforms and caps, but with Polish markings of course. This alone was a boost to their morale because, until recently, they had been feeling depressed about their situation: boredom, poor accommodation for the NCOs and lack of respect by the French who unfairly implied that the Polish fliers were ineffective against the Luftwaffe.

On January 7th, 1940, they left Lyon airbase and headed for Montpellier in the south. The French training facility there was well organized and equipped to handle the new Polish "students." In-class studies were followed by flights in MS 230 trainer aircraft (high-wing monoplanes); the pilots hadn't flown for a while so this was good just to get them back into being in the air again. Training on the MS 406-C1 began on February 3rd. It was a modern monoplane fighter that the Poles had no problem mastering. After completing about 20 hours flying time each—in less than two weeks with no accidents—the French instructors were duly impressed and said that their work was done. The fliers shocked officials at Lyon on the 16th by showing up early. With no place to stay and nothing to do, they were given two weeks off to go skiing.

When Polish pilots in France eventually completed their training, they were generally assigned to different French units such as Groupe de Chasses, Les Patrouilles de Protection and Groupe de Chasse de Défense. The fliers were sent to join these French fighter units in an effort to learn their organization and strategy, and ultimately some 190 Polish fighter pilots were to take part in the looming battle for France.

In early March, the "Montpellier Squadron" as they were now called, took part in more intense training on their Morane fighters at the Bron base. The pilots were then divided up into six three-aircraft flights. Sadly, they never flew again together as a unit. In this case, the Montpellier Squadron was split up into six different Groupes de Chasses[3] (GC) with three Polish pilots attached to each.

One of the 19 pilots, Captain Mieczysław Wiórkiewicz took up residence at Lyon-Bron as an instructor and flight commander so the math worked out perfectly. The six French/Polish squadrons would be the first units to be sent to the front ready to meet the Luftwaffe as and when the invasion took place. On March 27th, 1940, the Polish pilots were allocated thus: GC III/2 (at Cambrai-Niergnies): assigned to this unit were

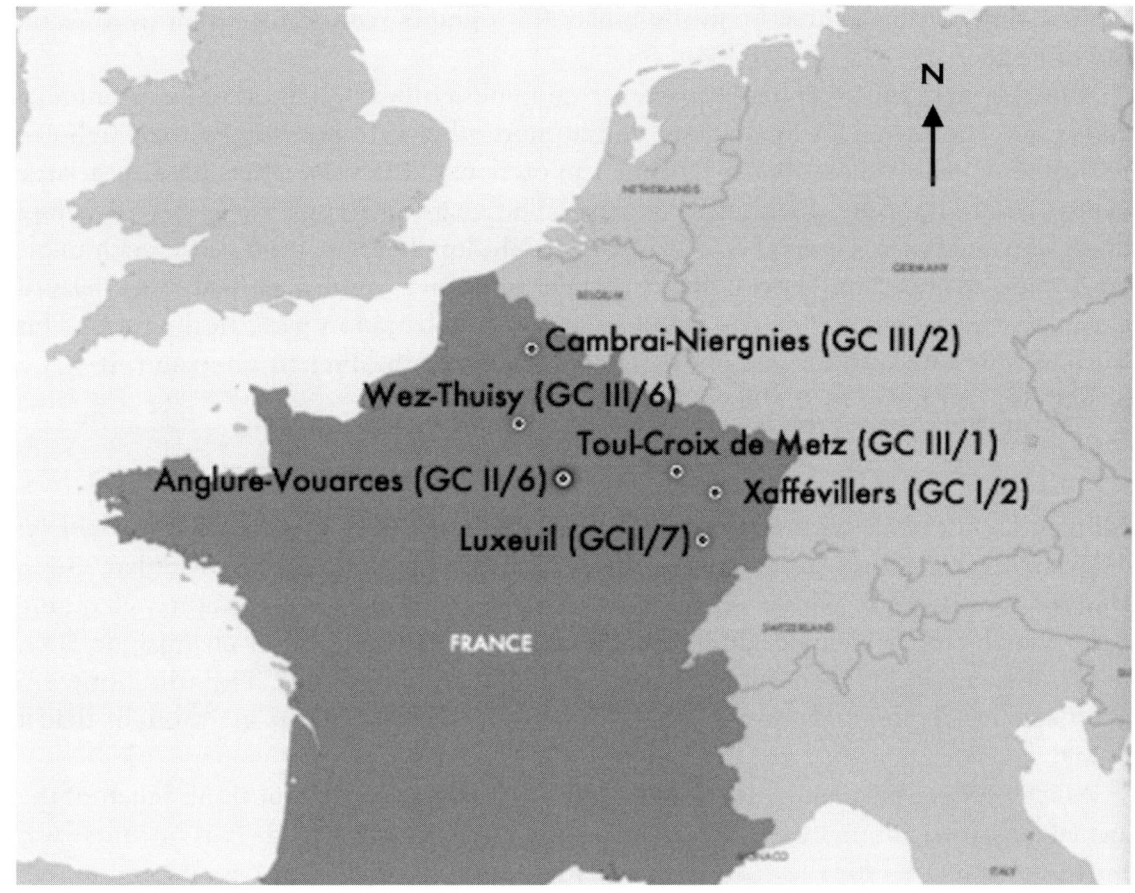

Airfields on the front line of defense.

(C.O.) Cpt Stefan Łaszkiewicz, Lt Stefan Zantara and Sgt Leopold Flanek; GC II/6 (at Anglure-Vouarces): assigned to this unit were (C.O.) Cpt Jan Pentz, S-Lt Bogdan Anders and S- Lt Włodzimierz Karwowski; GC III/6 (at Wez-Thuisy): assigned to this unit were (C.O.) Cpt Mieczysław Sulerzycki, S-Lt Erwin Kawnik and S-Lt Bolesław Rychlicki; GC III/1 (at Toul-Croix de Metz): assigned to this unit were (C.O.) Lt Kazimierz Bursztyn, S-Lt Władysław Gnyś and S-Lt Władysław Chciuk; GC I/2 (at Xaffévillers): assigned to this unit were (C.O.) Lt Józef Brzeziński, S-Lt Stanisław Chałupa, and Cpl Antoni Beda; and GC II/7 (at Luxeuil): assigned to this unit were (C.O.) Lt Władysław Goettel, S-Lt Wacław Król and Cpl Eugeniusz Nowakiewicz.

March 27th, 1940 and the weather couldn't have been worse. It was a cold, rainy wet day. However, the base was spotless, the aircraft were aligned, the band was ready and everyone's spirits were high. Supreme Polish leader General Władysław Sikorski had arrived. With other high-ranking Polish and French officials, it was a day of solidarity. It was the official opening of the Polish Training Centre and the ceremonial assignment of PAF personnel to French fighter units. The Montpellier Polish pilots were ready to help defend France. Each Groupe de Chasse section had its own team of 11–12 ground crew and had three brand-new MS 406 fighters with Polish identification on the fuselage.

After the meet and greet between French and Polish officials, there was the ceremonial flag raising and review of French and Polish pilots who were lined up by their fighters. French and Polish pilots then exchanged pilot wings. Mass was then held in a large hangar before the official handover of arms. The guard of honor was reviewed before the final parade march-past. The flypast by the Montpellier Squadron and French pilots who came to meet and escort them to their respective combat airfields was delayed because of the weather. The day culminated with a celebration party in the mess. This was probably one of the most photographed events of the French campaign. It was a proud moment for both the Poles and the French.

★

After the rendezvous with Groupe de Chasse III/1 at Toul-Croix de Metz airfield on March 29th, a situation arose between the French and Polish pilots. Once settled, Gnyś, Bursztyn and Chciuk with their eleven mechanics were made guests at a welcoming party which was held under a large enclosed tent. Many bottles of champagne later, the smartly dressed French pilots became very loud and boisterous. They did not seem at all concerned about the impending German invasion: in fact, many thought that it would never happen.

As the evening progressed, it became clear that the French did not think much of the armed resistance put up by the PAF fliers during the Battle of Poland. This of course was hurtful to the Poles for they had fought fearlessly with outdated planes and equipment and were vastly outnumbered. Many had sacrificed their lives in defense of their country.

Enough was enough: section leader Bursztyn turned to the French C.O., Commandant Paoli, and said, "Sir, I would like your permission to check out just how good your pilots really are tomorrow." His challenge was enthusiastically accepted.

The next morning, the entire squadron was assembled. Kazek Bursztyn went up against Gagnaire, one of the best French pilots for a mock dogfight. In this duel, the two aircraft approached each other head-on over the aerodrome within view of all spectators. The objective was to maneuver as quickly as possible and get on the opponent's tail, simulating a kill. Scoring was the best out of three.

Without the slightest trouble, Kazek managed to win both bouts. Next, Władek went up against Adj Bassaget, a French warrant officer and the outcome was 2:1 in Władek's favor. At this point, Chciuk who was paired up with S/Lt Jacques du Boucher won the match without trying as the French pilot at this point accepted defeat after seeing what had happened to his colleagues. This was the Poles' revenge for the French "sport" of the previous night. At the end of the day, bruised egos were massaged over numerous glasses of bubbly. Now good friends, they were able to concentrate their efforts on protecting France from the inevitable Nazi invasion.

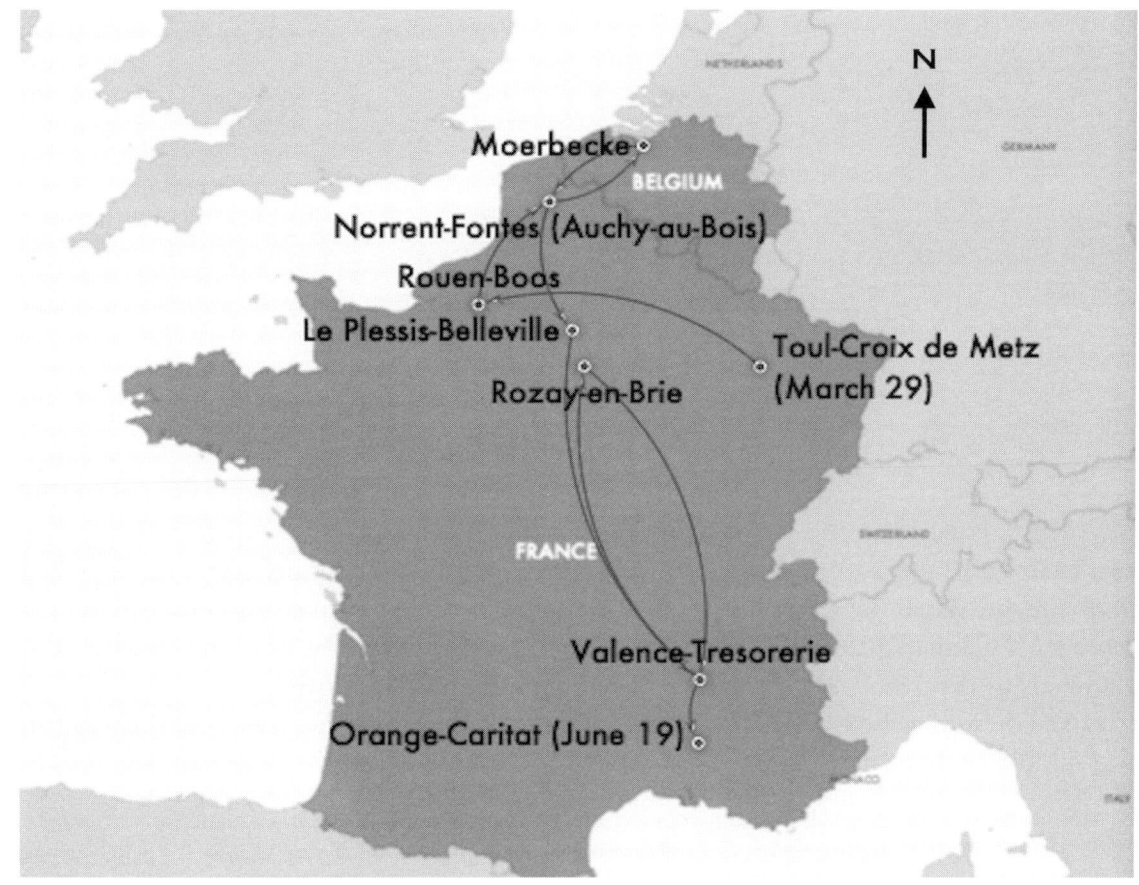

GCIII/1: From airfield to airfield, March 29th–June 19th, 1940.

At Toul-Croix de Metz during the first two weeks of April, there wasn't much to do except patrol the Luxembourg border area and provide escort protection for French reconnaissance aircraft (Potez 63s) that flew in and around the French–German border area. The Germans were also sending in their reconnaissance planes to photograph French airfields and military activity, but none was encountered by GC III/1. The squadron's flying formation was well established with the flight of three Polish fliers flying above the French squadron providing a protective umbrella. There was a language barrier, but many Poles picked up the French language quickly, especially when it came to basics in flying communication.

Interestingly, Władek's friend S-Lt Stanisław (Staszek) Chałupa was with Groupe de Chasse I/2 based at Xaffévillers airfield near Toul-Croix de Metz. By the end of the French campaign, Chałupa was a real contender in becoming one of the highest scoring pilots.

On April 16th, the unit flew to the Rouen-Boos airfield to protect the Rouen–Le Havre area just in case the Luftwaffe launched an attack. Then they moved again, on May 5th, to Auchy-au-Bois near Norrent Fontes on the Belgian border.

CHAPTER 5

The Battle of France

On May 10th, the explosive German blitzkrieg began. French airfields were attacked and damage was done not only to the aircraft, but to the runways themselves which were left pockmarked with large craters. Auchy-au-Bois was not immune and was also bombed on the 10th with a number of Moraine fighters destroyed.

S-Lt Gnyś described what it was like to be on the ground, defenseless and caught in the middle of a German bombing raid:

> I looked up and noticed a large formation of German aircraft coming in low and fast toward the airfield. I started to run across the field to my MS 406 fighter. Half-way across, I saw a German bomber coming directly towards me. I dropped to the ground, bombs bursting all around me. Machine gun bullets were breaking the earth inches from my body. I saw the earth spray up from their impact. The noise was deafening. I was literally shaken up and off the ground by the force of the explosions. A large bomb fell no more than 50 feet from me. Instinctively, I began to roll away from it. For some reason, the bomb did not explode. If it had, I would have been killed instantly. It was a miracle. Was God watching over me again?
>
> It is difficult to describe what it is like when you are being bombed on the ground. In the sky, you can do something … you have some kind of control in your aircraft … you can make a choice. But lying exposed and vulnerable on the ground, you are helpless. You feel like hiding behind a single blade of grass and just disappearing.
>
> I thought the raid would never end. I saw my own aircraft lifted bodily into the air and disintegrate. The devastation was tremendous, aircraft were burning, the wounded and dead lay all around … it was a nightmare.[1]

In 1998, Gnyś's friend and comrade in GC III/1 S-Lt Władysław Chciuk wrote to this author:

> Your father and I spent some time together and it is obvious to me that I benefitted from that more than he. He is a fine man and colleague. Although we did not know each other too well at first, I found in time that I could depend on him in the air, as well as on the ground. That was not the only good side of his though, but it was an important one during the war.

After the French Campaign our ways separated—we had been transferred to different units.

To answer your question: There were several outstanding and exceptional moments in his wartime adventures, so I will choose one of the many and that one is: his behavior, fast thinking and disregard for personal safety one day [June 3rd, 1940] during the strafing [and bombing] of our aerodrome [Le Plessis-Belleville airfield] in France by German bombers.

As it happened, the pilots had just finished their lunch when the Jerries surprised us. Everybody tried to avoid being a target, but not him. He ran to his aircraft and off he went after the enemy.

After a few seconds I tried the same, but could not start the engine in my aircraft, abandoned it, jumped into another one, started it and during the takeoff fell into a bomb crater—tried another— but then it was too late—the bombers were gone and I could only sit in my cockpit and look at the destruction they caused.

After the attack on Auchy-au-Bois on May 10th, the French fighter squadron, less a few Moraines, was able to pull itself together and be on the watch for the Luftwaffe in case they returned. On May 12th, the Polish section of three provided top cover as usual over the French in a patrol over Belgium. The squadron encountered an He 111 which they attacked.

Lt Bursztyn was the first to attack, but received a direct hit from the rear gunner. The engine of Bursztyn's Moraine fighter (no. 1031, L-621, numeral 'I') started to burn and smoke badly. He went down and crash-landed on a patch of Dutch terrain. It was then S-Lt Gnyś who attacked the bomber at close range. In a combat report he wrote: "I attacked a Heinkel and having killed the gunner and setting both engines on fire, we made him splash down on a river near Antwerp, Belgium."[2] Władek decided to continue the pursuit to make sure that the bomber was completely incapacitated. As he turned around and came in with guns blazing, he noticed a German crewman standing on the tip of the port wing waving not to shoot … but it was too late … the smoking engines had obstructed his view from above … he was cut down … it was war. The other crewmen who survived were captured and made PoWs.

Meanwhile, Lt Bursztyn's Morane which had crashed upon impact, was out of commission and so was he. Władek flew low over the landscape and watched for some sign of life. He then saw Kazek struggle from the cockpit and drag himself across the field—he had great difficulty walking. He looked up and waved at Władek to go back. Relieved, Gnyś returned the wave and headed back to Auchy-au-Bois which was no easy matter in itself as his machine was holed and damaged. He made it, but crash-landed, luckily unhurt.

Thanks to locals, Bursztyn was taken to a hospital in Ghent where he was treated for an injured knee. It would take almost two weeks before he rejoined his comrades Gnyś and Chciuk and the rest of the French squadron.

The victory was credited to the three Poles and eight Frenchmen.

During the move, their motor transport vehicles were attacked by a formation of He 111s. Without hesitation, Corporal Stefan Lisiak, an armorer, grabbed a heavy machine gun from one of the trucks, set it up on the roadside and shot down one of the Heinkels. He was decorated with the Croix de Guerre for his bravery and quick thinking.

Later that day on May 12th, GCIII/1 was instructed to move to Moerbecke airfield in Belgium. As it happened, due to the advancing Germans, they were ordered back to Auchy-au-Bois the next day.

During the move, their motor transport vehicles were attacked by a formation of He 111s. Without hesitation, Corporal Stefan Lisiak an armorer (weapons/armor expert) uncovered a heavy machine gun on one of the trucks, set it up on the roadside and shot down one of the Heinkels. Later, he was decorated with the French Croix de Guerre for his incredible bravery and quick action.

On May 13th, the squadron was back at Auchy-au-Bois, but continued to patrol Belgium. Since Lt Bursztyn was out of action, Lt Marche took the leadership position with S-Lts Chciuk and Gnyś flying on his flanks.

While carrying out a sweep over Brussels on May 16th, they came upon a formation of Dornier bombers—Do 17s. The pilots attacked the rear one and did damage to the engines, but S-Lt Chciuk was hit in a fuel tank by the gunner and his plane started to

After attacking a Do 17, S-Lt Chciuk got hit by the gunner and his plane started to burn and go down.

burn and go down. Unknown to anyone at the time, he glided in for a rough landing as his engine had stopped. After hitting some trees, he crash-landed at Braine-le-Comte southwest of Brussels. He was shaken, but unhurt. He counted over 20 bullet holes in his plane! It was a write-off.[3] Chciuk was lucky to be alive. At the time Gnyś did not see Chciuk crash and therefore was not aware if his friend was dead or alive. Right after this Lt Marche twice came under attack in the pursuit and was forced to drop out. The Do 17 put up quite a fight.

Meanwhile, Władek took up where Marche left off. He followed and attacked the Dornier as it dropped low to the ground. In a filed report at the Polish Institute and Sikorski Museum in London, S-Lt Gnyś is quoted:

> I followed him until we were hedgehopping and kept attacking from behind. The gunner stopped shooting and I noticed that his right engine started to smoke. I could see that the wings and cabin were riddled with bullets. Both engines were smoking, the right one soon caught fire. The chase continued for a dozen or so kilometres. Then the speed of the enemy's aircraft decreased and he [force] landed in a field. I ran out of ammunition so I was unable to finish him off.

French Lt Marche, S-Lts Chciuk and Gnyś were each credited with the destruction of a third of the Dornier. S-Lt Władek Gnyś was now the lone Pole flying with the French.

Later on May 16th, with Chciuk's fate still unknown, during a patrol over the front, the squadron confronted a formation of He 111s previously hidden by cloud cover. Władek shouted, warning the others. However, the French did not react so he decided to attack them himself. He gave chase to the last bomber in the formation and came up behind it, now face to face with the enemy gunner who was firing furiously at him. Firing back, Władek made a sweeping pass to the right side of the Heinkel's path. At close range, he gave it two short-distance bursts and saw his bullets exploding into the bomber, but during his attack he was suddenly taken by surprise when the joystick was wrenched from his hand with a powerful jerk. Gnyś regained the stick and kept firing. Then, the Heinkel showed its belly and took a nose dive. He was unable to follow it down as he saw a squadron of Messerschmitts off in the distance coming out of the clouds heading his way. Not standing a chance, Gnyś did an immediate 180° arc-like turn away from the Heinkels and, as luck had it, he saw some billowy clouds directly ahead. This was very fortunate as he needed to hide from the German fighters which were closing in quickly: the lead plane was already firing his guns. Władek successfully disappeared into the white "pillows" and flew back to base.

Upon landing, he discovered that a bullet had entered his MS 406 fighter and had actually hit the steel shaft of his stick then ricocheted to the other side of the cockpit. The thin stick in his hand had saved his life. Was God watching over him again? On inspecting the exterior of his plane, Gnyś also noticed that there were many holes from the Heinkel's gunner, amazed that his plane did not go down too. Because he didn't see the Heinkel crash, he was credited with "damaged."

During combat with an He 111, a bullet entered the cockpit and struck the joystick, knocking it out of Władek's hand. It was sheer luck that the stick "got in the way," probably saving his life.

After Gnys's attack, the Heinkel showed its belly and took a nose dive. Then the squadron of Messerschmitts closed in.

Having survived his crash on May 16th southwest of Brussels, Chciuk's objective was to get back to the Auchy-au-Bois airfield to rejoin the others. However, after waiting for a day for a ride that never showed up, he decided to walk. Three arduous days later, he made it back only to find that the unit had moved on to another base: Le Plessis-Belleville.

The question was, how would he get there? To Władysław Chciuk, the answer was obvious: take one of the unserviceable Morane fighters and fly there. Fortunately, there were several mechanics still at the base ready to torch the unusable aircraft before evacuating. With bits and pieces from various aircraft, the mechanics assembled a barely usable Morane. It had numerous deficiencies and was a sitting duck if attacked by the Luftwaffe. With no parachute, helmet or guns he took off and flew just above the trees. To make matters worse, his plane was shot at and hit by German troops as he went over enemy lines.

Over 170 miles later, via Paris, he eventually made it to Le Plessis-Belleville airfield on May 21st. Relieved, he rejoined his unit who was ecstatic to see him. The squadron had been there in its new location since the 17th.

There was no rest for Chciuk as he went up the same day in a French section and patrolled the area north of Paris. The three pilots encountered and attacked six Do 17s.

However, while coming in for the kill, Chciuk looked around and found himself alone in the attack without his French counterparts. Meanwhile, the Dornier gunners had been accurately shooting at him, hitting his MS 406 many times. Fortunately, in his badly damaged fighter, he landed safely near Clermont unknown to the French pilots who reported that he had been killed. In the eyes of his squadron back at base, Chciuk was missing and presumed dead.

The next day, out of nowhere, Władek Chciuk appeared on a bicycle and returned to his unit. It was another emotional "homecoming." However, Bursztyn their section leader, was still not with them, but at least they all knew that he was alive and was being treated for his knee injury.

On May 25th, Kazek Bursztyn returned from hospital to Le Plessis-Belleville airfield and joined his unit who were most anxious to see him. The "Three Musketeers" were together again; they hugged each other like brothers. However, this wonderful moment did not last, especially for Bursztyn.

His knee was swollen and he limped badly, but insisted he could resume flying duties that day. Władek urged him not to take a chance so soon, as his stiff right leg could interfere with movement in the cockpit if the action got hot. But he was determined and brushed the advice aside and said he was definitely flying and would lead his section once again.

Later in the day, GC III/1 (12 Moranes—nine French, three Polish) took off to escort a couple of Potez 63s on a reconnaissance mission. Near Bapaume, just west of Cambrai in northern France, about 50 miles from the Belgium border, is where they were attacked by 14 Bf 109 Messerschmitts. This was the position of the German front lines at the time. The Poles who were flying the top vic got involved immediately but at the same time, another six German fighters surprised them from above. The French fighters realized that they were outnumbered and fled the scene along with the Potez 63s. It was now up to the Poles to make the best of the battle.

Lt Bursztyn who had never before displayed any suicidal tendencies decided to take on all 20 German fighters He headed straight up toward them firing his guns. S-Lt Gnyś was not far behind, but realized that it was hopeless and pulled back along with S-Lt Chciuk. Bursztyn continued head on even though the German fighters had the advantage of height and collective firepower.

Gnyś yelled into his mouth-piece, "Kazek, turn back, turn back!"

But it was too late, he was hit almost immediately. His aircraft went over on its back and began to spiral downward.

Again, Władek yelled, "Bale out, bale out now!"

It was very likely that Bursztyn was badly wounded as it was observed that he attempted to recover from the spin, but did not succeed.

Władek did not see Kazek's plane crash as he was attacked from all directions and had to save himself. He flung his Morane fighter around, twisting and turning, never allowing himself to become a target. The situation was deadly, he was firing his guns without aiming as the Messerschmitts swarmed around him like angry bees. Putting his

Lt Kazimierz (Kazek) Bursztyn, Polish section leader of GC III/1, didn't stand a chance. It was suicide to try to take on about 20 Messerschmitts by himself. No one really knew why he left the Gnyś–Chciuk section so abruptly to attempt such an attack. He was killed almost immediately, May 25th, 1940.

machine on its back, he headed towards the ground still being pursued by a persistent enemy who finally let up above the trees. With their planes peppered with bullets, Chciuk and Gnyś returned to base but without their brother.

Kazek had been a good friend, a skilled pilot and a gutsy leader, but for a split second, he just "lost it." After the loss of Bursztyn, Władek, still shaken, took over command of the Polish section.

While still stationed at Le Plessis-Belleville, the Luftwaffe made a surprise bombing raid on the airfield on June 3rd. Much like the attack on Auchy-au-Bois airbase on May 10th, the Germans bombed and strafed the base without warning. All pilots frantically ran for cover except for S-Lts Chciuk and Gnyś who dashed for their Morane fighers in an effort to counterattack. Gnyś took off amidst the chaos, but by the time Chciuk found an aircraft that would start, the raid was over and the bombers were long gone. The result: several Moranes destroyed, buildings damaged and the airfield pockmarked by many craters.

Without too much more prompting, GC III/1 mobilized what they could and pushed on the next day to Valence-Trésorerie airfield in the south of France for some desperately needed R&R. It did not last long—a day in fact—as the Germans were rapidly advancing in the north. The squadron was needed back at the front so they flew on the 5th to Rozay-en-Brie, near Paris.

On June 8th, Chciuk, Gnyś and French Sgt Gagnaire were out on patrol northeast of Paris when they came across a Stuka Ju 87 and shot it down. However, French pilots had earlier attacked this Stuka and were subsequently given full credit for its destruction even though S-Lt Chciuk and S-Lt Gnyś actually shot it down. S-Lt Chciuk's report stated: "On 8.VI. with Gnyś and Sgt Gagnaire, who was killed two days later, we shot down a Ju 87 northeast of Paris, but because a French Lt with his section had fired at it before us, he was credited with it."[4]

Elsewhere, the German juggernaut advanced rapidly through Holland and Belgium into northern France and westward toward the English Channel trying to cut off the retreating Belgian, French and British forces. Fighting hard, the British Expeditionary Force was unable to fend off the Germans and it was evident that the Channel ports were being occupied one by one. Dunkirk became the most viable port left to facilitate the defense and evacuation of Allied forces. From May 26th to June 4th, 1940, almost 340,000 (out of some 400,000) Allied troops were rescued from the coast by an armada of military and civilian craft which took them to safety across the Channel to Britain.

On June 10th, Italy declared war on France and Britain. Dictator Benito Mussolini, with his ill-equipped and poorly trained forces attacked France on two main fronts: through the Alps at the Alpine Line and along the Mediterranean coast. The French fought with great courage and gave the Italian forces a hard time, but were considerably outnumbered.

On June 12, 1940 GC III/1 was back in Valence-Trésorerie. The squadron, undertaking patrols and reconnaissance missions, was scrambled a few times, but in the main things were quiet.

On June 18th, one of the areas that Gnyś and Chciuk flew reconnaissance over was the airfield of Lyon-Bron. This was a very nostalgic moment for them as this is where it all started: March 27th, a few short weeks before. It had been a time of excitement and of adventure but, most of all, it was an opportunity to have their revenge on the Nazi invaders.

However, it seemed that at this point, France was in jeopardy of being defeated just like Poland. It was evident that France and her allies were no match for the well-oiled German machine that crushed everything in its path. Plus, once the Italian forces occupied the far south and southeast, France was surrounded and stood no chance at all.

On the same day, June 18th, the Supreme Leader of Poland's Armed Forces in Exile, General Władysław Sikorski, reluctantly gave the order for all Polish personnel to evacuate France and make their way to England, the last place to make a stand.

When GC III/1 received the order to withdraw, they moved to their final airfield at Orange-Caritat in southern France on June 19th.

Two days later, on the 21st, S-Lts Gnyś and Chciuk with their ground crew wished a fond *adieu* to their French comrades. Władek, who was now the commander of the Polish section, went to the French C.O. Commandant Paoli and requested permission for him and Chciuk and their crew to leave the French squadron. Permission was granted. They were provided with road transportation, food, arms and ammunition for their trip to the coast. With his small Polish unit standing at attention in front of the French, Władek said, "*Vive la France! Vive la Pologne!*" as he saluted the injured C.O. who was in a wheelchair. Władek leaned over toward him and they kissed each other on the cheeks. With tears in his eyes and emotion in his voice, Paoli said, "*Bon voyage et bonne chance, Dieu soit avec vous.*"[5]

After saying goodbye to the Groupe de Chasse III/1, Gnyś, Chciuk and ten Polish ground crew piled into an open-roofed truck and headed for Port Vendres in southern France. The Germans and Italians were not far behind.

With approximately 4,300 Polish airmen and many Polish and Allied troops on the run, French, British and Polish vessels were sent to take part in this hasty exodus from a number of ports on France's Mediterranean and Atlantic coasts. President Raczkiewicz and members of the Polish government were among the evacuees. Some of the vessels that took part at different times were MS *Sobieski*, MS *Batory*, *Ile de France*, HMS *Arethus* and the British *Arandora Star*. The main destinations were Glasgow, Plymouth and Liverpool.

Like the exodus the previous year in the Black Sea, the evacuation was a déjà vous moment for Władek and many others.

On June 22nd, France capitulated, and an armistice was signed to take effect on June 25th. Driving solidly for three days, Gnyś and his party of 12 reached Port Vendres on the French coast on June 24th.

★

Approximately 190 Polish fighter pilots took part in the conflict, but there were many more who had just completed aircraft conversion training who were never used in the latter parts of the campaign due to logistical problems. Despite not being allowed to fly as 'pure' Polish squadrons, the Polish pilots were still extremely effective. The largest and only complete Polish unit was Groupe de Chasse Polonaise I/145 that was initially created and stationed in Mions to fight in Finland against the USSR. However in June 1940, they were broken up to fly with French squadrons who were in desperate need for reinforcements. The Polish pilots made as many operational sorties as the French pilots, if not more. They were experienced, fearless, persevering and were generally first to attack.

The French Air Force had no combat experience as of May 10th, but performed as well as they could under the circumstances. They of course had a lot to learn and in the process suffered unnecessary loss of aircraft and lives. However, like Poland, France did not know how to deal with the concept of a 'lightning war' or 'blitzkrieg'. Not only was Germany superior in terms of numbers, weapons, aircraft and tactics, but the element of surprise was stupendous. The Battle of Poland lasted 35 days while the Battle of France lasted forty-four.

Casualties among the original Polish Montpellier pilots (May 10th–June 24th)

- GC III/2: Sgt Leopold Flanek (killed)
- GC II/6: (C.O.) Cpt Jan Pentz (hospitalized)
- GC III/1: (C.O.) Lt Kazimierz Bursztyn (killed)
- GC I/2: (C.O.) Lt Józef Brzeziński (hospitalized), S-Lt Stanisław Chałupa, (hospitalized)
- GC II/7: (C.O.) Lt Władysław Goettel (hospitalized)

Casualties among the French pilots of GC III/1 (May 10th–June 24th)

Four French pilots who flew in combat with Bursztyn, Chciuk and Gnyś were killed during the French campaign. Including Tariel who was wounded, all five fought gallantly and contributed to a total of 21 victories. Gagnaire was top scorer. If there were on average, at any one time, ten French pilots/aircraft in GC III/1, then the casualty rate was 50 percent.

- Lt Jean Tariel (hospitalized) (4 victories)—Wounded May 18th, 1940
- Lt Paul Marche (1 victory)—Killed May 19th, 1940
- Sgt Chef Auguste Paulhan (3 victories)—Killed May 21st, 1940
- Adj Edgar Gagnaire (7 victories including 1 individual)—Killed June 10th, 1940
- Sgt Kleber Doublet (6 victories including 3 individual)—Killed June 11th, 1940

Victories of 9 Polish pilots from among 51 who saw action (May 10th–June 24th)

- NCO E. Nowakiewicz: GC II/7, individually destroyed 4, shared 1, damaged 1
- S-Lt E. Kawnik: GC III/6, individually destroyed 3
- S-Lt W. Król: GC II/7, individually destroyed 2, shared 2, damaged 2 (1 shared)
- S-Lt S. Chałupa: GC 1/2, individually destroyed 2, shared 2, damaged 1 (shared)
- Mjr M. Mümler: GC II/7, individually destroyed 2, shared 2
- S-Lt W. Gnyś: GC III/1, shared 3 destroyed, damaged 1
- S-Lt W. Chciuk: GCIII/1, shared 3 destroyed
- Lt K. Bursztyn: GC III/1, individually destroyed 1, shared 1
- Cpl A. Beda: GC I/2, individually destroyed 1, damaged 2 shared

Victories of S-Lt Gnyś (May 10th–June 24th)

- May 12th: Aircraft—Heinkel 111. Location: Antwerp, Belgium. Lt K. Bursztyn, S-Lt W. Gnyś, S-Lt W. Chciuk. In collaboration with: Lt du Boucher, Lt Leenhardt, S/Lt Calmel, Adj Crémieu, Adj Gagnaire, S/C Cazade, S/C Paulhan, Sgt Pralon (Gnyś 1/11 share)[6]
- May 16th: Aircraft—Dornier 17. Location: Moerbecke, Belgium. S-Lt W. Gnyś, S-Lt W. Chciuk in collaboration with Lt Marche (Gnyś 1/3 share)[7]
- May 16th (some sources say 12th): Aircraft—Heinkel 111. Location: Antwerp/ Brussels, Belgium. S-Lt W. Gnyś alone was credited with one damaged (most likely destroyed)[8]
- June 8th: Aircraft—Junkers 87 (Stuka). Location: East of Paris. S-Lt W. Gnyś, S-Lt W. Chciuk in collaboration with Lt Tariel, Sgt Doublet, Sgt Durand, Adj Gagnaire (Gnyś 1/6 share)[9]

CHAPTER 6

The Battle of Britain

"There will be no more running … from now on it will be the Royal Air Force who will go to meet the Germans … first on the English coast and then, as our strength grows, over France and eventually over Germany itself."

ANON

Port Vendres, near the Spanish border, teemed with Polish servicemen some of whom Władek recognized. They boarded the French SS *Président dal Piaz* which was to take them across the Mediterranean to Oran, Algeria, in North Africa. Incidentally, some brave pilots flew directly to England or to North Africa.

Playing cards while on a long voyage was a logical and fun thing to do. It was also a relaxing way to pass the time. One card game that Władek loved was poker. He found it to be not only entertaining, but a way to take his mind off the war and perhaps win a little cash along the way. He and his friends and many other servicemen had lots of free time on their hands especially while in transit from Port Vendres to Liverpool. So, card games were popular.

One sunny afternoon while in Oran, Władek and others found a nice shady spot beneath a large tree and threw a blanket down to use as a table on which they could play poker. The group consisted of over a dozen military personnel from different Allied nations all of whom were waiting to catch the train to Casablanca in western Morocco. What a better way to spend an afternoon than playing a game of chance with your allies. As luck had it, Władek couldn't lose!

Once in picturesque Oran, in the Gulf of Oran, Gnyś and his unit headed west by train to Casablanca, Morocco, in northwest Africa. The temperature was scorching hot at 135°F (57°C)—in the shade. At one point the train stopped due to a malfunctioning wheel. Since it was going to take a while to do the repair, they decided to wander over to a cluster of attractive white buildings in search of a cool drink of water. The compound was surrounded by a fence but the gate was not locked. Upon entering,

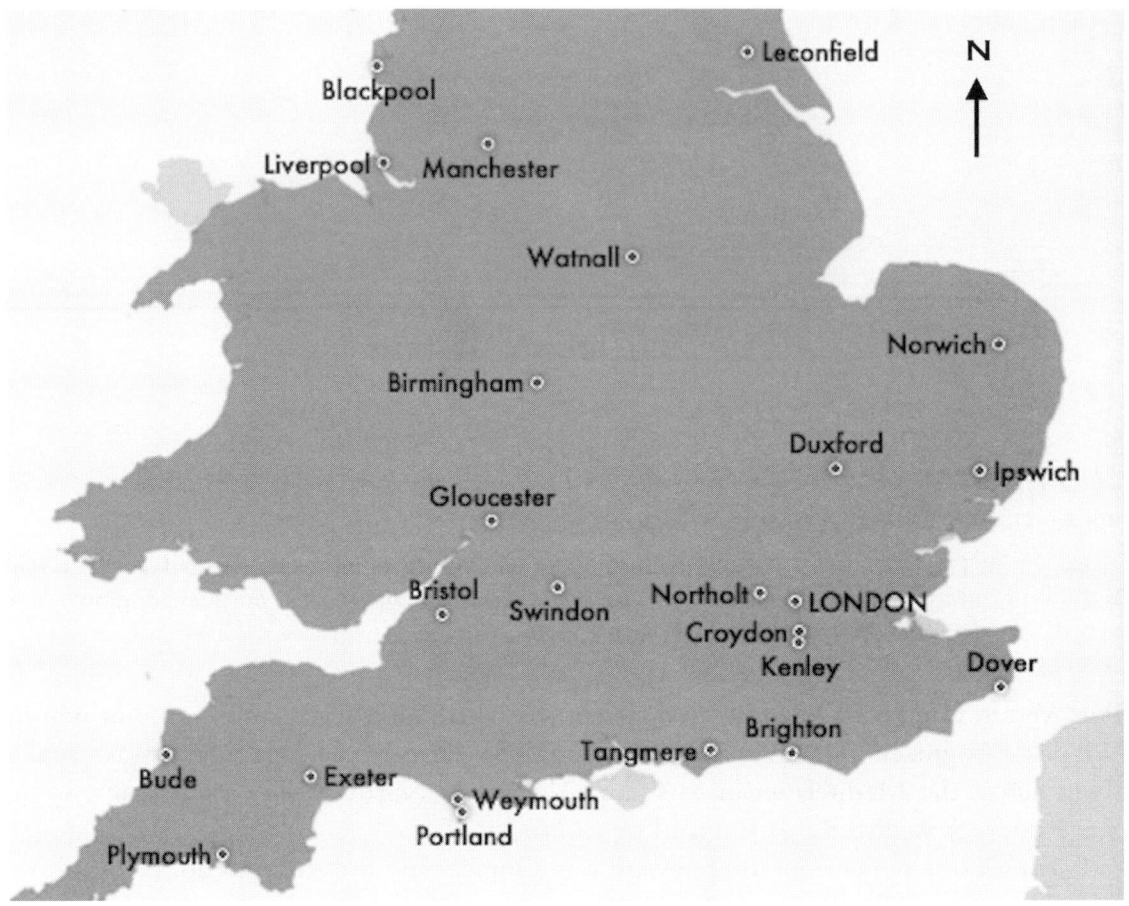

Great Britain—the place of last hope—1940.

they found a swimming pool and since no one was around, they stripped down and jumped into the refreshing water.

Then out of one of the buildings came a number of beautifully dressed, veiled Arab women escorted, as it turned out, by a eunuch. Władek and the others came to the conclusion that the compound was the home of a sheik and the women were his harem. The women squealed with excitement when they saw the interesting male strangers. The men, likewise, were more than thrilled to see them. However, this moment of bliss did not last long as the sheik himself appeared. He was most upset with them barging into his property and yelled at the eunuch to get the women inside. The Poles apologized and returned to the train disappointed but rejuvenated. They chuckled all the way to Casablanca.

The one-way ticket from Oran to Casablanca proved to be a very interesting journey. As could be expected, the train was filled to capacity with military evacuees from France, making the trip painfully slow. It was so slow in fact, that many rode on the top of the cars to avoid the crammed interior.

Not all pilots kept a personal diary, but S–Lt Władysław Chciuk was one who did log certain events. One entry he made on June 27th, 1940 while on the way to Casablanca was about Gnyś's love of cards. He said, "I spent the (entire) journey on the roof of our train car with Gnyś playing poker."[1] Obviously, Chciuk and others loved playing poker too. It was common for the men to sometimes jump off this slow moving train to obtain food and drink. S–Lt Chciuk in his diary also wrote, "I remember the train being so slow (at times) that some soldiers jumped off, bought fruit and still got back on the (same) train!" Because money was scarce, some men sold their personal weapons (for a good price) to the local Arabs and bought drinks, oranges and other food items.

Eventually the slow train from Oran arrived on June 28th at Casablanca, Morocco, their second to last stop before departing for England. They were quartered in a comfortable hotel and had a chance to rest up for a couple of days in this beautiful city before the next ship arrived to take them to Gibraltar.

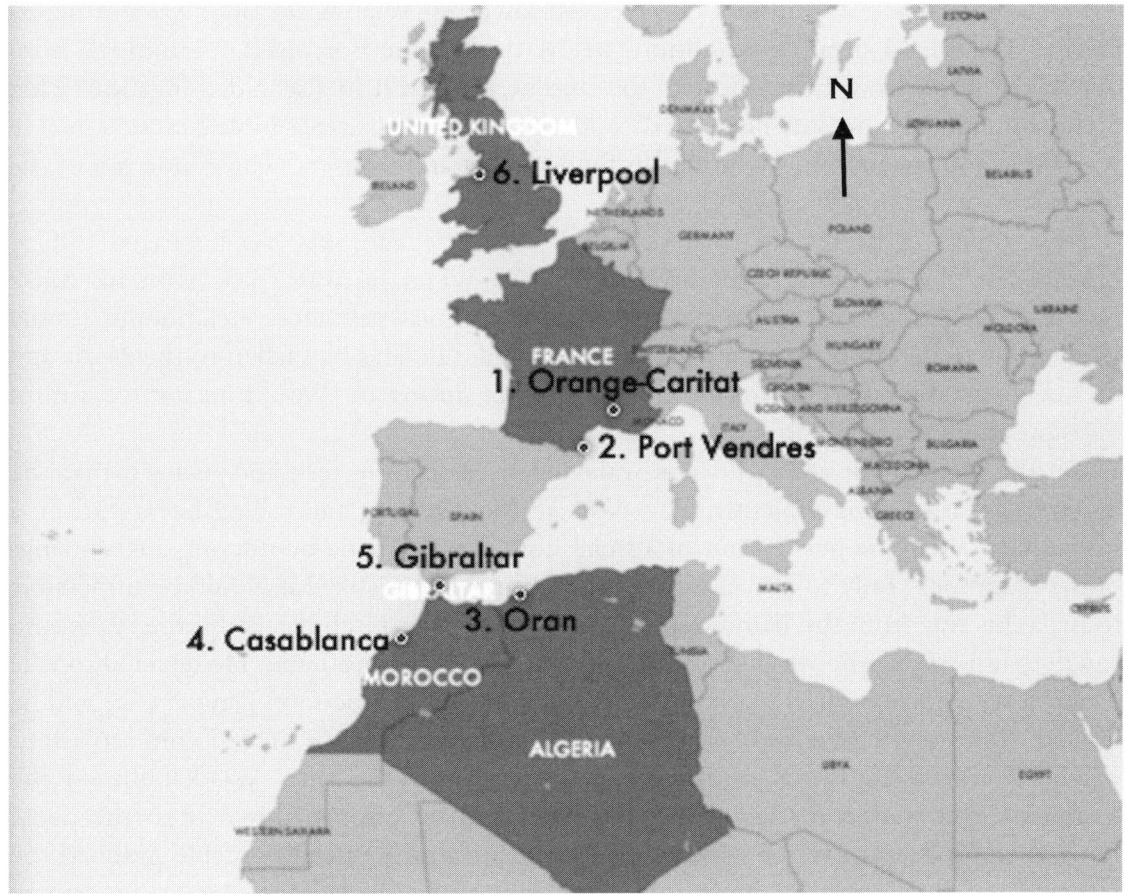

Escape route from France to England, June 21st–July 12th, 1940.

Escape from North Africa, particularly from Port Casablanca, was very chaotic at this time as thousands of Allied servicemen—French, Polish, Czech, etc.—were fleeing France, converging here on their way to Britain and elsewhere not yet occupied by the Nazis.

The name of the vessel upon which Gnyś and his group sailed to Gibraltar is not available, but was transport ship no. 3. What is known is that there were four big ferry boats and one smaller one all transporting soldiers out of North Africa.[2] Transport ship no. 4 was the Polish ORP (Ship of Republic of Poland) *Wilja* and ship no. 5 was the Polish ORP *Iskra*. The first three ships contained 143 officers, 357 soldiers and high-ranking PAF officers. Ppłk (S-Col/Lt Col) Pniewski for example, was on ship no. 3 which departed for Gibraltar on June 30th, 1940.

On July 2nd, 1940, the transport ship SS *Neuralia* departed from Gibraltar and headed into the vast Atlantic Ocean with a course set for Liverpool, England. It was fortunate that the *Neuralia* was able to join a convoy from Canada heading east as there were German U-boats lurking in the deep Atlantic waters. Gnyś, Chciuk and ground crew were happy to get underway on the final leg of their circuitous route that had begun in southern France.

Since cabin space was limited due to overcrowding, Władek for one, was not happy with the crammed sleeping conditions below deck so he borrowed a hammock from one of the ship's crew. In the bow of the ship he secured it in a secluded location. That night, he climbed into his new "bed" and closed it up so it resembled a cocoon. He was warm and comfortable wearing his flying jacket and trousers. The gentle roll of the ship soon rocked him to sleep.

Next morning he awoke to a beautiful day and calm seas. As he gazed out to the horizon, his thoughts went back to Sarnów when he was a boy with his horse Kasztanka and dog Asik and prayed that his family was still alive. He thought fondly about Constanta, Sonja and her mother. France, like Poland had fallen to the Nazis and he knew very well that his future in England was uncertain. Would he survive a third invasion and live to talk about it?

On the third night at sea he was wakened by a terrible jerk and realized that the hammock was swaying violently. The *Neuralia* was pitching and rolling like a cork in a storm. Cautiously he peeked out of a small hole that he made by untying a few strings of the hammock, only to get an eyeful of salt water. He realized it would be impossible to make his way from the hammock to the cabins. It was pitch black and the sea was so rough that he would be washed overboard without anyone noticing. He decided to ride it out. It seemed an endless night of violent rocking in his "cocoon." Dawn broke and he looked out to see the forms of friends waving and gesturing for him to come to safety.

The deck was awash as gigantic waves swept over the ship. Władek untied the hammock and waited for his chance; it came and he jumped down onto the deck. He was waste deep in water which swept him to the side of the bow. He grabbed the rails and fought his way to the outstretched arms that pulled him to safety. The storm

It sounded like a great idea at the time, to sleep in a hammock on deck of the SS Neuralia *in the fresh Atlantic sea air, until a storm blew up, almost washing Władek overboard, July 1940.*

did not let up for several days and nights during which time the cozy hammock was washed overboard.

Many of the airmen suffered from seasickness and were weak from vomiting. The sight of a distant land mass boosted their spirits considerably. Finally, the SS *Neuralia* docked in Liverpool on July 12th … the place of last hope.

It seemed like a fading dream that the SS *Neuralia* left Gibraltar on July 2nd. They had been at sea for about ten days battling Atlantic storms and avoiding enemy submarines.

By early July, main centers were set up in Blackpool, Gloucester, Kirkham and Weeton to accommodate the mass numbers of Polish aviation personnel after the disintegration of France. Władek and his group were directed to Blackpool.

By the end of July, 6,220 Polish airmen had reached the UK; Blackpool became the largest Polish center. The new evacuees increased the Polish Air Force strength to a total of 8,384 men on British soil.[3] For Władek and others, this was the first encounter with the English people who had their own customs and language—another new challenge for the Poles.

The first Polish pilots started reaching England in December 1939 after the collapse of Poland in early October. British authorities agreed to accept only 300 Polish pilots and 2,000 support personnel. The British were at first uneasy about using them, but just before the collapse of France, it was agreed to form two Polish bomber squadrons as part of the RAF Voluntary Reserve, but Air Chief Marshal Hugh Dowding (Fighter Command) objected to the formation of Polish fighter squadrons.

After the Fall of France, the beaten British Expeditionary Force with its contingent of RAF fighters only had several weeks in which to recuperate and reorganize for the next onslaught. In the meantime, even more Polish pilot evacuees arrived in England from France. It was apparent in early July 1940 that the Luftwaffe was increasing its pressure on Britain and Fighter Command had little time to beef up its strength to protect the island nation.

As a result, the first two Allied (Hurricane) fighter squadrons were created under British command, being No. 302 Polish Fighter Squadron at Leconfield and No. 310 Czech Fighter Squadron at Duxford. Certain command positions would be doubled up with British personnel in order to control aircraft training and the teaching of RAF operational methods.

As part of Hitler's long-range plan of conquest, his intention was to invade Britain with the same intensity as he did with Poland and France. The use of force was inevitable because there was no way that England would surrender without a fight. As a precursor to the cross-Channel invasion (Operation Sea Lion), the Luftwaffe would first soften up and overpower Britain's air defenses. Then his navy would "distract" the Royal Navy in the North Sea and Mediterranean which would allow his ground forces to move across unimpeded and take London, forcing an armistice or a surrender. In theory, it all sounded like a good plan, but in practice it would prove to be a nightmare for the Führer. He had the vision and the might to complete his European takeover, but this was not a normal blitzkrieg as before. His plan would only succeed if he was successful in all stages of Operation Sea Lion. The fact that the UK was separated from the European mainland by a narrow stretch of water, prevented a quick and perhaps easy victory.

In comparison to previous campaigns, the Battle of Britain was the first to be fought entirely by aircraft. Not only that, but it was the only battle that boasted the largest and most continuous aerial bombardment to date. Initial targets were coastal port facilities, docks and shipping. Then the Luftwaffe attacked RAF airfields, aircraft factories and ground infrastructure. Inaccurate bombing of these targets led to continuous bombing of urban centers. Its objective here was to terrorize civilians that would in turn force its government to give in and give up.

Hermann Göring, the ace fighter pilot of World War I, was appointed the Commander-in-Chief of the Luftwaffe. He and Hitler both knew that knocking out the RAF and Fighter Command was the key to victory over Britain.

Fighter Command was very well aware of this. Its headquarters was located at Bentley Priory in Stanmore, northwest London. Hugh Dowding knew the critical importance of organized, geographically placed defense groups. Each group contained many squadrons made up of British, Polish and other Allied airmen. The four fighter groups were 10 Group which covered southwest England and Wales and provided relief to 11 Group; 11 Group protected London and southeast England which was most threatened by the enemy and took the brunt of the German air offensive due to its close proximity across the Channel from occupied France; 12 Group was the second most active group (after No. 11) and covered the Midlands and East Anglia. It also provided support to its southern neighbor 11 Group. (P/O W. Gnyś was part of 12 Group); 13 Group defended the rest of northern England, Scotland, Scapa Flow and Northern Ireland.

Each of these groups in turn was sub-divided into geographical sectors. Each sector had its own well-equipped airfield and operations room. All relevant information from these sectors eventually found its way to Bentley Priory HQ which was at the heart of this complex defense system and was responsible for disseminating information to the relevant sector(s) about incoming hostile aircraft. At that point pilots would be scrambled to their waiting aircraft to intercept the enemy.

No. 12 Group RAF, of which P/O W. Gnyś's 302 Fighter Squadron was part, had its operational headquarters, an underground command bunker complex, at Watnall, near Nottingham). Air Vice-Marshal Trafford Leigh-Mallory as commander was responsible for the aerial protection of the Midlands, Norfolk, Lincolnshire and North Wales.

The quality of leadership during the Battle of Britain was extraordinary. Winston Churchill for example, was a superb military leader, but he also knew how to lead the British public giving them a reason to live and keeping their spirits up in the darkest of hours. Even his body language was representative of his great words of wisdom and his ever-present cigar was the torch that never went out.

Then there was Hugh Dowding who was the brains behind RAF Fighter Command who masterminded the defensive shield that the Germans were unable to penetrate. Even leadership rivals worked together … Leigh-Mallory and 11 Group's Keith Park had one thing in common: they had to stop Hitler and the Third Reich. It was touch and go for a while, but they got the job done.

Women contributed with vim and vigor. They volunteered by the tens of thousands and the resulting Women's Auxiliary Air Force was an army unto itself. They worked tirelessly in the many jobs that needed doing to support the men on the front lines. The number of British women who contributed to the war effort made a significant difference helping to keep the enemy at bay. Working together, the British collective was in great hands.

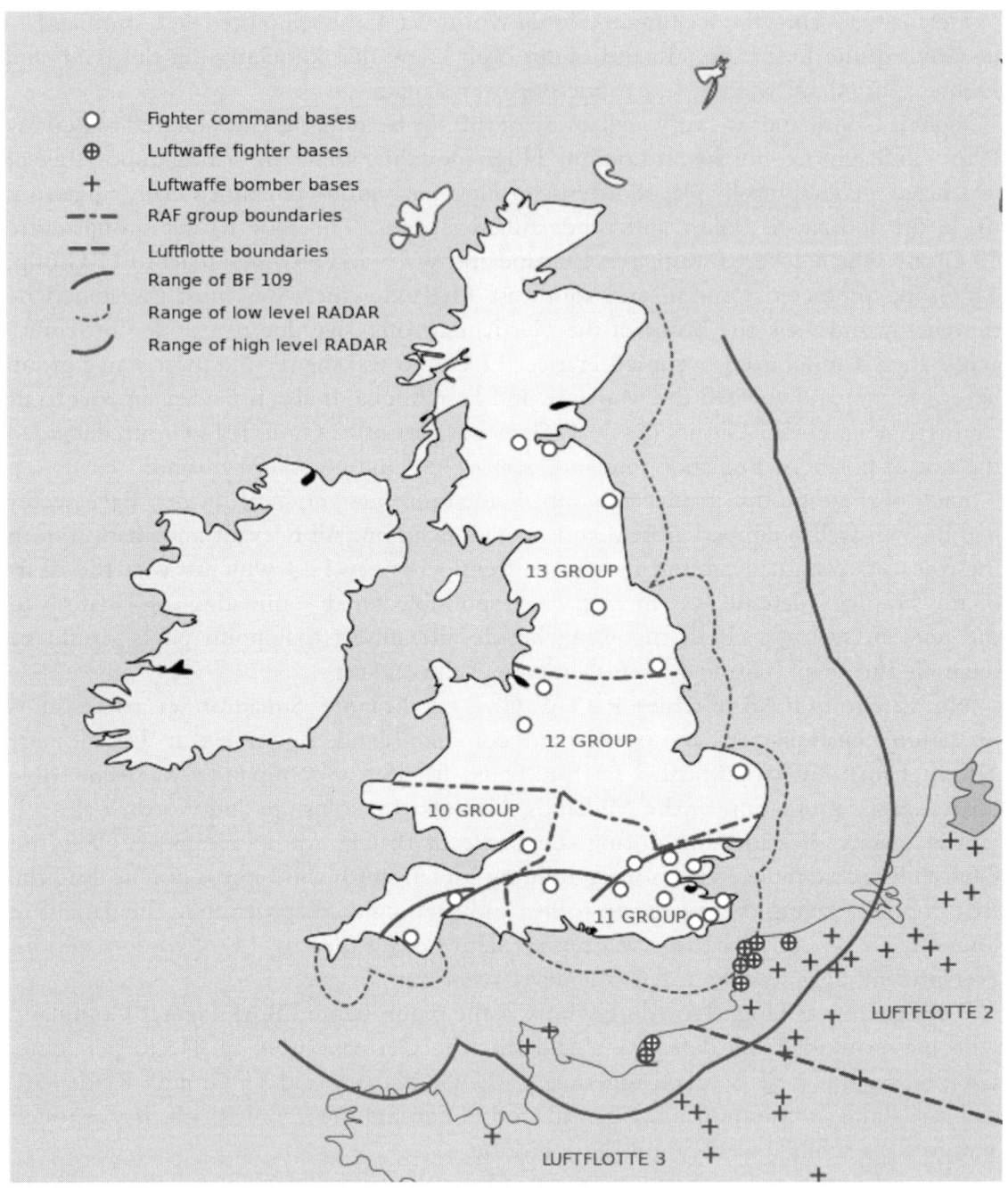

The location of fighter defense groups in the UK, 1940. Sir Hugh Dowding, commander of RAF Fighter Command during the Battle of Britain, played a crucial role in Britain's defense. The UK was broken up into four specific geographical areas. Each area was assigned a group number (10–13) as can be seen on the map. Each group sector had its own internal organization and squadrons at the ready. (No. 13 Group also protected Northern Ireland.) All sectors were linked to Fighter Command at Bentley Priory, London. P/O W. Gnyś in No. 302 Polish Fighter Squadron was part of 12 Group.

Phases of the Battle of Britain

Preliminary phase: June–July 10th, 1940. During the Battle of France, the Luftwaffe used a small part of its air force to fly over the UK to observe airfields, factories, ports and urban centers. It gave the German aircrews experience in navigation methods and in night flying. Another objective was to trigger air raid warnings, to institute fear as well as disrupting industry. The following phases and dates are endorsed by the Imperial War Museum.

Phase 1: Attacks on coastal shipping: July 10th–August 12th. Even in early July, there were encounters over the English Channel and North Sea with British ships coming under attack.

Phase 2: Attacks on fighter airfields and radar stations: August 12th–18th. Systematic attacks were made on the more immediate airfields and on countless radar installations (eye to the sky), the very heart of Fighter Command. Fortunately for the UK, the Luftwaffe did not generally follow up with more raids on these radar sites.

Phase 3: Attacks on 11 Group Sector airfields: August 24th–September 6th (bad weather 19th–23rd). The Luftwaffe pounded southeast England with the hope of shutting down Fighter Command. Both sides suffered heavy loses.

Phase 4: Assault on London and other cities: September 7th and beyond; the 15th was perhaps the climax of the Battle of Britain as Fighter Command was able to match and repel massive large-scale Luftwaffe attacks. In Hitler's eyes, Göring started to lose credibility.

302 Fighter Squadron

Leconfield is located near Beverley in the East Riding of Yorkshire, England. It was first opened in December 1936 as part of RAF Bomber Command. On the night of September 3rd, 1939, Whitley bombers from Leconfield were the first British aircraft to cross into German airspace, dropping propaganda leaflets over Germany. In October 1939 (until 1942), it was taken over by Fighter Command and during the Battle of Britain, the station became temporary home to many of its squadrons. They stayed here for short periods of time to rest and regroup after periods of combat in the front-line airbases of southeast England. Polish 303 "Kościuszko" Fighter Squadron is one example of the many squadrons that rotated through here.

After the reopening of the newly paved runways in December 1942, heavy Wellington bombers of 196 and 466 Squadrons made the first raids from these runways against the Germans. From then on, it developed into a major Bomber Command base once again.

It was here in Leconfield that Polish 302 Squadron was born. It was the first of several squadrons with which Gnyś would serve and the longest in duration. Polish Air Force veterans such as Piotr Kuryłłowicz referred to it as "the old squadron".

No. 302 (City of Poznań)[4] Polish Fighter Squadron RAF—302 Dywizjon Myśliwski "Poznański"—was the first Polish fighter squadron assembled in England as part of an agreement between the UK and the Polish government-in-exile under the leadership of General Sikorski.[5] No. 302 Squadron was formed on July 10th, 1940 at Leconfield (northeast Yorkshire) and became fully operational on August 15th. It was assigned to the No. 12 Fighter Group RAF and was given code letters WX (painted on fighter fuselage) under the command of S/Ldr (Mjr) M. Mümler. A good percentage of the Polish pilots came from the previous French squadrons who were former members of the "Montpellier Squadron" (2nd Poznań Fighter Wing) and Group de Chasse I/145.

No. 302 was one of several Polish units that fought with the RAF during the war, others being No. 303 "Warsaw Kościuszko's" Squadron (scored most kills in the Battle of Britain), No. 306 "Toruń" Fighter Squadron (became operational after the Battle of Britain), No. 307 "Lwów" Eagle-Owls Night-Fighter Squadron (became operational after the Battle of Britain) and No. 308 "Kraków" Fighter Squadron (became operational after the Battle of Britain).

Being part of No. 12 Fighter Group RAF, 302 was responsible for defending a good portion of north/central England. Initially, they flew routine patrols and guarded ship convoys on the east coast with little chance of engaging the enemy. Then on August 20th, they came across a Ju 88 bomber and S/Ldr Satchell was given credit for its demise. This was the first time an enemy was encountered by 302. At this point, P/O Gnyś was not yet with 302 Squadron.

The next day, over the sea, approaching Hull Harbour, F/Lt Riley and P/O (S-Lt) Chałupa claimed one bomber each. During the exchange of gunfire, Chałupa was forced down and had to make a belly landing.[6]

During the last week in August, P/O (S-Lt) W. Gnyś with F/O (Lt) W. Król, Sgt A. Beda and nine other comrades joined P/O (S-Lt) S. Chałupa who was already at Leconfield. With pilots (Polish and RAF) plus support personnel, total strength was approximately 219. It was the first Polish fighter squadron to enter the Battle of Britain.

Unknown to Władek who had just joined 302 Squadron, an application for him to receive the Cross of Valor for his participation in the Battle of France, was being completed in Blackpool:

For Decoration: 1st Cross of Valor

Rank: Pilot Officer

Surname and Name: Gnyś, Władysław

Distinguished by: "Courageous and tenacious pilot. Impressed the French [pilots] and gained their respect. Physically and morally strong. Flew and fought a great deal and with eagerness. It has been confirmed that while operating inferior equipment, he shot down 2 aircraft … allegedly, shot down 1 more. Decorated [by the French] with Croix de Guerre."

Signed: "I hereby support the application." Inspector of the Polish Air Force, S. Ujejski, Air Vice Marshal

Signed: Camp Commandant, S. Pawlikowski, Group Captain, Blackpool, September 2nd, 1940[7]

Bucharest, Romania, October 1939. Pilots Władek (right) and Jan Błażejewski are seen wearing civilian clothes. Along with many other Polish pilots, they tried to blend in with the crowd and not be noticed by Gestapo agents. Once in England, in the fall of 1940, Jan joined No. 304 "Silesian" Bomber Squadron flying Wellington bombers. In December 1941 on a mission to attack the docks at Ostend, Belgium, S/Ldr Błażejewski crashed into the sea off Margate, north of Dover, and tragically the whole crew drowned. It was his 27th operational flight.

Above: The "Montpellier pilots" from left: Goettel, Brzeziński, Treger (tech officer), Kawnik, Sulerzycki, Łaszkiewicz, Gnyś, Rougevin-Baville (French instructor), Bursztyn, Król, Nowakiewicz, Rychlicki, Karwowski, Beda, Anders, Chciuk, Flanek. Pentz, Chałupa and Zantara are hidden. *(PISM)*

Left: General Władysław Sikorski, Prime Minister and War Minister in the Polish government-in-exile and Commander-in-Chief of the Polish Armed Forces 1939–43.

Above: Inspection of the Polish sections at the Lyon-Bron base, March 27th, 1940. From left: Gen Zając, Col Pawlikowski, Gen Sikorski (lighter colored coat), Gen Denain, and the tall Frenchman Gen Picard. The six Polish flights or sections each contained three "Montpellier pilots" who had completed conversion training on French aircraft, mainly on MS 406-C1 fighters (as seen in photo). The flights were fully self-contained with each having Polish ground crews (specialty mechanics, technicians) of 11 or 12 men. These six sections were presented to Sikorski before departure to join six French squadrons at the front.

Top right: Gen Sikorski saluting the guard of honor in front of the Polish Forces Headquarters at Lyon-Bron. Notice the Polish banners, flags and eagles. *(PISM)*

Right: Gen Sikorski shaking hands with Lt Bursztyn. S-Lt Chałupa is saluting while S-Lt Gnyś raises his arm in salute, ready for the handshake, S-Lt Chciuk is next. Gnyś and Bursztyn probably have maps in their pockets. *(PISM)*

French pilot wings s/no. 31297. Gnyś was given these wings at Lyon–Bron, France, on March 27th, 1940 by French officers.

Cpt Stefan Łaszkiewicz, C.O. of the Montpellier Squadron, receives French wings from a French officer during the exchange of badges between the French and Polish pilots, Lyon-Bron, March 27th, 1940. Others from left are: Lt Bursztyn, Cpt Sulerzycki, S-Lt Gnyś, S-Lt Chciuk, S-Lt Chałupa, Cpt R-Baville, and S-Lt Kawnik. *(PISM)*

Right: A priest celebrates mass inside a hangar at Lyon-Bron with hundreds in attendance. The tail of a Potez 63.11 is used as an altar. Gen Sikorski is front-row, center. Aircraft such as the Caudron C.635 fighter are in the hanger. (*PISM)*

Center right: No. 4 Flight crew. Standing are S-Lt Gnyś (second from left), and Lt Bursztyn, C.O. (third from right) in front of his MS 406 "I" c/n 1031 at the GC III/1 airfield, May 1940.

Below: Polish Section No. 4 was attached to Group de Chasse III/1 (Fighter Squadron III/1) based at Toul-Croix de Metz airfield in northern France on the front line of defense against Germany. From left: Lt Kazimierz Bursztyn (C.O. of this section), S-Lt Władysław Gnyś and S-Lt Władysław Chciuk. They were more than ready to teach the French pilots a thing or two about flying and they did just that in a mock dogfight during the early days at Toul-Croix de Metz.

Above: S-Lt Gnyś with GC III/1 taking a break at Le Plessis Belleville, France, May 1940. An M.S. 406 is in the background.

Left: Wreckage of Lt Bursztyn's MS 406 C1 c/n 1031 (L-621) when he crash-landed May 12th, 1940 in Belgium. He received a direct hit from the gunner of a Heinkel. Hospitalized, he suffered only a broken knee. *(B. Belcarz)*

Below: S-Lt W. Chciuk leaning against his MS 406-C "III" fighter between "Winking Fox" and Polish checker. *(B. Belcarz)*

Once in Gibraltar, Gnyś, Chciuk and mechanics boarded the S.S. *Neuralia*, which had its course set for Liverpool. Władek was almost washed overboard, hammock and all.

Władek (third from right) with colleagues on board the S.S. *Neuralia* on the Atlantic headed for Liverpool. German U-boats were a real danger.

For bravery, S-Lt W. Gnyś was awarded the Croix de Guerre avec Palm for his role during the Battle of France. Around the portrait are the words République Française. On the reverse of the medal are the dates of the conflict: 1939–1940. On the ribbon is a bronze palm which represents the highest award. (Gnyś collection). He also received citation Ordre C no. 38 de 28 Mai 1940 l'Ordre de l'Armée de l'Air, a mention of a praiseworthy act or achievement in an official report during the Battle of France. (B. Belcarz)

Winston Churchill is widely regarded as one of the greatest wartime leaders of the twentieth century and most certainly this was true in the eyes of the British public during World War II.

Air Chief Marshal Sir Hugh Dowding (1882–1970) was the commander of RAF Fighter Command during the Battle of Britain.

Marie Earney (19) was a WAAF (Women's Auxiliary Air Force) during the war. She married Jan Kurowski of 306 and 308 squadrons, who was killed in action on May 21st, 1944. Marie worked in the operations room at RAF Northolt, London. *(John Kaye-Kurowski)*

Operations rooms were where WAAFs plotted the incoming Luftwaffe. A response was then planned using RAF fighters. Here is a plotting table at Fighter Command Headquarters, Bentley Priory, London (RAFM).

Sir Trafford Leigh-Mallory (1892–1944) was the controversial commander of No. 12 (Fighter Group) during the Battle of Britain—where he developed the "Big Wing" fighter formation theory with Douglas Bader—before assuming command of No. 11 (Fighter) Group. He was killed in an aircraft crash in November 1944, en route to his new command as C-in-C of Allied air forces in Southeast Asia.

New Zealand-born Air Vice-Marshal Sir Keith Park (1892–1975) commanded No. 11 (Fighter) Group during the Battle of Britain, responsible for the defense of southeast England. 11 Group bore the brunt of the Luftwaffe assault, but it was Park's brilliant decision-making that helped prevent Britain's demise.

No. 302 "Poznań" (Polish) Fighter Squadron, RAF Leconfield, September 4th, 1940 pose in front of a Hawker Hurricane. Seated from left: P/O Jerzy Czerniak, F/Lt Franciszek Jastrzębski, F/O Peter Carter, F/Lt James Farmer, F/Lt James Thomson, F/Lt Piotr Łaguna, S/Ldr Jack Satchell, S/Ldr Mieczysław Mümler, F/Lt William Riley, F/O Julian Kowalski, F/O Tadeusz Czerwiński and F/Lt Antoni Wczelik. Back from left: Sgt Bronisław Bernaś, P/O Władysław Gnyś, P/O Stanisław Łapka, P/O Edward Pilch, P/O Wacław Król, F/Lt Jan Czerny, Sgt Antoni Beda, P/O Jan Maliński, Sgt Antoni Łysek, Sgt Wilhelm Kosarz, Sgt Marian Wędzik, P/O Aleksander Żukowski, Sgt Stanisław Markiewicz, P/O Stanisław Chałupa, P/O Zbigniew Wróblewski, Sgt Eugeniusz Nowakiewicz, P/O Włodzimierz Karwowski, Sgt Zenon Kleniewski and Sgt Jan Załuski. *(PISM)*.

The Poles were trained on the single-seater Hawker Hurricane fighter. It was well armed, maneuverable, and dependable. Władek thought: "If only we had them in Poland."

Observer Corps posts were situated all across the country. Their job was to report Luftwaffe aircraft to Corps centers once they had crossed the coast and were behind the radar. This information was passed down to their sector control rooms, Group Headquarters and to Fighter Command where plotters kept progress up to date.

This photo shows tracer ammunition from a Spitfire Mark I striking a Heinkel 111 above Bristol, England, in late September 1940. Tracer bullets created a visual pathway for the attacking aircraft and increased target accuracy. Not every bullet was a tracer. *(PISM)*

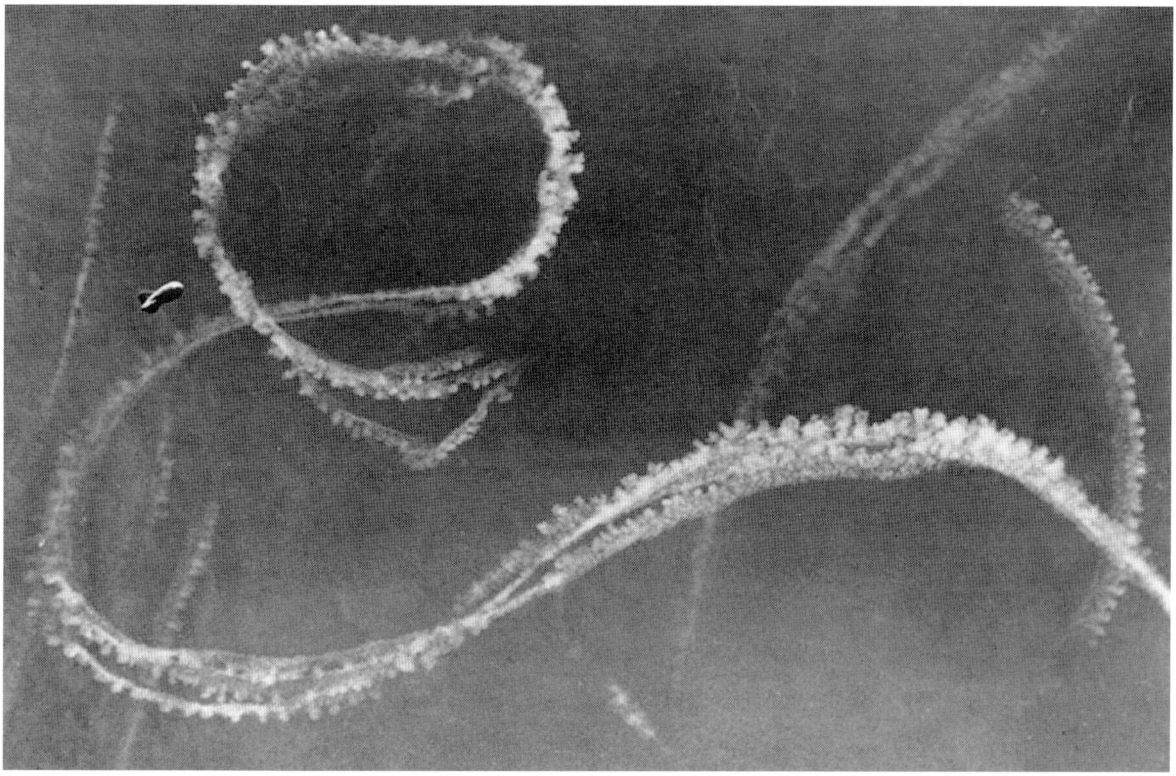

Above: Fighter contrails show the path of a dogfight above London during the Blitz. Note how close the aircraft came to a defensive barrage balloon with its dangerous cable wires.

Below left: Families did their best and for safety lived in the underground tube system for extended periods of time, although very uncomfortable and inconvenient.

Below right: An eastern suburb of London, September, 1940. Emotional children sit in front of what is left of their home which was randomly destroyed during a night raid by Nazi bombers.

Northolt, Squadron 302, October 1940. From left: T. Czerwiński; B. Bernaś; M. Neyder; unrecognized; W. Gnyś; a British doctor or English instructor but not a pilot; N. Nestorowicz; W. Kamiński; M. Wędzik; R. Narucki; S. Łapka; A. Łysek and S. Markiewicz.

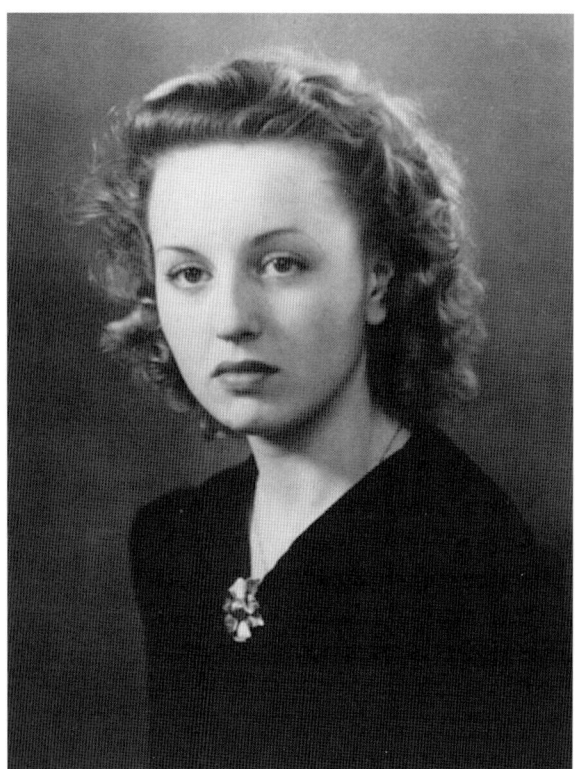

P/O Władysław Gnyś (30) met his future wife, beautiful 19-year-old English girl Barbara Simmons, in October, 1940 at The Orchard pub in Ruislip.

Like Władek, Barbara was no stranger to the personal consequences of war with the loss of her uncle Private B. E. Simmons (No. 77175) in the trenches of France during World War I. *(Cherrie Taylor)*

F/Lt (Cpt) Franciszek Jastrzębski (1905–40). Władek and friends affectionately called him Franek. He was a friendly, outgoing man who always liked to laugh and joke and who became an excellent pilot and commander. He was killed on October 25th, 1940.

The 1939–1945 Star was awarded for operational service between September 3rd, 1939 and September 2nd, 1945. The Battle of Britain Clasp was awarded to aircrew on fighter aircraft who took part in the battle between July 10th and October 31st, 1940. *(Gnyś coll.)*

Bristol Blenheim Mk 1 was a British light bomber used extensively in the first two years of the war. During daylight bombing operations, despite its powerful gun turret, it stood little chance against the Messerschmitt 109. It suffered many loses in the early stages of the war, though it proved more successful as a night-fighter.

The Junkers 88A was a fast Luftwaffe twin-engine, multi-functional aircraft. It was extremely versatile as a bomber, dive-bomber, torpedo-bomber, night-fighter and reconnaissance aircraft.

The Messerschmitt Bf 109 was one of the most advanced fighters of the era. It was the backbone of the Luftwaffe fighter force. Its combat record was monumental and it was literally a killing machine. The Spitfire was its only equal. F/O Gnyś's Hurricane was shot to bits by Bf 109s on May 21st, 1941.

After settling into his new surroundings at Leconfield, Władek started training on September 2nd, 1940 with No. 5 Operational Training Unit (OTU).[8] On the 4th he spent one and a half hours in the North American Harvard Dual Trainer under the guidance of RAF P/O Maloney. He then put in over four hours' flying in the Miles Master advanced trainer, practicing flying circuits and landings and formation flying.

On September 9th, P/O Gnyś flew a Hawker Hurricane (P 3603) for the first time. He experienced takeoff and landings over a period of an hour and a half. The next day he performed aerobatics (in P 2522) and formation flying (in P 1958) for two hours in total. The Hurricane was easy to maneuver, dependable and had amazing firepower. "It was unfortunate that we didn't have this type of fighter in Poland during the September 1939 invasion!" he exclaimed. (Władek continued flying the Hurricane until October 6th, 1941 when he flew the even more impressive Spitfire.)

His conversion training with OTU lasted about three weeks after which he returned to No. 302 Polish Fighter Squadron. The assigned British flight commanders to 302 were F/Lt James Farmer and F/Lt James Thompson while the two main instructors were F/Lt William Riley and F/O Peter E. G. Carter. Maloney, Farmer, Thompson, Riley, Carter and S/Ldr Jack Satchell played a significant role in the lives of Gnyś and the other Polish pilots, helping them in all aspects of conversion training. Despite the language barrier, they were very grateful to the British pilots for their skill, patience and commitment and for then leading them into combat. All were excellent pilots and fine gentlemen.

As of October 11th, 1940 until June 14th, 1941, Gnyś spent time with No. 302 going back and forth between RAF stations Leconfield, Northolt, Tangmere and Halton.

Needed where the action was much hotter, 302 Squadron was moved 126 miles south to Duxford (still within No. 12 Fighter Group) on September 14th. They stayed here until the 25th and at that point Władek's OTU program was over. Duxford is 55 miles north of London. Here, they joined the "Big Wing" under the command of the illustrious Douglas Bader. The Big Wing involved the use of three to five squadrons (a squadron had nine to 12 aircraft) in a wing-sized formation to meet approaching Luftwaffe bombers and deliver a big "punch" in a potential knock-out situation. So at maximum, there could be as many as 60 Allied fighters in the air at once. Both Group Captain Douglas Bader and 12 Group commander Air Vice-Marshal Leigh-Mallory were big advocates of this tactic.

Douglas Bader

Group Captain Douglas Bader (1910–1982) was one of the most famous aces and respected RAF pilots of World War II. Despite the fact that he lost the lower parts of both legs while performing aerobatics in 1931, he never lost hope or the desire to fly again. After many obstacles and much retraining, he was reactivated as a pilot. Bader took part in the Battle of France (Dunkirk) and the Battle of Britain. By late summer of 1941, he had been credited with over two dozen aerial victories. In August 1941, he was shot down over France and captured. After a number of escape attempts, Bader was sent to the high-security POW camp at Colditz Castle in Germany. There he remained until liberated by the Americans in April 1945. In the years that followed, he went back to work in the oil industry, but continued to fly. A crowning moment for him in later life was being knighted by the Queen for his crusading efforts for the disabled.

★

It is widely accepted that September 15th was the climax of the Battle of Britain. Göring threw everything he had at London: wave after wave of bombers and escorting Messerschmitts. (The "Blitz" falls within Phase 4 of the Battle of Britain.) It was a time of the most intense, continuous and focused bombing of the UK by Nazi Germany during the Second World War. It was a new kind of warfare: the attempted annihilation of urban populations. The Luftwaffe's night bombers (in mid-August 1940) while aiming for RAF targets, accidentally hit homes in London, killing civilians.[9] This event escalated the war on urban centers very quickly when Churchill responded by bombing Berlin the following night. On the afternoon of September 7th (first stage of the Blitz), almost 1,000 German aircraft descended on London. Between September 7th 1940 and May 21st, 1941, thousands of tons of bombs were dropped on 16 British cities. Over almost 37 weeks, London was attacked over 71 times, Birmingham, Liverpool and Plymouth eight times, Bristol six, Glasgow five, Southampton four, Portsmouth and Hull three and there was also at least one big raid on another eight cities, including the notorious destruction of Coventry.)[10]

On September 15th, 1940, No. 12 Fighter Group, part of the Big Wing at Duxford, was scrambled twice and for the first time 302 Squadron engaged in large-scale combat over London.[11] Hurricane and Spitfire squadrons from No. 11 Fighter Group were also involved in the interception of Dornier and Ju 88 bombers with their escorting Messerschmitts (Bf 109s). WAAF plotters at Fighter Command in Stanmore and other sub-control stations such as in Uxbridge were worked furiously to keep track of the numerous aircraft, friend and foe, on their plotting tables.

The skies over London became a vista of deadly scenes: fighters turned and twisted trying to both deliver and avoid attack, dogfighting at the ultimate. Tracer bullets sprayed everywhere as the planes tangled from all over the sky. Some aircraft collided at full speed and flipped onto their backs, bits of their machines flying off to the ground below. There was the constant danger of shooting one's own comrade if he came into the line of fire. Pilots on both sides were fighting like men possessed as they climbed and dove. People below could not always see the struggle if the planes went into and above cloud cover, but they could hear the screaming engines and machine-gun fire and witness empty shell casings, shrapnel and debris raining down on them. Not only did they see the falling, burning aircraft, but they witnessed parachutes slowly floating to earth. The skies were filled with contrails—the trails of condensed moisture from engine exhaust—left behind at high altitudes in spaghetti-like shapes.

At the end of the day, 302 Squadron achieved 11 victories and seven probables, but lost three Hurricanes and unfortunately one pilot. P/O Stanisław Chałupa destroyed two of the 11 enemy planes himself.[12] All pilots gave a magnificent account of themselves.

At RAF Duxford No. 302 found Douglas Bader to be a pleasant and congenial man who took a direct personal interest in his pilots. After returning from operations they would gather in the officers' mess for a few drinks and discuss the experiences of the day. Władek just made it to Duxford after his conversion training ended, and was able to be with 302 before they departed on the 25th. They talked about their involvement with the French Air Force and what tactics had worked for them personally when battling the Luftwaffe. The Poles questioned the British procedure of their very close formation method, because the pilot's complete attention was directed to keeping the wing of his aircraft even and level with the aircraft in front and at the side. The Poles' method differed. Their procedure was quite simple, yet effective. A section of three would fly approximately 200 feet above the (French) squadron, safeguarding the main flight below. The squadron would fly in a much looser formation, enabling a sudden break. This method gave far more flexibility during an attack.

Leaning in his chair, artificial legs crossed, puffing on his pipe, Bader listened intently. "Good idea," he would say and "Good show," nodding periodically in complete agreement. The Poles also described their technique of attacking enemy bombers head on (when possible) at close range causing panic and the breaking up of the bomber formation, making them more vulnerable. These tactics were put under consideration for implementation by Bader and the RAF. Overall, Bader made a lasting impression with the pilots and was certainly an inspiration to No. 302 Squadron.

On September 18th, the wing was scrambled three times; for 302 Polish Squadron it was a day of outstanding success. On their third sortie with the rest of the Duxford Wing, they encountered a formation of approaching Ju 88 bombers on their way to bomb London. Since Spitfires were even matches for the escorting Messerschmitts, two Spitfire squadrons left the wing to deal with them. In the meantime, S/Ldr Bader led his three Hurricane squadrons in an almost 90° dive on the first formation of German bombers, breaking them up and forcing them to do an about-face. As they retreated, the Poles attacked with great resolve.

The following ten pilots from 302 were credited with victories on this day: S/Ldr Satchell, S/Ldr Mümler, F/Lt Riley, P/O Karwowski, P/O Pilch, P/O Wapniarek, Sgt Paterek, F/Lt Jastrzębski, F/O Kowalski and F/Lt Farmer. There was no loss of life for 302. Air Vice-Marshal Leigh-Mallory personally congratulated the Poles for their "keenness and gallantry displayed in these combats."[13]

Even though pilot casualties were high collectively, Fighter Command under Dowding's direction was able to counterattack sufficiently and repel the Luftwaffe assaults, downing many German aircraft in the process. As a result of these successes and the accumulative efforts of the many fighter squadrons in Britain, it was no big surprise that Hitler, on September 19th, terminated Operation Sea Lion.

★

As of September 7th, London was bombed by the Luftwaffe for 57 consecutive nights (less one). Between one and two million homes were damaged or destroyed and more than 40,000 civilians were killed, almost half of them in London.[14] Overall during this conflict, industry and ports not in London were also heavily bombarded. Liverpool for example was heavily hit resulting in almost 4,000 deaths. The port of Hull in northeast England which is on the North Sea was attacked many times killing about 1,200 civilians. Other ports raided were Bristol, Plymouth, Swansea, Southampton, Cardiff and Portsmouth. Industrial cities were also prime targets for the Luftwaffe such as Manchester, Coventry, Birmingham, Glasgow, Belfast and Sheffield.

Despite all this chaos and destruction, the war economy of the UK was diminished, but not devastated and the people kept a "stiff upper lip" under Churchill's guidance. By May 1941, the threat of an invasion of Britain had passed with Hitler's attention now focused on the Soviet Union in the east with Operation Barbarossa.

In September of 1940, the capital was a massive sprawling city, a target not too hard to miss. It was the heart of the country with the greatest density of urban population and it had a well oiled but vulnerable infrastructure.

As protection, certain safeguards were put into place, like the incredibly loud air raid sirens or "Moaning Minnie" which warned of approaching enemy aircraft. These sirens gave the people time to run into local shelters. They also announced the anticipated all-clear sound. London's famous "tube" (underground rail) system became a temporary home for many thousands during the raids as they were usually deep enough and large enough to provide protective shelter. However, the living conditions were poor and they became overcrowded and unsanitary. There were a few direct hits and flooding from broken sewers and water mains added to the death toll. Numerous barrage balloons with heavy steel cables were strategically placed around the city to discourage low-level bombing. Gas masks were provided to all citizens just in case the bombs contained lethal gas. Blackouts were imposed to decrease target visibility. Massive searchlights swept the night skies over London locating targets for the AA guns. All in all, these safeguard measures did save lives, but they also unified the British people and gave them a feeling of solidarity. Petrol was rationed and vehicles were not allowed to use their headlights after dark so driving was slow and risky, but one became used to the conditions.

After bombing raids, civilian casualties were atrocious. If not killed, countless Londoners became trapped under collapsed homes; local neighbors and volunteers worked frantically to dig them out. In addition, water, electricity, gas mains and sewers were broken, and roads were blocked by demolished buildings.

Causing great fires, incendiary or fire bombs were also dropped along with high explosives. Once buildings caught fire, they were very difficult to extinguish as firefighters could not logistically and safely handle such massive blazes. In fact, many firefighters were killed during the war with thousands seriously injured. The Nazi objective was to create deadly firestorms to not only consume city blocks but to act as beacons to guide in subsequent flights of bombers.

Day after day, week after week, the bombs continued to fall. The RAF did their best to shoot down as many of the raiders as possible, but still many got through. Churchill shared the public's rage and scornfully announced, "He [Hitler] has lighted a fire which will burn with a steady and consuming flame until the last vestiges of Nazi tyranny have been burnt out of Europe."

★

On September 25th, 302 Squadron returned to Leconfield and for the next several weeks, until October 11th, no enemy was encountered.

On September 28th and 29th for example, P/O Gnyś participated in five flights in formation flying and climbed as high as 25,000 feet and as low as 5,000 feet performing aerobatics. While on October 6th, he tested his guns by firing them into the sea ensuring that all armaments were in working order.

During this time, and according to Władek's log book, he made a total of 14 flights (average of one per day) flying Hurricanes WX code letters: D, Q, E, J, Z, B, V, T (he flew Q, E, J, and B more than once each). Along with the squadron's two code letters in large print (e.g. 302's WX), the large single code letters of the alphabet were painted on the fuselage on one side of the roundel. This was of course for identification purposes.

On October 11th, No. 302 switched places with Polish No. 303 Squadron who moved up from Northolt airbase to "quiet" Leconfield in the north for a well-deserved rest. This sort of rotation was commonplace especially during the Battle of Britain.

Activity in Northolt was initially very limited due to the deterioration of weather conditions: cloudy with rain, gusty winds and invading fog made flying very dangerous if not impossible. The ever-present balloon barrages with their heavy grounded cables made flying even more dangerous over London and, as such, the pilots had to be extra careful not to run into them when landing. Władek had a close shave once when returning home from a combat mission during inclement weather. Visibility over southeast London was poor and the wires from the barrage balloons were very difficult to see. Without warning, he felt a violent jerk on his right wing. "Oh my God, I've hit a wire!" he shouted. Fortunately he was able to land safely, after which he noticed that a chunk of the wingtip was missing.

Over this six week period, P/O Gnyś was kept very busy with 302 patrolling the skies on the look out for enemy planes. According to his flight log book, they had nine encounters with the Luftwaffe. Even though there were exchanges of gunfire, he was not credited with any confirmed kills. Władek's philosophy was that if he didn't see a German aircraft with which he was fighting either explode, crash or forced to land, he did not report a victory.

Specifically, on October 15th, waves of about 100 Bf 109 Messerschmitts carrying bombs, headed for London. The weather was dreadful with thick cloud cover resulting in very low visibility. The British 229 Squadron joined the Poles in a fierce dogfight. F/Lt Riley and P/O Król had confirmed victories. Fortunately, there was no loss of life on their side, but several Hurricanes were destroyed: Sgt Wędzik baled out, P/O Maliński crash-landed, S/Ldr Satchell's plane was damaged and Sgt Kosarz hit a barrage balloon wire and clipped his starboard wing in bad visibility, but managed to land safely. Only two pilots landed back at Northolt while the rest landed elsewhere. Once the weather cleared, they went back to base.[15]

Between combat sorties and bad weather, the pilots would patronize a fashionable restaurant called The Orchard, in Ruislip, West London. Even though the Northolt airbase had a handsome, well-equipped and spacious officers' mess, the pilots looked forward to going to The Orchard on their time off. It was a friendly destination for young men and women to have a drink, a meal, make new acquaintances and dance to a live band. The Orchard was just a couple of miles north of the Northolt airfield. It had always been a well-frequented establishment before the war, but it then became an even more popular spot as it provided a very close and convenient social destination for the squadrons at Northolt during the war. In particular, Polish Squadrons 302 and 303 "adopted" The Orchard as their own.[16]

Barbara Simmons's close friend Muriel Lauther came to live with Barbara and her mother in Pinner not too far away from The Orchard Hotel in Ruislip. The two girls had grown up together and had attended Northwick Park College.[17]

The girls shared a bedroom, except during the air raids when they slept on a mattress in the cupboard under the stairs. More often than not, this area would stay intact even if the rest of the house collapsed as a result of a bomb exploding nearby.

One Saturday evening in October 1940, Barbara and Muriel went to The Orchard with Muriel's brothers John and Billy. The softly lit lounge had an atmosphere of excitement for them with the glamor of many Allied uniforms from such countries as Canada, Poland and Czechoslovakia.

Blackout regulations called for lowlight and absolutely no interior illumination to be visible from the outside. This only added to the allure of the well-furnished room with its white tablecloths and waiters in tails serving patrons. In one corner of the room was a three-piece band and couples danced to the popular music of the times. It was easy to forget that a war was going on outside and people paid little heed to the occasional air-raid siren and the explosion of a distant bomb.

Barbara noticed a group of Polish officers sitting at a nearby table close to the dance floor. They appeared to be in high spirits, laughing and raising their glasses. One of the Poles, Władek, was staring at her intently. She pretended not to notice, but then his eyes met hers causing her face to flush and her heart to race. He was infatuated by this beautiful English girl. When Barbara got up to dance with Billy she could feel the dark-haired man's penetrating gaze boring into her. She was intrigued with this handsome stranger. When the evening came to an end, with a slight nod, Władek smiled at Barbara.

The following Saturday evening was a repeat of the last but this time Barbara deliberately looked across the tables and solidly met his gaze. With a cigarette in one hand and a glass in the other, he smiled, raised his glass ever so slightly and put it to his lips. She flashed a quick smile in return, then turned her attention to her friends who suggested that they get up and dance.

Just as the song was ending, three of the Poles jumped up and made their way to the microphone. Władek was one of them. They briefly spoke to the leader of the band who nodded approvingly. The music changed to a popular French song of the time called "J'attendrai" (I will wait). To everyone's surprise, they started to sing it which got Barbara's attention—as planned. Władek continued to look at Barbara and directed the refrain at her. Before the song ended, he quickly left his two friends, crossed the dance floor and tapped her dance partner on the shoulder.

Smiling from ear to ear and in broken English, he said, "Pardon! Scuse please!" Barbara's date graciously stepped to one side and handed her over to the good-looking Polish officer. He then slid his arm around her waist, took her hand and immediately stepped on her foot; he was most embarrassed. Barbara started to laugh which seemed to break the ice.

"Me Władek ... your name?"

"Barbara," she replied.

"Oh, Bar-bar-a! Nice name ... in Polish ... Baśka [Bashka]."

When the band stopped playing, he led her back to their table, pulled the chair out for her and said, "*Dziękuję*—thank you!" He then gave a little bow to Barbara and her friends and returned to his group. Her table was most impressed!

Later as the evening drew to a close and they made their way to the cloak room, Władek was waiting in the lobby.

"Baśka, you see me tomorrow, please?"

In time of war life tends to move along fairly quickly. In fact, the next day, Barbara introduced Władek to her mother Eva Simmons with whom she lived. Their comfortable home at 44 The Avenue was located in Rayner's Lane in a suburban district in the Borough of Harrow in northwest London between Pinner and west of Harrow. It was near The Orchard, RAF Northolt and Stanmore where Fighter Command Headquarters was based.

When he met Eva, he bowed slightly and kissed her hand. She was impressed by this chivalrous foreign gentleman. His splendid manners won her over completely. The coffee and biscuits were good, but the conversation was difficult. However, dispite the language barrier, both women were thoroughly charmed. Not overstaying his welcome, Władek said goodbye to Eva inside the parlor, then Barbara walked him to the door. He gently kissed her on the lips and to his surprise, she put her arms around his neck and returned the kiss. At that point, they both knew that they were falling hopelessly in love.

They had about six happy weeks together while Władek was stationed at Northolt. Whenever he was not flying or had days off, he would see "Baśka" and they enjoyed walking, cycling, sitting in Eva's garden and sometimes went to The Orchard. On those occasions, as soon as they sat down, the band would start to play "J'attendrai." This became their favorite song especially since it was the catalyst that brought them together.[18]

Barbara got to know "Teddie" (Tadeusz Czerwiński) and "Eddie (Edward Pilch)," two of Władek's pilot friends and their English girlfriends, Joyce and Jean. They all got along extremely well and went out together to dine and dance at The Orchard. The girls all shared the same fears regarding the dangerous missions their men flew. Often, they would watch the pilots fly overhead, get into formation and be off on their sorties. Anxiously, they would wait for their return counting the number of planes returning to base.

Barbara lost her uncle Bernard Simmons in World War I fighting in the trenches in France. In his early twenties, he was killed on August 8th, 1918 three months before the war ended at Démuin on the Somme. His death was very hard for the Simmons family. With the death of her uncle on her mind, one of the last things in the world that Barbara wanted, was to lose the love of her life. She spent many sleepless nights thinking about what her life would be like without her "white knight in Polish armor" who called her Baśka.

★

It was bad enough being outnumbered in a dogfight, but flying in inclement weather could sometimes be more frightening … and disastrous. When a pilot lost visual contact with the ground and/or his comrades, he could become disoriented and in the pursuit of a suitable landing site, he could collide with another plane, objects or features on the ground or simply run out of fuel and crash. Władek said, "The worst part about flying in bad weather was the descent."

Two consecutive days in 1940 proved to be devastating for 302 Squadron.

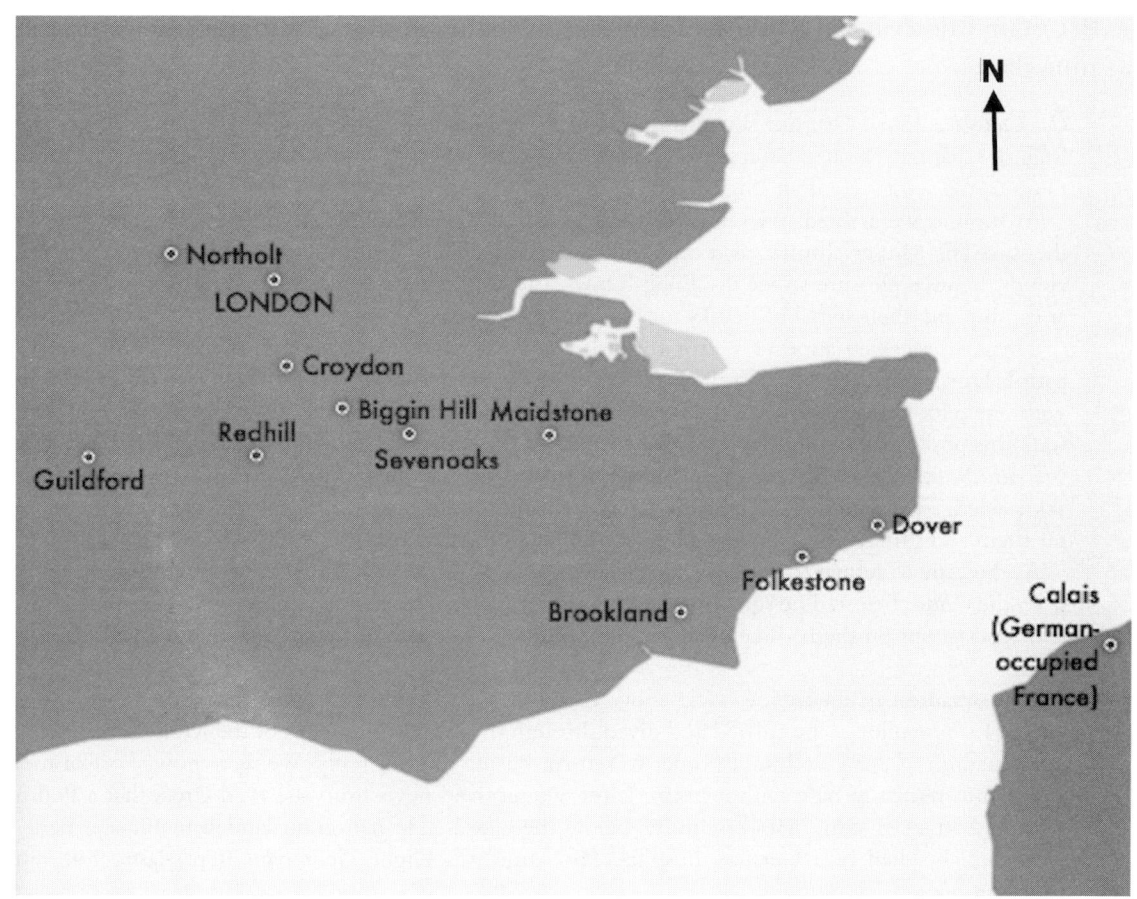

Locations patrolled by P/O Gnyś and 302 Fighter Sqn: According to his flight log book, nine interceptions were recorded from October 11th–November 23rd, 1940.

On October 17th, during an operational flight Sgt Załuski lost his bearings in the clouds above ground level and was forced to land as he was running out of fuel. He died when he crashed in rugged terrain.

On October 18th, 302 was scrambled to intercept a formation of German aircraft. The weather conditions at ground level were abysmal. After a brief encounter downing a Ju 88 above the thick fog cover, returning back down to base was marked with tragedy. F/O Carter, F/O Borowski, P/O Wapniarek and P/O Żukowski (one of Władek's friends) all crashed and were killed! These four young men were lost apparently as a result of poor decision-making at the operations room level to scramble the squadron in such bad weather conditions.[19]

Despite the blow to morale, the Poles had no choice but to resume their flying duties. During the next several days, the squadron continued its operational flying. Three new pilots fresh from 5 OTU joined 302 Squadron: P/O Antolak, P/O Sporny and Sgt Rytka.

P/O Gnyś describes a day of combat and how they lost a sixth comrade and friend in nine days:

> On October 25th 1940, our squadron took off from Northolt with the task of patrolling over the English Channel. We had been patrolling for some time when the operations room gave us an order to go to the assistance of an English squadron fighting under heavy odds.
>
> As soon as we arrived, we climbed to attack the enemy from above and from the direction of the sun. The Messerschmitts, as if on command, immediately went down and disappeared into the clouds. It was a pleasure to see the English boys waving the wings of their aircrafts from side to side at us, showing their signal of thanks for coming to their aid.
>
> Then we received another vector towards the area where we were supposed to continue our patrol. During this type of patrol, one section of the squadron would fly above the other section with one pilot flying singly over them to guard against any surprise attack. I was usually the one who took this position. I would fly faster that the rest of the squadron constantly keeping watch towards the sun. Suddenly, I noticed a few Messerschmitts "around the sun." I informed my leader who acknowledged my message. Then the Messerschmitts swept down upon us but we were prepared for them and suffered no damage. They continued going down and disappeared into the clouds.
>
> As the time to return to the base approached, once again we saw more Messerschmitts emerging from the clouds below. The squadron went in to the attack. The first few pilots who were the closest managed to fire on them, [likely] shooting one down. The rest of them took refuge in the clouds again.
>
> Our squadron made a wide circle above the clouds, gathering our pilots into closer formation, except for one pilot … he turned and dived through the clouds in pursuit of the Messerschmitts … our squadron leader gave him an order to return, but he did not reply. We were now short of fuel and had to return to base without him. Later, we received news from the Red Cross that a Polish pilot had attacked some Messerschmitts below the clouds. He had crash-landed in France. Badly wounded, he died in a German hospital. His name was Flight Lieutenant (Cpt) Jastrzębski, an excellent pilot.[20]

Despite the loss of Franek Jastrzębski, the squadron was up and running the next day—business as usual.

October 26th came quickly for P/O Gnyś who logged three sorties in which the last patrol flight over Maidstone, with an interception over the French coast, took two hours; any longer and fuel would have been an issue. Total flying time for him that day was a stressful three hours, 45 minutes. Over the next few days they also patrolled over Croydon, Brookland and Northolt. For the month of October, 302 Squadron made five enemy interceptions over the southeast region and coastal France.

Allied countries that took part in the Battle of Britain[21]

Participant Eligibility: A total of 2,937 (updated from 2,936) airmen[22] from 15 countries around the world took part in this conflict against Germany. They were awarded the Battle of Britain clasp for having flown at least one authorized operational sortie with an accredited unit of RAF Fighter Command during the period from July 10th to October 31st, 1940.

National representation

Great Britain 2,342
Poland 145 (largest non–British contributor)
New Zealand 127
Canada 112
Czechoslovakia 88
Australia 32
Belgium 28
South Africa 25
France 13
United States 9
Ireland 10
Rhodesia 3
Barbados 1
Jamaica 1
Newfoundland 1 (an independent dominion in 1940, became part of Canada in 1949)
Palestine 1
During this conflict, 544 lost their lives (18.5%), almost 1 in 5. A further 795 were to
die before the end of the war, in total, almost half.

Unit participation[23]

Squadrons: 1, 1(RCAF), 3, 17, 19, 23, 25, 29, 32, 41, 43, 46, 54, 56, 64, 65, 66, 72,
73, 74, 79, 85, 87, 92, 111, 141, 145, 151, 152, 213, 219, 222, 229, 232, 234, 235,
236, 238, 242, 245, 247, 248, 249, 253, 257, 263, 264, 266, 302, 303, 310, 312, 501,
504, 600, 601, 602, 603, 604, 605, 607, 609, 610, 611, 615, and 616 (66 in total)
Flights: 421, 422 and 1 Fighter Interception Unit
Fleet Air Arm: 804 and 808 Squadrons
Grand total: 71

The controversy of rank

In 1940 when the organization of the Polish Air Force in Britain was in its early stage, all
Polish officers had to start with the lowest Royal Air Force rank, i.e.: P/O Pilot Officer.
Even though the Polish pilots were already seasoned fighters having taken part in the
Polish and French campaigns against Germany, they were not allowed by RAF authorities
to hold equivalent ranks to the British pilots who had little or no combat experience.
The British (like the French) had never seen the Poles in action and couldn't understand
how the Luftwaffe defeated them so quickly, thus assuming that the Polish pilots were not
highly skilled combatants. This was of course unfair and untrue. The RAF soon changed

their tune once they witnessed how fearless and tenacious the Polish fighters really were during combat. In fact, the most successful Hurricane squadron in the Battle of Britain was No. 303 ("Kościuszko") Polish Squadron RAF, which scored the highest number of kills.

No. 302 Squadron Pilots Who Participated in the Battle of Britain

BRITISH

S/Ldr Jack Satchell
F/Lt John Farmer
F/Lt James Thomson
F/Lt William Riley ‡‡
F/O Peter Carter ‡ Oct 18

POLISH

S/Ldr Mieczysław Mümler
F/Lt Piotr Łaguna ‡‡
F/Lt Franciszek Jastrzębski ‡ Oct 25
Sgt Antoni Beda
P/O Bronisław Bernaś
F/O Jan Borowski ‡ Oct 18
P/O Stanisław Chałupa
F/Lt Tadeusz Chłopik ‡ Sept 15
P/O Jerzy Czerniak ‡‡
F/Lt Jan Czerny
F/O Tadeusz Czerwiński ‡‡
P/O Władysław Gnyś
P/O Włodzimierz Karwowski
P/O Stefan Kleczkowski
Sgt Wilhelm Kosarz ‡‡
F/O Julian Kowalski
P/O Wacław Król
P/O Stanisław Łapka
Sgt Antoni Łysek ‡‡
P/O Jan Maliński
Sgt Antoni Mierkiewicz
Sgt Eugeniusz Nowakiewicz
P/O Edward Pilch ‡‡
P/O Stefan Wapniarek ‡ Oct 18
F/Lt Antoni Wczelik
Sgt Marian Wędzik

P/O Zbigniew Wróblewski
Sgt Jerzy Załuski ‡ Oct 17
P/O Aleksiej Żukowski ‡ Oct 18
Total: 34
‡ 7 killed in Battle of Britain (1 in 5)
‡‡ 7 killed by the end of 1942

Battle of Britain Top 10 RAF Aces[24]

Name	Squadron	Nationality
P/O Eric Lock	41	British (killed Aug 1941)
Sgt James Lacey	501	British
F/Lt Archibald McKellar	605	British (killed Nov 1940)
Sgt Josef František	303	Czech (killed Oct 1940)
F/O Brian Carbury	603	New Zealander
P/O Robert Doe	234/238	British
S/Ldr Witold Urbanowicz	145/303	Polish
F/Lt Paterson Hughes	234	Australian (killed Sept 1940)
F/O Colin Gray	54	New Zealander
S/Ldr Michael Crossley	32	British

CHAPTER 7

November 1940–June 1944

"I bow my head in humble respect to my many fighter pilot friends for their individual and courageous accomplishments. They were young, proud and fearless."

W. G.

According to his flight log book, over the five-month period November 1940 to March 1941, Władek made 40 flights in his Hawker Hurricane doing routine patrols, testing his guns, scrambles, Luftwaffe interceptions and high-altitude flying. Activity in the colder months was limited by adverse weather conditions. His busiest month by far was March where he logged 20 flights. He logged 20 hours, 45 minutes, made three interceptions and tested the engine capabilities of his plane by flying at 35,000 feet, the highest to date. His Hurricane of choice was code 'W', flying it 12 times in March. From January 1st to April 11th, 1941 (including March) he flew 'W' a total of 21 times and 'T' nine times.

With regard to high-altitude flying, and jumping ahead to 1943 while on a sortie in his Spitfire, he blacked out and was almost killed. Usually, there was never a problem, but sometimes, unusual things can happen at that height. On one fighter sweep over France, Władek's squadron flew low overland to prevent the Germans from picking them up on their radar. On the squadron leader's signal, they climbed steeply, their engines at full throttle. Somewhere over 25,000 feet Władek blacked out. Moments passed and then he seemed to hear voices, faintly at first and then growing louder. His engine was roaring, but he was too weak in his semiconscious state to fully realize the gravity of the situation as his aircraft dove rapidly.

Gradually, the haziness of his mind began to clear. All the time the voices seemed to be forcing him back to consciousness. Finally he distinguished the words: "Władek! Władek! Wake up! Pull up! Pull up your aircraft!" The urgency in the voices hammered at his brain and his mind returned to almost full comprehension. With horror, he realized that his Spitfire was diving towards the sea. He closed the throttle and reduced the speed and pulled on the joystick with all his strength. He managed to bring his plane out of its deadly dive just above the water. That was too close for comfort. He climbed to a suitable height, and, after giving himself time to recover, returned to base. After landing, the mechanics examined his plane. There was no mechanical problem, but speculation was that there could have been condensation in his oxygen line that froze and blocked the flow of air. This occurrence did not happen to him again for the rest of the war.[1]

On April 7th, 1941, 302 Squadron moved to RAF Kenley a district in the South London Borough of Croydon. RAF Kenley was a strategic airfield during and after the Battle of Britain. It was in close proximity to RAF Biggin Hill and Redhill just outside Croydon. All three stations south of the capital contained Allied squadrons responsible for the air defense of London and the East End. Northolt, northwest of London was also part of this defense effort. The Germans called Croydon the "second line of defense" for London and warned that they would bomb it into submission. From October 7th, 1940 to June 6th, 1941, almost 1,400 high-explosive bombs were dropped on Croydon.

Gnyś described conditions during a bombing raid on Croydon when he and others were on the ground near Kenley:

> Every day we were taking off for the interception of any approaching enemy aircraft or patrolling the English coast or protecting our sea convoys against Luftwaffe attacks. In the evenings after flying duties, we would often go to the local pub for supper and drinks. One night in May 1941, four of us (close friends since the start of the war in Poland) were sitting at a table waiting for the waiter to bring our order. The small band was playing when suddenly their music was drowned out by the mournful wailing of the air raid warning siren. Almost immediately, our ack-ack [AA] guns could be clearly heard. We got into our car to return to the station immediately. The air raid was extremely heavy. The German bombers were immediately overhead. Incendiary bombs completely lit up the town of Croydon. Houses received direct hits and exploded like match boxes. All around us was an inferno.
>
> It was then that I met the real English people, the true heroes. People were under tremendous stress—their homes being destroyed before their very eyes. Although there was chaos with people running for cover, the way they handled themselves filled me with admiration. Neighbors were helping neighbors to carry or dig out friends and relatives from the damaged houses and rubble.
>
> We stopped our car and ran to help dig out those who were trapped. All the while we were tripping and falling over broken bricks in our haste and effort to rescue the unfortunate victims.
>
> During this time I noticed one man in particular. Regardless of the terrific danger from the bombs exploding everywhere, he was running continuously with others carrying women and children out from burning houses.
>
> I was close to him as he carried out a little girl—she couldn't have been more than three. I took the terrified child from him and he turned towards a pile of burning rubble that was once a house. He looked at me, tears streaming down his dusty cheeks, "That was my home. My wife and three children were inside." He brushed the tears from his face, turned quickly and continued to help his neighbors in their plight.
>
> This gentleman was indeed a real hero of the war and one I will never forget.
>
> A large section of Croydon was razed to the ground that night and we had difficulty in getting through the destruction to the base early next morning. We took with us a mental picture of these wonderful British people's fantastic courage under heavy fire. I knew that they would not be defeated easily.[2]

One night in May, 1941 while in Croydon for dinner with his pilot friends, the Luftwaffe rained bombs down on the borough, killing and trapping civilians in their homes. Without hesitation, they all helped free survivors. Here Władek helps rescue an hysterical young girl from what used to be her home.

302 Squadron roster (May 1st, 1941)[3]

C.O.: S/Ldr Piotr Łaguna

A FLIGHT

F/Lt Julian Kowalski C.O.
F/Lt Włodzimierz Karwowski
F/O Stanisław Łapka
F/O Zbigniew Wróblewski
F/O Jan Maliński
F/O Aleksander Narucki
F/O Władysław Kamiński
F/Sgt Eugeniusz Nowakiewicz
F/Sgt Marian Domagała
F/Sgt Antoni Łysek

B FLIGHT

F/Lt Tadeusz Czerwiński C.O.
F/Lt Wacław Król
F/O Zygmunt Kinel
F/O Władysław Gnyś
F/O Marceli Neyder
F/O Zbigniew Janicki
F/Sgt Antoni Beda
F/Sgt Marian Rytka
F/Sgt Marian Wędzik
Sgt Bronisław Malinowski

F/Lt Marian Duryasz and F/O Stanisław Chałupa were detailed off to the operation room of the Kenley sector.

★

Sometime in mid-May, Barbara got a call from Władek who explained that he had a three-day leave and wanted to come over and discuss something with her and Eva. Her curiosity was really piqued, but he wouldn't say anything more. She told him that Eva was just getting ready to leave for Newport and wouldn't be back until Tuesday. Barbara filled her in with Władek's call just before she left the house.

When he arrived at their home and without any warning, he blurted out in broken English, "Would you like go with me to public registry office in London?"

Too astonished to speak, Barbara sucked in a deep breath and the words came tumbling out: "You mean, get married? You mean, you want me to be your wife? You mean, now? Right now?"

"Yes, my darling!"

On May 17th, they walked out of the registry office as man and wife.

Since the war was still roaring overhead, there had been no time for a formal wedding, and Barbara felt that her mother who was recently widowed, could not afford it anyway.

So when Eva came back on the Tuesday she almost fell over with shock: her nineteen-year-old daughter was now a married woman. However, she gave them her blessing, love and total support. They couldn't have been happier. Four years later they were remarried in a church with close friends and family around them.

★

By the end of February 1941, Polish Hurricane squadrons were flying close protection for English bombers over the English Channel on their way to targets in occupied France. Usually, the Hurricanes escorted the bombers while Spitfires flew top cover as they were a better match for the Messerschmitts. By May, the action was warming up again:

May 8th—Flight B: attacked five Bf 109s at 10,000 feet, dogfight resulted. F/Lt Król and F/O Kinel shot down one each and F/Sgt Rytka with one probable; Flight A: F/Sgt Nowakiewicz destroyed one from another group of German fighters but in the afternoon, S/Ldr Łaguna and F/Sgt (Sgt Maj) Domagała were attacked and forced to bale out; Flight B (evening): F/O Wróblewski downed one Bf 109, but F/O Kinel was killed.

May 11th—Another tragedy … when the squadron was returning from a late patrol, Polish pilots had to land in the dark … three aircraft smashed into each other at the end of the runway … F/O Narucki died as a result.

May 21st—"Shot to Bits!" For F/O Gnyś, this would be a day he would long remember. It all started with Circus 18, the order to bomb a "fringe" target in occupied territory across the Channel. With a small formation of nine Blenheim bombers from 21, 82 and 110 Squadrons, they set off escorted by a large fighter formation i.e.: No. 1 Polish Wing from Northolt. Squadrons 303 and 306 flew as an advanced party trying to bring German fighters to battle and take the heat off the vulnerable Blenheim bombers who stood little chance against the Messerschmitt 109. The task for 302 Squadron was to provide close escort for the bombers together with 258 Squadron RAF who, in April, had left Jurby (Isle of Man) on their way to RAF Kenley in preparation to take the offensive to the enemy. Over target, they met and fought many defending Messerschmitts. Sgt Rytka was shot down and had to bale out, F/O (Lt) Gnyś was up against a number of German fighters at one time which left his Hurricane badly damaged, but despite this, he managed to limp back to England. Gnyś describes what took place that day:

> As we approached the French coast, our ground control room informed the squadron leader of large numbers of enemy fighters above our formation. Moments later, our Spitfires were heavily engaged in combat with them but were unable to prevent them from closing in on our bombers. We were the last ones now to stop the Messerschmitts from their attack. Unfortunately, because of the position of our Hurricanes' formation, we had not enough room to maneuver or gain speed. Both Hurricane squadrons were now under attack and had broken into loose formation intercepting Messerschmitts diving down.
>
> It was a vicious dance. Our Hurricanes were holding well … tracer bullets were everywhere. I saw some Hurricanes smoking, turning and twisting constantly in combat. We were meeting the Messerschmitts in practically head-on collisions.
>
> Suddenly, I saw an enemy fighter diving rapidly at me, shooting furiously. I threw my plane to the right and managed to escape the deadly line of fire but received some bullet holes in my left wing. Instantly more enemy fighters appeared from nowhere.
>
> We were fired upon and were firing back in a frenzy. At the same time, I was attacking a Messerschmitt, I was also attacked by another German fighter. I saw him on my tail, but could not escape from his line of fire completely. My engine had been hit and became very hot and was smoking. It started to cough and lose speed. I looked around quickly for another enemy attack and saw the Messerschmitts disappearing into the horizon.
>
> My engine was now smoking badly and was shaking. I reduced my speed and turned towards home. The English coastline was still quite a way off and I was rather apprehensive that, without my engine, I would not be able to glide the distance and would have to ditch in the sea. The bombers were now on their way home, successfully having deposited their bombs on target.

Two of my friends, seeing my plight, joined me and while flying by my side kept a protective watch over me. They were waving and motioning from their cockpits, movements of rocking back and forth in the pretense of helping my spluttering aircraft make its way over the rough aqua-green swell below.

The gratifying sight of the White Cliffs of Dover gave me the reassurance that, with lady luck on my side, I might be fortunate enough to make the aerodrome.

The waves below me, tipped with white crests, seemed only a short distance beneath me. My Hurricane was spluttering and groaning. "Come on baby … come on." I glided over the cliffs, my engine smoking very badly, I switched it off to avoid it catching on fire. Then I saw the aerodrome in front of me and the landing strip. I was losing height rapidly, I knew I would not make the runway. I looked around … a large field was close … I guided her in cautiously. I did not want to damage my plane any more than necessary. I felt the wheels touch the ground. I patted the side of my plane, "Good old girl, I knew you could make it!" My friends flew over me waving their wings in happy relief that I had landed on dry land safely.[4]

When F/O Gnyś got back to England after his harrowing ordeal on May 21st, 1941 over France, he was admitted to RAF Hospital Halton suffering from shock and anxiety from a near-death experience. Even though not physically wounded, his mental state was affected. The doctors discovered that he exhibited symptoms of what is today known as post-traumatic stress disorder (PTSD), referred to then as COSR (combat stress reaction). In World War I the term was shell shock.

The following factors that day were most likely responsible for his COSR condition: that he was unable to fully protect the Blenheim bombers from the Messerschmitts; being attacked on all sides by numerous enemy aircraft; seeing tracer bullets all around him and knowing that his plane was shot to bits even losing parts of his wings and tail plus the fact that bullets could have entered his cockpit and killed him; his seeing and hearing his motor smoking, choking, stammering, losing speed and control; flying above the Channel's cold watery surface and not knowing if he could make it to the White Cliffs; not being able to make it to the airbase and having to make a crash-landing in a field.

All these contributed to his hospitalization. After treatment and rest for a little more than three weeks, he was discharged on June 14th, 1941. He resumed flying again on June 16th.

The Palace Hotel in Torquay is located on the south coast of England. Due to an anticipated number of casualties, the RAF converted the hotel into a recovery hospital with 48 beds for its officers by October 1939. By December, it was equipped with 249 beds. With its lush gardens, magnificent landscaping, accessibility and its mild Mediterranean-like climate, it was the perfect spot for convalescing.

From 1940 to 1942, the hotel-hospital was in full swing treating injured RAF officers. Eventually, German intelligence learned about this facility. Allied pilots who had recovered enough from physical and/or mental injury, were an obvious future threat to them, so it was put on the map as a target.

As one could see in a recently surfaced photo, F/O Władek Gnyś was indeed there, but it is not fully known if he was there as a patient for further PTSD treatment or

Dover looms. On May 21st, 1941, No. 302 Squadron with the rest of the 1st Polish Fighter Wing was escorting RAF bombers over France. A fierce battle with swarms of Messerschmitts ensued. F/O Gnyś managed to return in a badly shot-up Hurricane, but with a little help from his friends.

was there as a visitor. Inquiries at the hotel in 2015 revealed no such evidence: records could have been lost or destroyed in the bombings.

In 1942, it was in fact bombed, and convalescing airmen where killed or wounded. Four Polish officers were killed. The damage to the building was extensive and it had to be evacuated. Other accommodation was later found at the majestic Cleveleys Hydro (Golf Club) Hotel, near Blackpool. In the meantime, reconstruction of the bombed-out Palace Hotel swung into gear. The Germans realized that they would have to bomb it again, which they did in 1943. This time there were no casualties, but it had to be shut down. Today, it is a thriving hotel in all its reconstructed glory and a magnet for tourists.[5]

★

Before and even in the early stages of the Battle of Britain, British pilots and commanders were dubious about the competence of the Polish pilot escapees who arrived on British soil after the fall of Poland and France, not to mention the fact that most Poles could not speak English. However, they were quick learners and it didn't take them long to prove themselves as experienced fighters who demonstrated their deep hatred for the Nazi invaders.

On a social level, the Poles played hard as well. While off duty, they frequented the local pubs and restaurants where they drank, danced and chased English women. They were hot-blooded men who craved female companionship. As a bonus, the British women found them to be very exciting, romantic and handsome, especially in their Polish uniforms. Their broken English also added to their charm. Many, like Władek Gnyś, married English girls.

On other levels, they forged lasting friendships with members of the RAF and with non-military trained professionals such as doctors and clergy, who were, of course, an integral part of the support system of the fliers. The following are a few tangible examples from around 1941 that illustrate genuine camaraderie:

"OK!"
by S/Lt Palnam Goroom
Chief Controller, Operations Room, Tangmere

Oh these Poles who've come to stay,
So very blithe, so very gay,
All the English they can say?
OK, OK!

Jerry Hun from coast of France,
Leads Controller hellish dance
And to the Vectors they will bray.
OK, OK!

Are you airborne Pipsqueak in?
A Hun above you! Get at him!
Get a move on! Join the fray.
OK, OK!

When into the murk they fly,
You may beg them to reply,
But they go upon their way.
OK, OK!

The bomber's down, the fight is done,
Another score against the Hun.
You may land, you've earned your pay
OK, OK!

Then, they drink a mixture queer,
Gin and whisky in their beer,

But still upon their feet they stay.
OK, OK!

With the girls a great success,
A little kiss, a slight caress.
Then into her ear they say:
OK? OK!

If I must write something …
by Herbert E. Fry

"If I must write something, let it be a tribute to the grandest crowd of fellows I've worked with."

If you want a frank opinion of Hitler and his Hun,
The pedigrees of Goering and all the Reich's sons.
And you want it played to music of barking Browning guns,
Ask the Poles!

For these, who gave us Chopin and Paderewski's strains,
Have left their music, homes and friends and taken up the reins.

To fight, with us, oppression,
till nothing else remains of the Huns!

They've earned the fame that's theirs today for valour in the fight,
They've earned a place in every heart that's proud of British might.
And they'll give their shirts and trousers too, to bring their planes in sight of a Hun!

And when this war is over and the sounds of fighting end,
We'll still be proud to call them "comrade," proud to call them "friend."
And we'll raise our glass and wish that peace and happiness descend
– Forever—On the Poles.

To my very good friends of 302 Squadron—every good wish and blessing—happy landings and speedy return to your native land.
Long live Poland!
Father David L. Greenstock 5/4/41.

While at Leconfield, the pilots of 302 Squadron loved to party when they were not fighting the Luftwaffe. With the 303 Squadron pilots they constructed their own pub right inside one of the buildings on the base. It wasn't large, but it was, and still is, very ornate, well constructed and colorful. The brick fireplace was their pride and joy.

When they weren't there, they frequented a pub called The White Horse Inn in Beverley, East Riding of Yorkshire not far from the Leconfield aerodrome. It is a large 16th century original gas-lit pub which is still very popular, and nicknamed Nellies after the woman who used to manage it. Nothing much has changed for hundreds of years, it maintained its original charm and friendly atmosphere even today. This author can vouch for its vintage decor, delicious food and great beer. After spending an afternoon there, one can understand why the Poles loved it so much—P/O Gnyś was no exception. Naturally, it was also a great place to meet English women.

An adjutant to 302 Polish Squadron, D. W. A., worked with the Poles and got to know them well and became good friends. The following letter written on RAF letterhead (circa 1942) sums up their social behavior and supports the adage "work hard, play hard."

> Royal Air Force
> Tangmere,
> Chichester,
> Sussex

The fighter, being a "defensive" weapon, the Poles introduced into the station just that offensive spirit that was needed. They had, naturally enough, a wholesome hate for the Hun and they showed it magnificently when at last the trend of the war allowed them once more to close with the enemy.

This seemed always to be their chief characteristic, but I was also very strongly impressed by the vigor which they showed at the parties which we had while at Leconfield. Hospitality seems to be part of their nature: nobody seems ever to have seen a tired Pole, even in the summer, when they are on duty from 5 a.m. to 10 p.m., drank hard till the early morning and spent the rest of the night with a woman (perhaps more than one woman). They always seem keen to improve their English, and I suppose the R.A.F. are to blame if the first words they learnt were of the unprintable variety!

There was only one Air Force custom which the Poles could not absorb, the habit of good-humoured insult. It is, of course, a strange custom, but some of us British people found them unduly sensitive if a joke was made against them; they seemed rather easily to take offence.

They are grand people and I shall always be very proud of having worked for them.[6]

On October 26th, 1941 while with No. 302 Polish Squadron, F/O W. Gnyś was seconded (temporarily) to the Central Training Unit (CTU) Woodlands, Clamp Hill, Stanmore (Fighter Command) to take the (air traffic) controllers' course covering a variety of topics such as the principles of aircraft control, the organization of Fighter Command, the art of interception, R/T (Radio Telephony) speech and procedures, meteorology (the scientific study of the atmosphere), RDF (Radio Direction Finding—radar), AI (Airborne Interception—night fighter radar equipment) and GCI (Ground Controlled Interception) techniques.

The main training room was laid out like a normal sector operations room of the time with a large map table on the floor on which moveable plaques/blocks were used to indicate the position, altitude, heading and speed of both fighter and target aircraft. At the foot of this room was a raised dais from which the controller gave directions and orders to deputy controllers who radioed the relevant fighters to intercept approaching

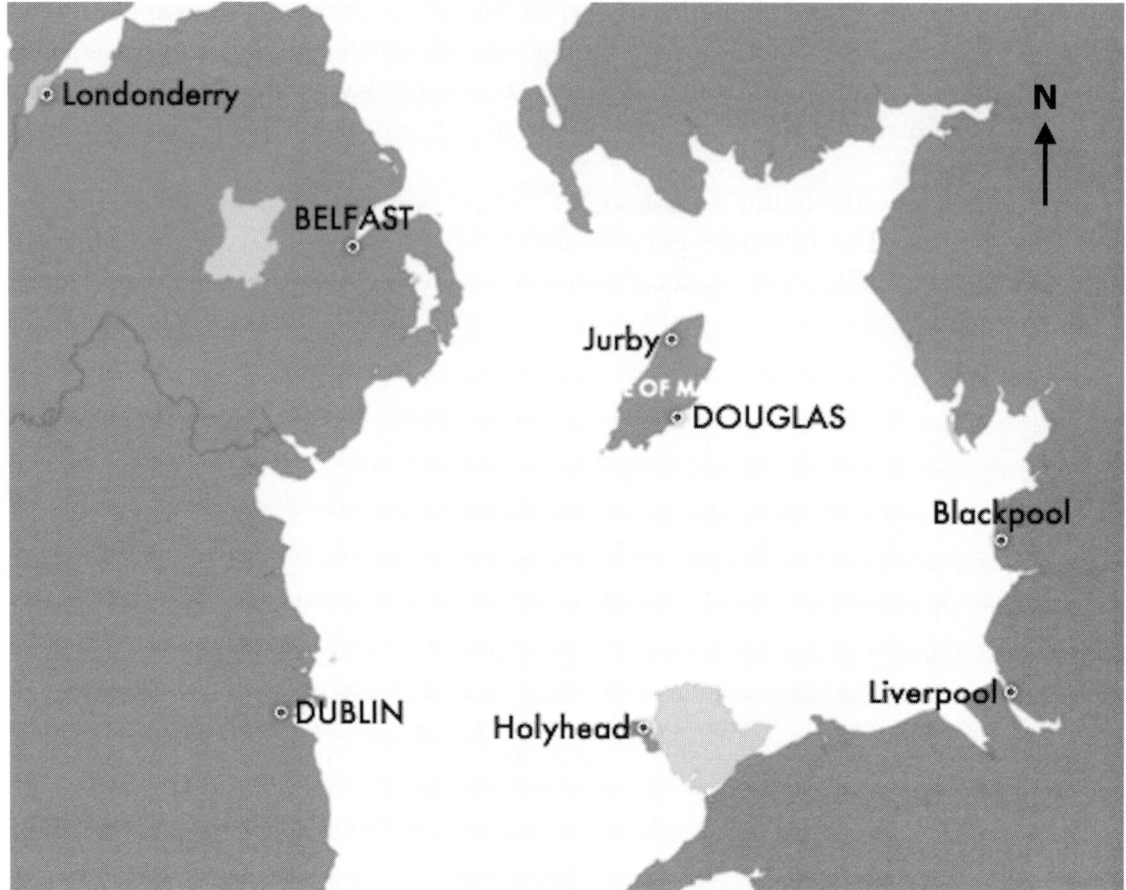

Gnyś and his unit were transferred to RAF Jurby (Isle of Man), May 28th–August 7th, 1941. Here they rested, did light patrol duties and trained new pilots.

Luftwaffe aircraft. The program objective was to simulate Luftwaffe interceptions. To add realism to the controller's task of directing the fighter plaque onto the target plaque on the map table, tricycles were peddled in the field (literally) to simulate fighter aircraft and their Luftwaffe targets. This unusual exercise also taught the trainee controllers some of the problems that their pilots had to face.

Gnyś completed the course (CTU Stanmore) on November 15th, 1941 and returned to No. 302 Squadron on November 18th. On January 23rd, 1942, he was assigned to the operations room at RAF Exeter as controller. On January 30th, he was rested and moved to No. 302 Squadron's operations room at Northolt until the end of July before transferring to 303's control room on August 1st, 1942.

No. 303 "Kosciuszko" Polish Fighter Squadron got its name from the Polish and U.S. hero General Tadeusz Kosciuszko and the Polish 7th Air Escadrille (Fighter Unit) that served Poland in the 1919–21 Polish-Soviet War. No. 303 was formed in July 1940 at Blackpool just after the formation of No. 302 at Leconfield, the first Polish Fighter Squadron RAF.

No. 303 was then deployed to RAF Northolt on August 2nd as part of an agreement between the Polish government-in-exile and the UK. It became operational on August 31st, 1940. Placed within No. 11 (Defensive) Group, they had the huge responsibility of protecting London and southeast England.

During the Battle of Britain, No. 303 Polish Squadron achieved fame and bragging rights for the most number of Luftwaffe aircraft victories when compared to the results of all other squadrons under the command of the RAF. i.e.: 126 destroyed; 13 probables; 9 damaged.[7] These figures include the 16–4–3 aircraft attributed to its British pilots. It became the highest scoring unit among the 66 squadrons of Fighter Command that participated in the battle.

12 pilots of No. 303 Polish Squadron and their victories in the Battle of Britain[8]

- Sgt Josef František, a Czechoslovakian, was one of the highest scoring pilots in the battle: 17 kills (died in landing accident October 8th, 1940)
- Acting S/Ldr Witold Urbanowicz: 15 kills plus 1 probable (including kills gained while in 145 Squadron prior to being posted to No. 303 Squadron, but still during the battle)
- Sgt Eugeniusz Szaposznikow: 8 kills plus 1 damaged
- P/O Jan Zumbach: 8 kills
- F/Lt Athol Forbes, British 'B' Flight commander: 7 kills, plus 1 probable
- P/O Mirosław Ferić: 7 kills plus 1 probable (killed in 1942)
- F/O Zdzisław Henneberg: 7 kills plus 1 probable and 1 damaged (killed in 1941)
- Sgt Stanisław Karubin: 6 kills (killed in 1941)
- F/O Ludwik Paszkiewicz: 6 kills (killed Septempeber 27th, 1940)
- S/Ldr Ronald Kellett, the first British C.O. of No. 303: 5 kills, plus 2 probables and one damaged
- F/Lt John Kent, Canadian "A" Flight commander: 4 kills plus 2 probables
- P/O Witold Lokuciewski: 4 kills plus 1 probable

Total: 94 kills plus 9 probables and 3 damaged

As of the end of July 1942, Acting F/Lt W. Gnyś was still exempt from combat sorties having served in No. 302 Squadron's Command Post. From August 1st until September 10th, 1942 (40 days), Gnyś went to work in No. 303's operations room, under the command of S/Ldr Jan Zumbach, not as a pilot, but rather in the control room directing pilots during operational sorties. This worked out well as Władek's wife Barbara was soon expecting their first child. This post allowed him travel flexibility to be at the birth: a son Haydn was born on September 1st. During this time with 303, he got to know the pilots personally and stayed in touch with a number of them after his 40-day term came to a close.

As of September 10th, he was posted back to No. 302 Squadron, RAF Northolt, but was rested until December 29th and resumed flying the next day for a total of three flights that month. This hiatus permitted him to be with his wife Barbara and their new baby.

In January 1943, he made 12 flights doing patrols and bomber escorts. One of the bombers he escorted on bombing raids over France and elsewhere during the war was the Avro Lancaster introduced in early 1942. It became the main offensive heavy bomber used over occupied Europe. Primarily a night bomber, it also excelled at daylight precision bombing, but was vulnerable to Luftwaffe attacks.

★

S/Ldr Juliusz Frey along with British S/Ldr C. J. Donovan (as advisor) were given the responsibility of forming No. 316. Frey was the first Polish commander of the new squadron.[9] No. 316 "City of Warsaw" Polish Squadron was one of several Polish

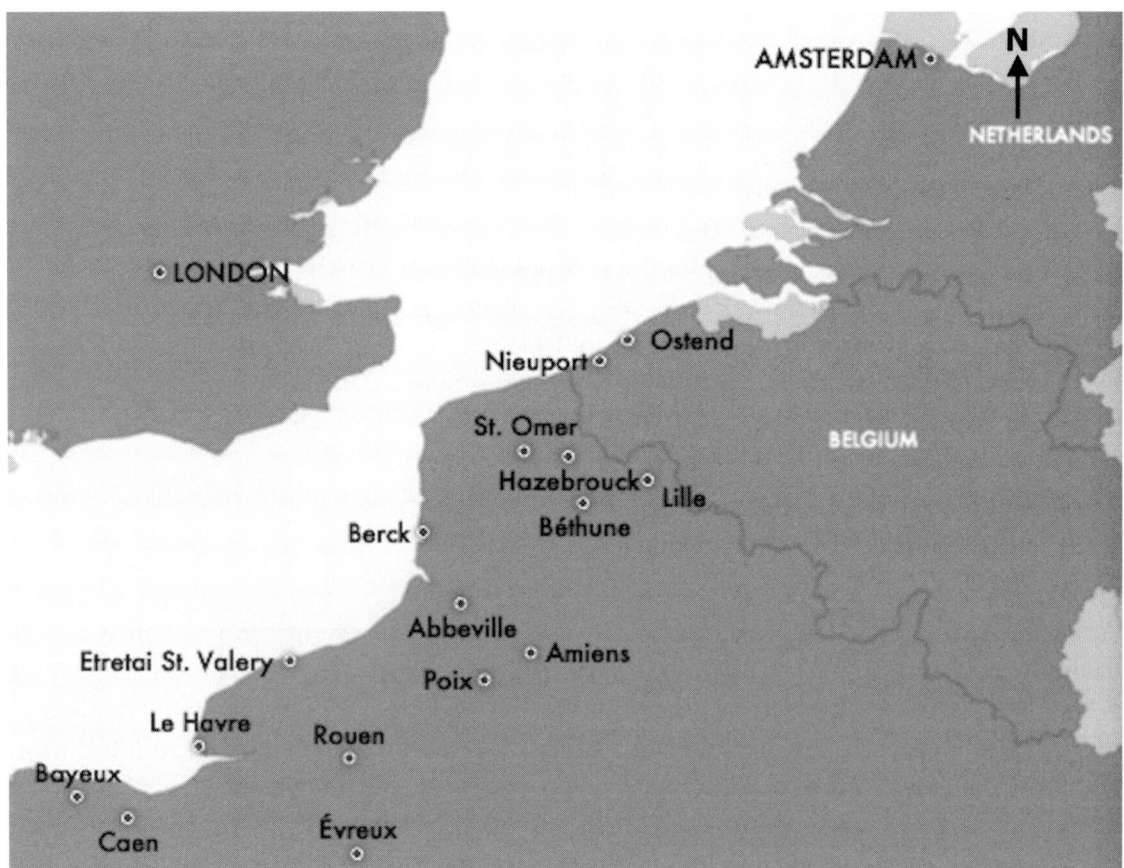

Many centers in German-occupied France, Belgium and the Netherlands were attacked by F/Lt Gnyś with 316 Sqn in 1943 by way of offensive fighter sweeps hitting targets of opportunity.

fighter squadrons fighting alongside the RAF. It was formed on February 15th, 1941 at Pembrey, Wales, as part of an agreement between the Polish government-in-exile and the UK and became operational March 25th.[10]

No. 316 initially flew Hawker Hurricane Mk Is and performed defensive duties over southwest England until it moved up to Mk IIs when it began offensive sweeps over northern France. It later re-equipped with Supermarine Spitfires and North American Mustangs. The Owl logo and the squadron code SZ appeared on their aircraft.

Over the course of the war, 316 Squadron flip-flopped between defensive and offensive duties. But in 1944 onwards, it got involved with fighter-bomber escorts and the battle against the German V-1 rocket bombs (Doodle-bugs) over the skies of London.[11]

Acting F/Lt Gnyś was posted to 316 at RAF Hutton Cranswick (East Yorkshire) on February 10th, 1943. On March 1st, he was made a full F/Lt Commander (Cpt) and served under C.O. Marian Trzebiński. In March the unit moved south to RAF Northolt where they remained until September. He stayed with 316 until August, 1943. Other notable commanders of this unit were Aleksander Gabszewicz and Janusz Żurakowski. No. 316 Polish Fighter Squadron dates and duties are as follows:

> February–August 1941: defensive fighter duties
> August 1941–July 1942: offensive sweeps over northern France
> July 1942–March 1943: defensive duties, Yorkshire
> March–September 1943: offensive sweeps
> September 1943–April 1944: defensive duties
> April–July 1944: fighter-bomber escort duties, East Anglia
> July–October 1944: anti-V-1 campaign
> October 1944 onwards: escort duties

★

On his way from Cairo to London, General Sikorski's plane stopped at Gibraltar. On the night of July 4th, 1943 it took off only to almost immediately crash into the sea killing all on board except for one of the pilots.

How could this happen to such a respected and essential Allied leader? It was incredulous. But as the news travelled round the world and back, the reality of his tragic death finally settled into the psyche of all those who believed in freedom and democracy: at 62, he was dead, a brilliant, charismatic leader was no longer.

Sikorski was probably the most prestigious leader of the Polish exiles working tirelessly with Allied leaders such as Winston Churchill to fight the Nazi threat of invasion. His death was a severe setback especially for the Polish cause. Pilot W. Gnyś and his Polish comrades who had the honor of meeting him on more than one occasion, were devastated along with the British armed forces and their Allies and millions of civilians, especially in Poland.

Was it an accident or was it a well-executed assassination? In terms of the latter, a vast number of conspiracy theories were presented about the cause of the suspicious plane crash. Perhaps the most popular was that Soviet leader Joseph Stalin was behind

Sikorski's demise. In April 1943, Stalin broke off Soviet-Polish diplomatic relations after Sikorski pushed for the International Red Cross to investigate the Katyń Forest massacre in which over 20,000 Polish officers (police and military) and educated professionals were executed by the Red Army in 1940. Logically then, Poland's prime minister of the Polish government-in-exile and Commander-in-Chief of the Polish Armed Forces was an obvious threat to Stalin and an embarrassment to his reputation. We may never discover the real cause of the crash. Meanwhile, Sikorski's body still lies in state in his magnificent stone crypt in Wawel Cathedral in Kraków in the company of other great Polish leaders.

★

February 15th to August 5th, 1943 was a busy period for Władek as he made a total of 115 flights. Many of these consisted of squadron and/or wing formations; high and low flying; practicing close escort with Typhoons and bombers; patrols over Wembley, South Coast, the Channel, and the North Sea; aircraft tests; scrambling; photography; sector reconnaissance; navigation flying; low-level attacks/sweeps, Ramrods, Rodeos, and Rhubarbs; rear support flying and testing of guns.

Combat missions over France included 21 "Ramrods" (includes 1 Target Support), 6 "Rodeos" and 4 "Circuses". All Circuses took place in March, April and May while the majority of Ramrods occurred in June, July and August as the Allies were really pounding German positions. During fighter sweeps of enemy territory, Władek had sympathy for the French who were forced to work for the Nazis war machine such as in the running of train locomotives carrying German troops and supplies to the front lines; working in alcohol distillation/fuel refining facilities sometimes hidden in farmers' barns; or driving lorries filled with troops and supplies. He attacked and destroyed his share of these, but could do nothing about collateral damage on military targets. The killing or wounding of non-combatants really bothered him. However, destroying enemy gun positions was another matter as he made a point of knocking them out of commission. He also attacked one or two "surface torpedoes" operated by frogmen whose job it was to sink anchored Allied shipping.

Apart from combat, many Allied pilot deaths were caused by such things as inclement weather, darkness, accidents, and limited or inadequate training.

Ongoing training was essential: in the case of the RAF, it promoted aviation innovation and the education of its aircrews. Defeating Hitler's Luftwaffe was paramount.

While with No. 316 Squadron, F/Lt Gnyś had already taken the Fighter Command School of Tactics Course in May/June, 1943. In his case, it sharpened his flying skills and also prepared him for a higher level of leadership responsibility.

In addition to this, from July 25th–29th, Władek began a Flight Training Course at Wittering, (north of London) and at the same time was involved with Link Trainer practices. But first, he had to fly in an RAF dual cockpit Tiger Moth biplane to Wittering. A basic training aircraft, the Tiger Moth was "easy to fly, but difficult to fly well." It was

Gnyś attacked French trains bringing German troops and supplies to the front. He felt bad for the captive French engineers who died as a result.

On several occasions Gnyś broke formation and silenced camouflaged gun placements firing at his squadron over France.

part of a family of other trainers such as the Harvard and Master aircraft that Władek first flew in early September 1940, before moving up to the Hurricane. The pilot instructor witnessed Gnyś's manual dexterity as control movements of the Tiger Moth required a positive and sure hand as there was a slowness to control inputs. However, this was not the first time Władek had flown in a Tiger Moth. In May, 1942, he flew with another instructor from Exeter to Tangmere and back for a total time of 3 hours and 15 minutes.

Eager to get started, he and instructor Jasionowski flew in the Tiger Moth from Northolt to Wittering on July 24th, 1943; at the end of the program, they would return to Northolt for a total of two hours in the Tiger Moth. Gnyś would be in Wittering for five days of intensive training. His time was divided up between the Link Trainer (flight simulator) and the Beam Approach Training (BAT) course involving the Oxford communications aircraft. But first, a word about this simulator.

An American invention created by Edwin Link in 1929 resulted from the necessity for a safe means to teach new pilots how to fly by instruments. The Link (Flight) Trainer is also known as the "Blue Box" and "Pilot Trainer." It allowed pilots to take some of their flight training on the ground. This life-saving simulator became famous in World War II and was used around the world.

Objective: to randomly strafe and hopefully destroy French barns hiding German alcohol distillation/fuel refining facilities.

The unit was a mock-up of the controls of a plane in which the pilot could be totally enclosed. The elaborate box with a plane-like appearance was mounted on a platform that responded (changed its angle) according to the pilot's use of the controls. By the early 1940s, Link trainers used movies (taken by real aircraft) along with interactive controls to simulate realistic situations.

For an experienced pilot like F/Lt Gnyś, this was an opportunity to learn the latest in blind-flying developments using given instrumentation. The Link Trainer was a mechanical engineering piece of genius.

The concept of the BAT was to guide tired and/or injured aircrews (with possibly damaged aircraft) safely onto their runway in the dark or in reduced visibility such as fog. It saved the lives of many pilots who would have otherwise missed their runway or made a crash/forced landing.

The system consisted of two main ground beacons on the runway, the inner and the outer, which transmitted radio signals or beams to a receiver set in the aircraft. The beacons emitted three different tones—dots, dashes and a constant tone—and each one told the approaching crew where they were in relation to the runway. The interpretation of these tones was rather complex and required in-depth training.

F/Lt Gnyś spent ten hours in an Airspeed As.10 Oxford aircraft with eight different instructors learning the BAT system of navigation. The twin-engine Oxford was used because it was a multi-functional aircraft able to train aircrews in a variety of areas such as in navigation, radio-operating, bombing, gunnery and camera operating. In terms of the BAT course, the Oxford had the necessary space to house the bulky navigational equipment. Gnyś flew with and was trained by each of the following instructors in July, 1943:

25th: F/O Winton—Aircraft and Equipment Orientation
26th: F/O Harincidn—Aircraft and Equipment Orientation
26th: H/O Bachurek—Beam Approach
27th: F/Lt Usman—Beam Approach
27th: P/O Crozier—Back Beam Approach
27th: H/O Bachurek—Beam Approach

Attacking and destroying German transport columns prevented troops and supplies from reaching the front.

Right: Born near Kraków, F/Lt Stanisław (Staszek) Chałupa (1915–2004) joined the PAF in 1936. He served in Poland, France and Britain, being the first Polish pilot to shoot down a German plane during the Battle of Britain. After a brutal crash-landing in September 1940, he was forced to give up operation flying, but not before he had notched up as many as ten kills.

Below: April 13th, 1941. Sgt Marian Rytka (left) gives his report after returning from an unsuccessful search for S/Ldr Zdzisław Henneberg of 303 Squadron who had to ditch in the Channel on April 12th and was last seen swimming from his plane; he was never found. F/Lt Łukaszewicz (center), P/O W. Gnyś (right) and others listen intently. *(PISM)*

January 1943, No. 302 Squadron, RAF Heston (West London). F/O Gnyś is in front of his Spitfire V WX-F with Polish checker. On February 10th, he would be with No. 316 Sqn. RAF Polish fighter units temporarily based at Heston included 302, 303, 306, 308, 315, 316, and 317. *(KARTA)*

No victory is without its unsung heroes. If it wasn't for the skilled work of ground crews, the aces of the war may not have been aces. Without a finely tuned engine and expertly woven ammunition belts, the pilot wouldn't stand a chance in combat. Mechanics, armorers and others worked their magic. *(PISM)*

Spitfire IX EN179 SZ-J "Jasia" (Jean) was flown by F/Lt (Cpt) Gnyś. He flew this fighter 24 times for a total of 33 hours, 40 minutes from February 27th to August 5th, 1943. It was "his" plane. No. 316 pilots are seen relaxing at the dispersal hut, Northolt, in mid-1943. Gnyś (far left) is talking to F/O Jerzy Szymankiewicz. *(PISM)*

R.A.F. Form 96.
S 575 (Naval)

MESSAGE FORM.

Office Serial No.

Call IN
and :—
Preface OUT

No. of Groups
GR

Office Date Stamp.

(Above this line is for Signals use only)

TO* Group Captain Bajan Polish Liaison Officer H.Q.F.C.

FROM* H.Q.F.C.

Originator's Number 5/7 Date Your/my

Please convey to all Polish Squadrons in Fighter Command my most sincere

sympathy for their irreparable loss in the death of General Sikorski and the

Staff who perished with him. The Allied cause has lost a great man and

Fighter Command mourns his loss alongside their brother pilots in the Polish

Air Force.

Leigh Mallory.

This message must be sent AS WRITTEN and may‡.................be sent by W/T.
Signature

This message must be sent IN CYPHER and may‡.................be sent by W/T.
Signature

Originator's Instructions.*   Degree of Priority.*

Time of Origin. 18.55

‡ Originator to insert "NOT" if message is not to go by W/T over any part of the route.

(Below this line is for Signals use only.)

T.O.R.

T.H.I.

| System in | Time in | Reader | Sender | System out | Time out | Reader | Sender | System out | Time out | Reader | Sender |

* The Signal Department is responsible what these details are transposed to the appropriate portion of the message form and that all possibility of compromising distinguishing signals, etc., by omitting to remove their signification from the address, etc., is avoided. Before delivery of the message these details are to be re-inserted in P/L.

The message from Air Vice-Marshal Leigh Mallory expressing his sorrow for the death of Gen W. Sikorski.

F/Lt Gnyś, cigarette in hand, with F/O Karnkowski. Both pilots are still wearing Mae West inflatable life vests. The grime on Władek's face and his body language illustrate the stress of combat. They have just returned from a mission over France with No. 316 Squadron, 1943. *(PISM)*

Above: From left: F/Lt (Cpt) Władysław Gnyś, Janusz Żurakowski and Józef Jeka. All three pilots served with No. 316 Squadron at one time or another in 1942 and 1943. This photo was probably taken in late July or early August, 1943. *(PISM)*

Left: Pilots in high spirits getting ready for a photograph, 1943. Władek (facing camera) is sitting next to Wing Commander Aleksander Gabszewicz (on his left) of the 1st Polish Fighter Wing at Northolt airbase.

The Airspeed AS.10 Oxford was a twin-engine aircraft with dual controls used for training airmen in the art of navigation, radio-operating, bombing, air gunnery and camera work. From July 25th–29th, 1943, Gnyś flew with eight RAF instructors for ten hours on a special navigational course.

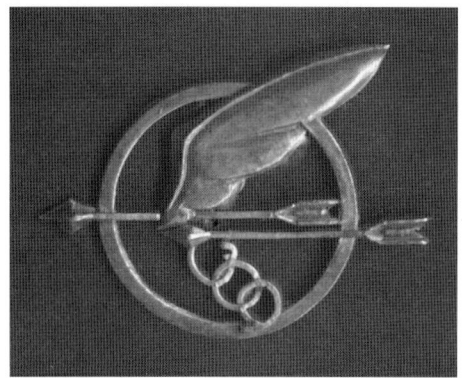

Left: This is the actual No. 309 Polish Squadron badge worn by F/Lt Gnyś.

Below: This rare autographed photo was taken of No. 309 Polish Squadron in September, 1943 at Snailwell, northeast of Cambridge. C.O. Jacek Piotrowski is front, fifth from left and F/Lt Gnyś is fourth from right. *(PISM)*

Above: A very proud moment. C–in–C of the Polish Armed Forces in exile in England, Kazimierz Sosnkowski decorates Władek with a bar to his Cross of Valor and two other airmen of No. 309 Polish Squadron, October 20th, 1943. From left: F/L W. Gnyś, F/Lt Janusz Lewkowicz and F/Lt Roman Jarema. *(W. Matusiak via P. Sikora)*

Right: The Cross of Valor (Krzyż Walecznych, KW) was awarded to Gnyś on February 1st, 1941 for deeds of valor and courage on the field of battle. It reads, "Na Polu Chwały" (On the Field of Glory) 1920. The reverse bears a sword and the word "Walecznym" (To the Valiant). As of October 31st, 1947 he had received three bars to his KW (one bar here is missing). *(Gnyś coll.)*

A V-1 rocket runs out of fuel and drops from the sky above Drury Lane, London, 1944. *(Public domain)*

Once the war began, millions of civilians (mainly children) were evacuated from London and other centers to safer environs away from the devastation of German bombs. Many were billeted overseas which ripped families apart, causing much loneliness and grief. *(Imperial War Museum, public domain)*

28th: F/O Robinson—Identifying Position by Measurement
28th: H/O Camwall—Identifying Position by Measurement
29th: P/O Crozier—Finding the Q.D.M.[12] of an Unknown Bearing
29th: S/Ldr Kinder—Finding the Q.D.M. of an Unknown Bearing

In this schedule, there were two flights per day except for the 27th (three); each flight averaged one hour for a total of ten hours of BAT training. After course completion, Gnyś and Jasionowski flew back to Northolt in the Tiger Moth where Gnyś hurriedly participated in two Ramrod sorties (#176 & #179—July 30th & 31st) over Tretot and Poix, France.[13]

As part of an agreement between the Polish government-in-exile and the United Kingdom in 1940, No. 309 Polish Fighter-Reconnaissance Squadron was formed. It was named No. 309 "Land of Czerwien" after a province in southeast Poland. The squadron was formed at the RAF base of Renfrew near Glasgow in Scotland on November 8th, 1940, part of Group 12. It was ready for combat in early December, 1940. In May 1941, 309 Squadron was transferred to Dunino in Fife on the east coast of Scotland, near St. Andrews, northeast of Edinburgh.

Initially, it was a reconnaissance squadron, but later it evolved into a fighter squadron for bomber escort and ground attack during the latter half of the war. After being posted to No. 316 Squadron on February 10th 1943 as a flight commander, Gnyś moved up to No. 309 on August 11th of the same year holding the same position.

The commanding officer of the unit at the time was S/Ldr Witold Jacek Piotrowski, RAF service no. 76687. He and Władek had known each other years before and worked well together as commanding officers in 309. After the war, like Gnyś, he immigrated to Canada but passed away in 1973 holding the rank of wing commander.

In 1940, the Westland Lysander (two cockpits) was used by this squadron until June 1942 when the North American Mustang was introduced. The squadron insignia on the planes was AR at the time, but from 1944 it became WC. The aircraft of choice was the long-range Mustang, but Hurricanes and Lysanders were reliable standbys for the unit.

While F/Lt Gnyś was with 309, there was a tragedy. On September 28th, 1943 during a camera gun practice, F/Lt J. Strusinski was accidentally shot down by an Allied fighter off Peterhead, which sits at the easternmost point of mainland Scotland.[14]

Władek was with No. 309 for almost two and a half months. There were no entries listed by him in his log book during this time, so it is unclear how much flying he did or details of his posting. He had, however, just completed a grueling six months with No. 316 Squadron, so he appreciated seeing less combat in a squadron that was more reconnaissance oriented.

His son was just approaching his first birthday on September 1st, and he really missed being with his wife Barbara and young Haydn: Scotland was a long way from London.

On February 1st, 1941, he was decorated with the Cross of Valor. But near the end of his tour with 309, he was awarded a Bar to his KW (Cross of Valor) from General

Sosnkowski on October 20th, 1943 and then posted to 18 Fighter Wing, HQ 84 Group two days later as a liaison officer. (After the war, two more bars were added to his KW on October 31st, 1947.)

General Kazimierz Sosnkowski (1885–1969)

Coming from an affluent family, Kazimierz was a nobleman and scholar. He loved the arts, mastered eight languages, was an artist, architect, freedom fighter, politician, a Polish Army general and commander. He held many military/political positions and was Poland's representative to the League of Nations where he initiated work on the prohibition of poisonous gases and germ warfare—weapons of mass destruction.

Being a loyal supporter of Józef Piłsudski, Sosnkowski refused to swear an oath of allegiance to Kaiser Wilhelm II of Germany. As a result, he spent most of the Great War in jail.

After World War I, Kazimierz became a successful commander in both the Polish-Soviet war of 1920 and during the invasion of Poland in 1939. When Poland was defeated, he escaped to France, then to England to work with the Polish government-in-exile. After the death of General Sikorski in 1943, he officially became the new C-in-C of Polish Armed Forces. Later, he and his family immigrated to Canada where he worked tirelessly on immigration policy.

F/Lt Janusz Lewkowicz[15]

F/Lt Witold Piotrowski (309 Squadron) made the first operational sortie on a Mustang on May 21st, 1942 flying a Rhubarb with two British pilots and attacking ground targets in the Le Touquet area of France. There was much talk about the operational range of this "new" aircraft. German-occupied Norway was a long way from east Scotland across the North Sea, and at the time, the belief was that it was too far for the P-51 Mustang Mk 1 to make an offensive attack against facilities there and, return to base.

Being an aeronautical engineer, Janusz Lewkowicz begged to differ with this assumption. After making numerous calculations, he was convinced that the Mustang was capable of making such a flight. So sure of his findings for the Norway sweep, that he presented them to HQ No. 71 Group, but they just ignored them. Not taking no for an answer, he made an unauthorized flight from Dalcross, Scotland to Norway on September 27th, 1942, where for good measure he strafed some military installations at Stavanger and safely returned to Dunino, Scotland.

Upon return, he was arrested and severely reprimanded for breaking regulations, but then was sincerely congratulated by Air Marshal Sir Arthur Barratt. Almost immediately, word spread of Lewkowicz's accomplishment and he became an overnight sensation. As a result of his action, the range of the Mustangs' operational sorties was increased the next month.

Over the two and a half months, Władek got to know and like Janusz who displayed great flying confidence and had a good sense of humor. The two of them along with F/Lt Roman Jarema felt privileged to receive the Cross of Valor together from C-in-C Sosnkowski on October 20th, 1943.

★

By September 1940, London had already felt the effects of German bombing. But the Blitz really got going on September 7th when the Luftwaffe blackened English skies with their first major daytime raid on the capital. The night-time raids that followed were as horrendous and devastating. Night after night for nearly two months, the bombers continued to do their best to cripple and demoralize the nation, hoping to force a British surrender; thousands of people died in the process. However, despite all the death and destruction, resolve strengthened.

The Luftwaffe had been making concerted efforts to continue to bomb London in strength. However, they never returned to the intensity witnessed in 1940/41, the reason being that most German bombers were needed on the Eastern Front when Hitler invaded the Soviet Union in June, 1941.

As the Allies continued to take the war to the Germans in occupied Europe and to Germany itself, Hitler realized that he would have to alter his tactics. As a result, he ordered his scientists to work on new, secret weapons—the V-1 and V-2 rockets— which they did feverishly. Hitler and Göring never gave up on the idea of pummeling the British Isles into the ground, especially London, and forcing a capitulation. The Luftwaffe threw everything it could at England. Realizing that a full-scale invasion was now out of the question, they still continued to attack despite the RAF's resistance.

By 1942, RAF Bomber Command was able to fly into German skies at night and dish out some of their own medicine. By the end of 1943, the Allied bomber offensive had done considerable damage to industrial cities.

Out of frustration with the failure of his Luftwaffe, Hitler ordered revenge attacks on British cities in southern England: of course London and the Greater London area were the main focus of attack. Operation Steinbock[16] was the last calculated air offensive by the Luftwaffe in the Western campaign; it took place from January to May 1944, coinciding with the Allied bombing campaign against Berlin (November 1943–March 1944).

Hitler's bombing offensive was propaganda to feed the despondent German population to assure them that he was doing something to halt the attacks on the Fatherland. In Britain, Hitler's air offensive was known as the "Mini" or "Baby Blitz" due to its smaller scale when compared to the Blitz of 1940/41.

During this five-month period, the Luftwaffe suffered heavy loses (over 300 aircraft) and achieved very little. In fact, Steinbock deprived the Luftwaffe of desperately needed

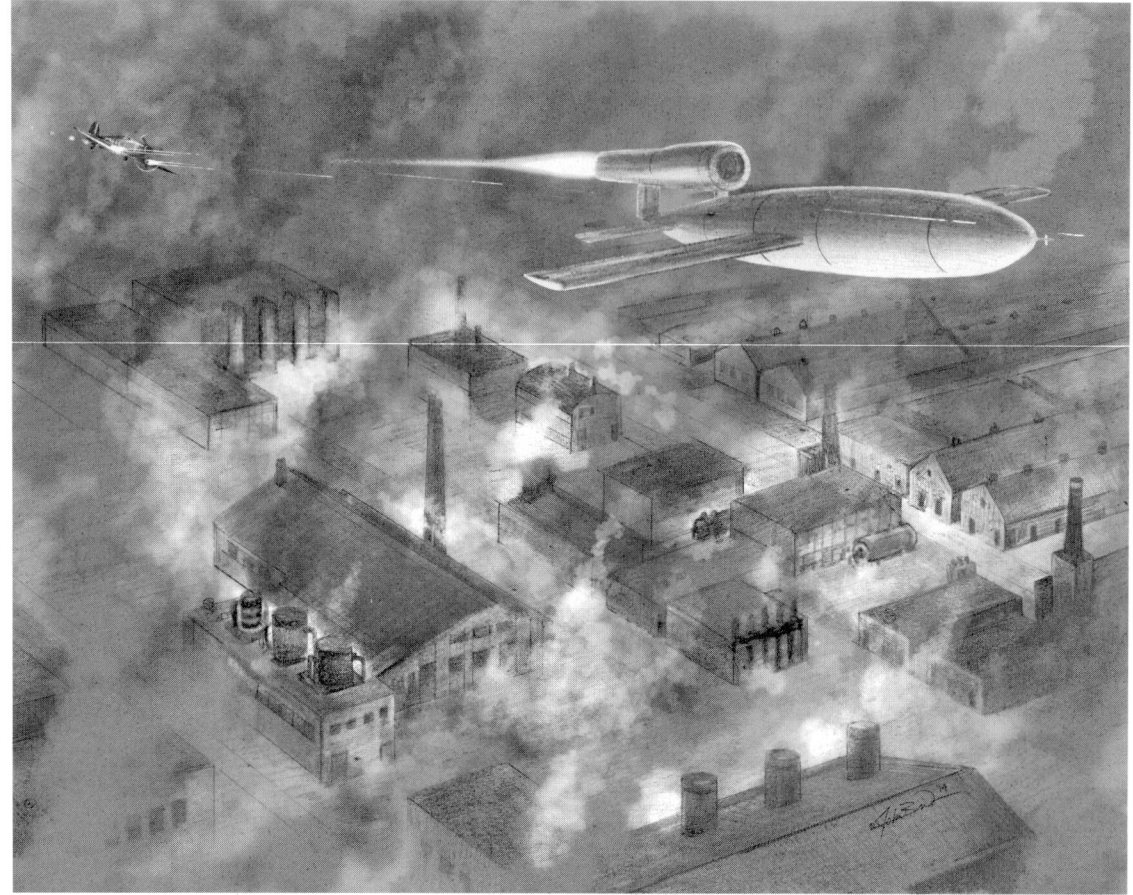

Allied fighter chasing a German V-1 flying bomb (also called a buzz bomb or doodlebug) over London in 1944.

aircraft to use in the anticipated Allied invasion of France. When the invasion of Normandy commenced on June 6th, 1944, the Luftwaffe counteroffensive was relatively insignificant.

As it turned out, Operation Steinbock was the last time that Hitler used traditional attack aircraft against Britain. What followed was the birth of the first cruise missile called the V-1 rocket, a pilotless high-speed flying bomb, followed by the V-2, a short-ranged ballistic missile. They were the latest "terror" weapons and launched mainly against London.

The first V-1 attack took place on June 13th, 1944. A new type of warfare began in earnest. The concept was simple: attach a motor and wings to a very large bomb, fill it with enough fuel to reach London, launch it from a coastal location in northern France and as soon as the fuel is consumed, the pilotless flying bomb falls to earth and explodes. This "buzz bomb" or "doodlebug" as coined by the British, was not necessarily accurate, falling randomly. Sometimes they malfunctioned and other times they were blown off course; it didn't take the RAF long to start chasing them in stripped-down Spitfires that could match their speed and shoot them down. However, these buzz bombs were frightening to the general public below, because as soon as they heard the engine cut out, they knew that the bomb was coming down on them.

As of September 1st, 1939, with Operation Pied Piper[17] Londoners in particular started to leave the city for safer havens within the UK and elsewhere. Vulnerable to attack and with the anticipated Nazi invasion, thousands of civilians, mainly children with or without their mothers, crammed trains and buses on a daily basis to get out of London and the port cities on the east and south coasts.[18] Many children were billeted outside the UK to countries such as the United States and to Commonwealth countries such as Canada. Ultimately, more than 3.5 million were evacuated.[19]

By June 1944, the buzz bombs coming across the English Channel were like swarms of attacking insects. There appeared to be no end to their numbers and frequency despite the defenses of anti-aircraft guns, barrage balloons and RAF fighter planes trying to shoot them down.

Władek and Barbara decided the best course of action was for her to leave London with baby Haydn and evacuate to the north coast of Cornwall—some 189 miles, a safe distance from London. When a cottage called the Salt House on the cliffs near Bude became available, Barbara rented it immediately. A close friend, Kay Hallowell, and her young son Nigel decided to join her in the move. Kay's husband was also in the military. Even while they boarded the crowded train at Victoria Station, several buzz bombs crashed and exploded nearby.

After a few weeks of complete safety from the bombs, Władek sent a telegram saying that he would be visiting on a three-day leave.

He came by taxi from Bude station which let him off at the end of the long path that led to the cottage. He stood for a moment looking around and then spotted her as she came outside. He waved and she waved back and ran up the path into his outstretched arms. He held her close to his side as they walked down the path to the cottage.

Władek and Barbara spent a blissful three days together. Little Haydn was thrilled to see his father again and the three of them loved to walk on the beach or on the downs together. It was a magical time; no one knew what the future held.

On the third day, Władek gently told her that his Polish Wing (131) was headed for France on July 12th; after the invasion on June 6th, the Germans where now on the run. Barbara was gripped with fear, tears rolled down her cheeks, she couldn't speak. She knew the dangers that lay ahead because everyone knew that the Germans would be fighting a defensive war now and would be throwing everything they had at the enemy. That evening they walked together as one with their arms around each other along the glistening shoreline and tried not to speak about the war.

Early the next morning, while waiting for the taxi to take him back to the station, they held each other close and cried. After kissing Barbara and Haydn goodbye, he left.

CHAPTER 8

Shot Down Over France

"My story is a lucky one—I managed to survive. Just how many gallant men, women and children fighting on the side of the Allies or in the underground during the occupation, gave their lives for the freedom of their beloved homelands, is unknown."

W. G.

On June 1st, 1943 the (former) RAF Second Tactical Air Force[1] was formed as 'HQ Tactical Air Force' from Army Co-operation Command. This air force was created in preparation for a full invasion of occupied Europe, one year hence. The 2TAF was one of three tactical air forces within the Royal Air Force during and after the war. It was composed of squadrons and personnel from the RAF, British Commonwealth air forces and the expatriated from German-occupied Europe.

Units from both Fighter Command and Bomber Command were utilized in order to form a sizable force capable of supporting ground forces (Allied armies) on the battlefield. Each tactical air force would have its own fighters, fighter-bombers, medium bombers, reconnaissance aircraft and night fighters.

On October 22nd, 1943, F/Lt Gnyś was posted to the HQ Tactical Air Force, No. 18 Polish Fighter Wing Sector, within No. 84 Group. Subsequently, he was a Liaison Officer at HQ No. 84 Group RAF. He continued his role with No. 131 Polish Wing as of July 12th, 1944. D-Day (invasion of Normandy, June 6th, 1944) was well underway at this point.

Over the years, No. 131 Wing RAF[2] went through many changes starting in early 1941. It was initially formed as the 1st Polish Fighter Wing, from two Polish squadrons No. 302 RAF (Gnyś's first squadron), No. 303 RAF and one British, No. 601 RAF. In May, No. 601 was replaced by another Polish Squadron, No. 308 RAF.

This new configuration would not last for long as the Polish squadrons were frequently exchanged between the three Polish wings: No. 131 (1st Polish) Wing, No. 133 Wing

RAF (2nd Polish) and the 3rd Polish Fighter Wing. Other Polish squadrons such as No. 315, No. 316, and No. 317 RAF soon entered the mix.

In early October 1943, the unit was renamed, No. 131 Wing. Finally in July 1944, it became more distinctive as it was named No. 131 Polish Wing (131 Polskie Skrzydło Myśliwskie). Its fighter aircraft was mainly the Supermarine Spitfire Mk IX with the Hawker Typhoon as its attack aircraft.

In December 1943, Wing Commander Stanisław Skalski (a top Polish fighter ace of the war) commanded No. 131 Polish Fighter Wing. F/Lt (Gnyś was transferred to No. 131 Polish Wing on July 12th, 1944, but from July 22nd he would be with No. 131 in northern France. The Polish squadrons in this wing were No. 302, No. 308 and No. 317 RAF. Aleksander Gabszewicz commanded No. 131 in February 1944 and led the wing during the invasion of Normandy.

With all the training and experience Gnyś had up to this point as a fighter pilot, further advancement and responsibility as a squadron leader, for example, required official evaluation and approval from his superiors. The following are the opinions of two higher-ranking Polish officers as of August 25th, 1943:[3]

Opinion #1 (nn)
1. Personality: "normal"
2. General Knowledge: "sufficient"
3. Mastered his trade to: "an outstanding degree"
4. Carries out his responsibilities: "sufficiently"
5. External appearance: "exemplary"
6. Command of English language: "good"
7. Suitable for the position of: "fighter squadron commander"
8. Distinguishing personality traits and soldierly qualities: "a very good fighter/combat officer, but too brusque towards subordinates—difficult to coexist with younger colleagues. Currently seems burnt-out due to having flown in a fighter squadron for years. Very well fit for an instructor in a pilotage school."
9. Character flaws: no entry as it is incorporated into 8. above.

Opinion #2 (from C.O. Aleksander Gabszewicz)
10. Positive character, but too impetuous, brusque, uncompromising. After a break, he will be fit for the position of fighter squadron commanding officer. This officer has been a fighter pilot for about 10 years and requires a longer break or transferring to do some non-operational work.

By March 24th 1944, Władek was still a contender for the position of squadron leader but as the previous evaluations stated, he needed a break from the action. The following opinions from Polish officers on March 24th and April 26th respectively, moved him a little closer to becoming a squadron leader. However, he still had some weaknesses to overcome:[4]

Opinion #1 (nn)
1. Personality: "normal"
2. General knowledge: "sufficient"

3. Mastered his trade to: "a sufficient degree"
4. Carries out his responsibilities: "exemplary"
5. External appearance: "satisfactory"
6. Command of English language: "good"
7. Suitable for the position of: "a squadron commander or an operations controller"
8. Distinguishing personality traits and soldierly qualities: ... no entry
9. Character flaws: "Tends to be easily overcome by excitement, which merely makes cooperation with people more difficult which causes problems."

Opinion #2 (nn)
10. "Ambitious, tenacious at work, self-reliant"

Regardless of his faults, A. Gabszewicz had faith in him all along: four months later on August 25th, he did indeed rise to the rank of Acting Squadron Leader of No. 317 Fighter Squadron.

Aleksander Gabszewicz (1911–83)

Aleksander Gabszewicz had many qualities that made him an outstanding leader in Poland, France and Britain. He was well schooled, had developed keen flying skills early on and was commissioned in 1934. Not only was he charismatic and well liked, but he was highly respected by his peers, superiors and those under his command throughout the war.

As a pilot and member of the famous Pursuit Brigade, F/O Gabszewicz (tactical officer of IV/1 Squadron) led his section on September 1st, 1939, making his first kill (shared) protecting Warsaw from the invading Luftwaffe, by downing a Heinkel 111. It was the first German aircraft shot down near Warsaw. Later that day, he was shot down himself, but managed to bale out of his PZL fighter.

On September 18th, he escaped Poland and made his way to France via Romania, Yugoslavia and Italy. He served in the FAF and led the Polish fighter section of GC III/10 in June 1940 before evacuating to Britain where he fought with No. 607 Squadron in October at the tail end of the Battle of Britain. Before the year was out, he was posted to the high-scoring No. 303 Polish Squadron. After a stay with them, he became 'A' Flight commander of No. 316 Squadron, taking total command by mid-November, 1941.

Taking a needed break, he went to HQ No. 11 (Fighter Group) as Polish Liason Officer in June 1942. In late September, Gabszewicz was sent to command the Polish Fighter School, RAF Grangemouth.

Aleksander continued to move up the ladder when he returned to frontline action in late January 1943, when he assumed the role of Wing Leader of the 2nd Polish Fighter Wing. On June 21st, he held the same position with the 1st Polish Fighter Wing based at RAF Northolt where F/Lt Gnyś was stationed. Never staying in one place too long, Gabszewicz undertook a three-month stint with the 61st Fighter

Squadron of the U.S. Army Air Force from December 1943 before returning to the PAF in February 1944 to command No. 18 (Polish) Fighter Sector (three wings). Then from July until the end of the war he commanded No. 131 (Polish) Wing. A highly decorated pilot, Aleksander Gabszewicz was an ace three times over with as many as 15 victories.

★

No. 317 "Wilno" Polish Fighter Squadron[5] (317 Dywizjon Myśliwski "Wileński") was formed on February 22nd, 1941 at Acklington, (northeast England) as a Polish Hurricane squadron and was ready for action two months later. It was part of an agreement between the Polish government-in-exile and the UK in 1941. It was not unusual for identification codes for squadrons to change over time and No. 317 was no exception. It went from WU to JH as of February 1941 to the end of 1946.

The squadron moved south in June 1941 and began to take part in sweeps and bomber escort missions over France. In October, No. 317 received Spitfires, a much superior fighting machine. They joined other Polish squadrons at RAF Northolt in April 1942, but were transferred up to northern England in September. Not unusual for squadrons to be juggled around, 317 returned to the south in April of the next year to fly offensive sweeps over northern France and later it joined the Second Tactical Air Force in preparation for the invasion of occupied Europe. After No. 317 flew ground attack missions in support of the D-Day landings, the squadron moved to Normandy in August 1944. Secured from the Germans, Plumetot became the jumping-off point into occupied Europe.

F/Lt W. Gnyś was with No. 131 Wing in northern France in late July before the arrival of 317 in August. So, as fate would have it, Gnyś was appointed Acting Squadron Leader of No. 317 Polish Fighter Squadron on August 25th, 1944. For the first time, he was now in charge of a fighter unit.

It was August 27th, 1944 and the Allies had the Nazis on the run. The main location was in northern France, upper Normandy, on the Seine east of Le Havre. The mission was to hit the retreating Germans hard as they pulled back out of France. The order from W/Cdr Gabszewicz of 131 (Polish) Wing to S/Ldr Gnyś of 317 Squadron was to lead, locate and communicate back to the Wing, the location(s) of where the retreating German forces were crossing the River Seine. The squadron took off at 1725 hours. The crossing points were heavily protected with AA artillery. When S/Ldr Gnyś saw thick, deadly flak in the distant sky, he asked for pilot volunteers to proceed with him. They were F/Lt Baran, F/O Hrynaszkiewicz and F/Sgt Winski; the others fell back to wait for the rest of the Wing to catch up.

W. Gnyś, officer commanding No. 317 was shot down by flak near Rouen, France on August 27th, 1944 and presumed dead.

In the morning of August 27th, 1944, S/Ldr Gnyś with his squadron (No. 317) attacked German shipping in the waters off northern France. This perspective is from the cockpit of Gnyś's Spitfire IX A.

The following, compiled by the Intelligence Section of No. 131 Polish Wing, summarizes the turning of the tide … the Nazi retreat:

This is to be the history of a unit of a group of men on their way back home—The Other Way Round. These few words hold a lot of meaning to us. The beginning was the war in Poland. Our trip through Eastern Europe, Africa, France to England. A journey made into a nightmare by the ever present Luftwaffe. It is to be the story of men hunted by the enemy all over Europe. Of men, whose only thought, only want, was a chance to fight, and so win the freedom of their country [Poland].

It is the story of their return, The Other Way Round. It is the story of their march from west to east, no longer hunted but hunting the enemy everywhere. The story of a hard fight, crowned by victory. Many of them have given their lives for that chance to fight but to those who live, they are not dead, for the memory of their deeds will always be fresh and living.

Roads were choked with enemy transport of all types and our pilots were taking their toll of it. 600 cars or lorries and about 30 self-propelled guns or tanks destroyed and damaged were the result of our attacks during the enemy's retreat.

One day a terrific number of Red Cross ambulances was reported by pilots. Intelligence was curious. Some of the ambulances were reported to be ordinary lorries, filled with surprisingly "agile casualties." When attacked, these "casualties" very quickly left the ambulance and took cover. The pilots received the order to open fire on these "ambulances." The result was unexpected. Terrific explosions took place and "casualties" transported in them, dispersed even quicker than normal troops usually do. Now the cat was out of the bag. The enemy had been using ambulances to transport ammo and troops. From then on it was everything on the roads is game. That of course proved to be, in some cases, unfortunate for some of our own pilots. The enemy flak was not to be disregarded at low level. It was very accurate and the enemy had lots of it all over the place. We had losses. One of our pilots had been shot down by the enemy, taken P.O.W. and, whilst being moved to the rear, the ambulance in which he was riding was attacked by our own aircraft. This pilot returned in the course of a few days to the unit and, according to his report, it was no fun being in the way of one of our fighters.

The Luftwaffe was seldom seen at that time. Within the course of a few months only two fights were recorded and our Wing claimed 4 enemy aircraft destroyed and 5 damaged. But the enemy had reached the River Seine and there were no bridges. He crossed the river whenever and however he could. It was a pleasure to disturb him as much as possible. But flak was especially intense and accurate in that area. We had losses and, the best way to illustrate things in that area will be to give the story of one of our pilots who was shot down over there, and eventually returned to us.

Here is S/Ldr Gnyś's story: "It was, as you know, my first day as commander of 'Wilno' Squadron. The whole wing, led by Gabszewicz, was out on the operation. When near the

"I went down ... but at about 2,500 feet my engine was hit by flak and started to burn ... The obvious thing to do was to bale out, but, trying to open the cockpit canopy [jammed by shrapnel], I broke the emergency handle!"

target I was told to identify and attack it with cannon and M/Gs in order to give the other two [Polish] squadrons [302 and 308] time to get ready for their dive-bombing attack."

Just before his Spitfire was hit by ack-ack fire, Władek transmitted the co-ordinates of where the Germans were retreating across the Seine.

"I went down with my squadron [section] but at about 2,500 feet my engine was hit by flak and started to burn."

At this point, due to very dense AA fire, he had already sent back the three pilots who had volunteered to go this far with him.

"The obvious thing to do was to bale out, but, trying to open the cockpit, I broke the emergency [canopy] handle. By the time I had the blessed thing open, it was too late and had to crash-land." In fact, the canopy opened fully upon impact with the ground. He said that under stress, he literally tore the inside handle off in desperation to bale out but realized he had to go down with the plane.

"I noticed a nice-looking field and made for it. At the last moment I saw it was anything but nice—there were stakes driven into the ground—but I just [braced], closed my eyes and hoped for the best. First one and then the other wing was left hanging on the stakes. The plane, what was left of it, made a few somersaults but I got out of it unhurt."

"… it was too late … I had to crash-land. I noticed a nice-looking field and made for it. At the last moment I saw it was anything but nice. There were stakes driven into the ground [and high-tension wires] but I just closed my eyes and hoped for the best."

"I got into a shallow ditch and was making my way along it towards a small wood near-by when machine gun and rifle fire was aimed at me from both sides."

Bullets were so close that he could feel them whizzing by, some passing through his clothing.

"I was about half-way by then, so did not stop but just ran as fast as I possibly could. The ditch ended and I had about 50 yards to go, but in front of me was an open field with absolutely no cover. I stopped for a moment, then jumped out of the ditch and ran again. Just before reaching the wood, one of the bullets hit me in the left side."

He said it was like getting punched really hard, knocking the air right out of him: it pierced both lungs as the bullet entered on an angle below his heart. "I fell and then saw some Germans running towards me, firing all the time."

The soil was "jumping" all around him from the bullets hitting the ground. "I swore [in Polish] at them, told them to stop firing and they did so." They were very young soldiers—teenagers, maybe 16 or 17. The older boy replied in Polish which suggested

"First one and then the other wing was left hanging on the stakes. The plane, what was left of it, made a few somersaults but I got out of it unhurt." S/Ldr Gnyś was shaken and disoriented as he quickly unbuckled himself and fell out onto the underside of the starboard wing.

S/Ldr Gnyś almost made it to the woods where he would have been safe from the German patrols chasing him. But a hail of bullets stopped him short: one struck him below the heart, fortunately on an angle as he was in a crouched position, but it "bounced" around inside before lodging in his liver.

that he had been forced into the German army. They laid down their guns and raised him to a sitting position and opened his blood-soaked flying jacket. Ironically they took pity on him and applied a handkerchief to his wound for him to hold. Władek said the blood pumped out like a fountain with every beat of his heart.

"They helped me to walk to their tank, a Panther, which was hidden in the very wood I had been making for."

Placing his arms around their shoulders, the boys half-carried him toward their tank. They passed a house where two young girls stood at an open window. They looked at him very sympathetically and one began to cry. Soon they arrived where their tank was parked. Władek realized then that they were part of a Panther crew. They gently sat him down on the grass. One fetched a bottle of cognac from the tank and offered him a drink: he accepted and took a couple of sips.

"There I had my first sample of Herrenvolk good manner and chivalry! One of them [not the tank crew, but rather an infantry soldier with rank of corporal] with an SS flash on his tunic, kicked my side as he walked past. Luckily it was my right side."

Two frightened young girls cried as they watched the scene unfold. They lived in a a hamlet called Hameau Le Wuy near the crash site not far from La Mailleraye-sur-Seine.

Initially, this German corporal (large and in his thirties) who joined them, stood shouting and swearing and waving his revolver. "Shoot him, kill the bastard! He is *kaput* … he will die anyway!" But the two young soldiers stopped him from firing and one of them even drew his revolver to protect the wounded pilot: the irony of war.

"I was then allowed to rest a little on the grass but soon had to get on the tank [with their help] and the journey northeast started."

On their way to the Seine, however, the Panther tank was spotted by either Typhoons, Mosquitoes or American Thunderbolts. Fearful, the crew ran for cover leaving Władek exposed next to the hatch opening. With all his strength, he tucked in his legs as bullets ricocheted all around, luckily missing him. The Allied fighters disappeared as suddenly as they arrived. The two young soldiers who had shown kindness before now appeared sullen and angry as they climbed into the tank and started down the road.

"After what seemed to me to be days but in fact were only hours, we arrived at the banks of the Seine."

Władek's radio message obviously got through to the base as the death and destruction the Allied aircraft left behind at this crossing was staggering. Along the shore vehicles burned everywhere, bomb craters pockmarked the area and hundreds of German soldiers lay dead and dying. The tank changed direction and rumbled into a field, eventually

The Panther tank was parked behind them next to the trees. "There, I had a first sample of Herrenvolk good manners and chivalry … [an army corporal] kicked my [right] side." He said, "Shoot him, shoot the bastard." However, the two young tank crew stopped him from killing the wounded pilot.

coming to a large tent erected among the shelter of some trees. It seemed to be some sort of command post.

Władek was taken down from the tank and laid on the ground while the two boys went to report his capture. A German general and a young SS officer came out of the tent and stared for a moment, then bent down to examine the still bleeding wound: "Kaput!" they agreed.

The general asked, "What is your rank?"

Hoping his Polish accent would not be noticeable, Władek replied in his best English, "Squadron leader."

The general nodded and gave an order to his adjutant. An army jeep was brought up and the officer and two privates lifted the squadron leader into the back seat.

The car pulled away and drove onto the road. Wounded laid everywhere. Recognizing the RAF uniform they shouted, "Shoot him!" Some became threatening, blocking the path, swearing and shaking their fists. The SS officer yanked his service revolver from its holster and ordered sharply, "Get back! Let us pass!" They reached the bank of the Seine where hundreds of German military waited for transportation to the other side

After a drink and a short rest, Władek was lifted onto the tank to begin their journey to the River Seine. On their way, however, the Panther was spotted by strafing Typhoons and Thunderbolts. Fearful, the crew ran for cover leaving Gnyś exposed. With all his strength, he tucked in his legs as bullets ricocheted all around, but luckily missing him.

of the wide river. Gnyś had no choice, he was going to be included in the masses of retreating evacuees.

"The river was literally choked with barges full of Huns, all making their way north. Some of our aircraft attacking the place made the whole thing like a nightmare."

Several barges loaded with trucks, infantry, ammunition and other supplies were bombed and strafed: fuel fires and floating debris including bodies covered the surface of the river. It was an unforgettable scene of carnage. Fortunately for the retreating enemy, darkness was closing in, masking other German barges trying to cross the Seine; however, flares were dropped lighting up the river for short periods and exposing targets to the attacking Allied aircraft.

"I was transferred to an ambulance ... we got across somehow."

Here, S/Ldr Gnyś was put into a narrow ambulance with six bunks. The back door was locked making it a "do-or-die" situation for the wounded inside. It drove onto an available barge which chugged its way across the river. However, the journey across was a nightmare: Allied bombs exploded in the water very close to the barge, violently rocking it from side to side; torrents of water came down on men and machines soaking

German trucks carrying troops, munitions, food, fuel and other cargo are hastily crammed onto large flat barges retreating across the Seine. On one such barge, countless soldiers, including the wounded (plus Gnyś), fill any remaining space. Allied bombs almost sank the barge.

everything on board. As luck would have it, the flat-bottomed vessel made it to the other side. Or was God watching over him again? Władek had experienced what it was like to be on the receiving end of Allied airpower—for the second time.

"There were five seriously wounded German soldiers in it [ambulance] and, to the accompaniment of their cries, the trek towards Amiens continued."

The ambulance inside was dark, claustrophobic and tightly packed. Władek was overpowered by the putrid stench of sweat, urine and excrement as he lay on his confined narrow canvas stretcher surrounded by the dead and dying. Constant cries of pain and anguish filled the small compartment, needing no translation.

They were frightened young men calling for their mothers. One above in particular was bleeding profusely, dripping over Władek's face. Conscious of his own wound and applying pressure to it with only a handkerchief, he knew his chances of survival and seeing his loving wife and baby boy again were extremely slim.

As he lay there for what seemed like hours, thoughts of his Polish family in Sarnów flashed through his head. The noise of the ambulance engine became more noticeable as the cries of the wounded diminished ... eventually there was no sound from them at

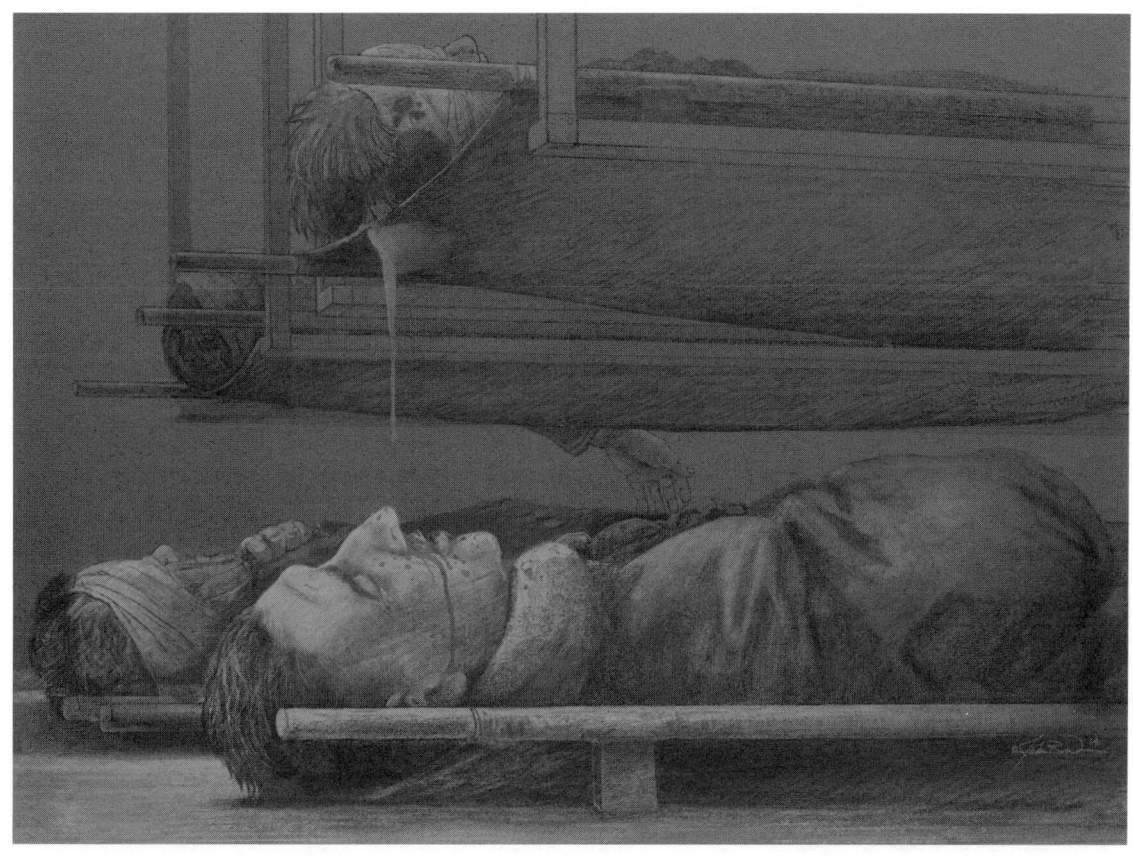

In the ambulance the sickening metallic taste of warm blood was not only gagging, but suffocating for Władek. He managed to turn his head slightly away from the blood dripping from the wounded German above. The groans and cries for their mothers soon faded: he was now alone.

all: he was the only one breathing. As the vehicle hit every bump, the constant jostling and rough ride added to his exhaustion. Water for his parched, bloodied lips was not to be had as the drivers of the ambulance did not stop to check up on their human cargo.

"Nobody appeared to take any notice of me. There was no interrogation and no doctor to see my wound. Jerry was too busy trying to get away and only worried about his own skin."

"We continued to travel northeast and on the 29th [of August], I saw the first [German] doctor."

It was a long night. They reached a large French château that was used as a field hospital. Władek was carried inside and laid in a hallway with dozens of other wounded. An orderly went from one to another checking wounds and making notes for an attending doctor. Triage determined the degree of urgency and treatment. It was a hideous scene as doctors removed infected or shattered limbs which were carried outside past the wounded squadron leader. There were few doctors and limited medical supplies. Because the Germans were on the retreat and being pursued, complex surgeries just didn't happen; treatment was basic.

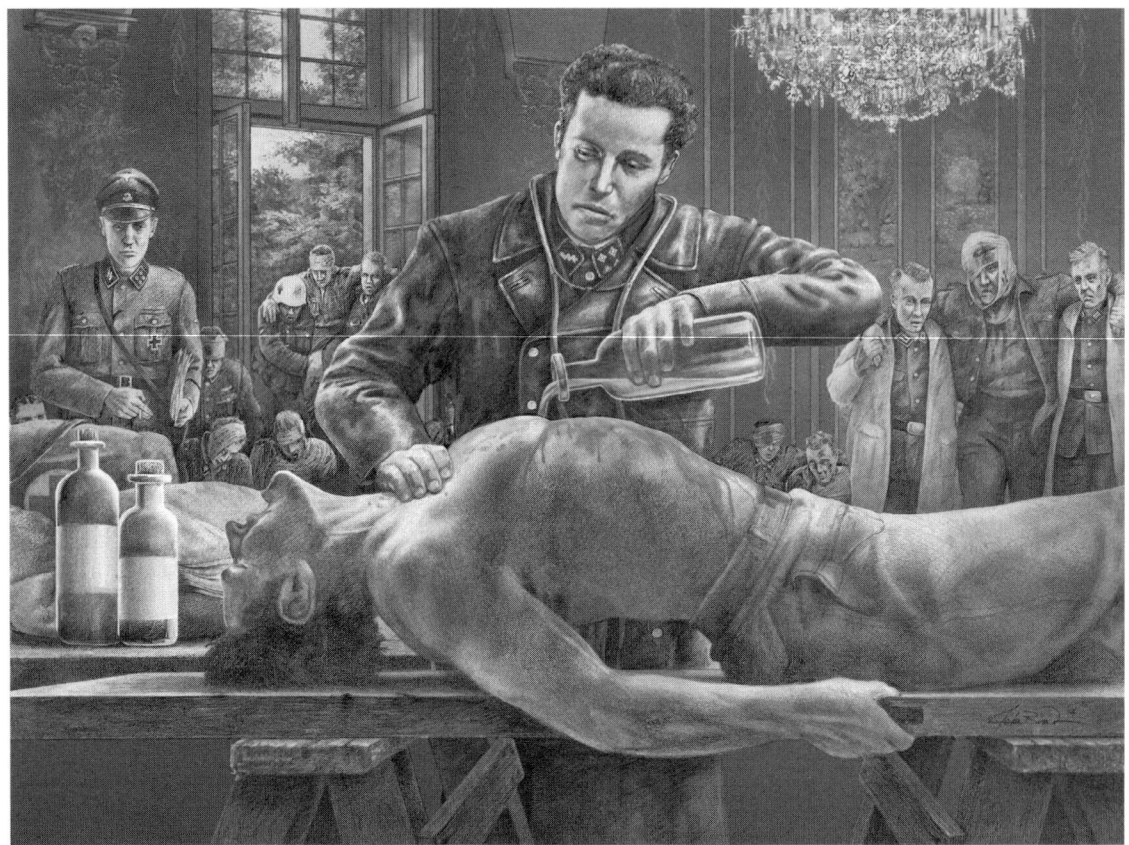

Grimacing with pain, Gnyś savagely grips the makeshift operating table as German Dr. Graham Lindemann cuts away gangrenous flesh from around the wound and disinfects it with neat iodine. In a château used as a field hospital, wounded soldiers and an officer look on.

Finally, a doctor got round to him. Two strong men picked him up and laid him out on an old door used as a table. Since there was no anesthetic, the doctor ordered the men to hold him down because the pain would be unbearable. Gnyś declined the support but instead, gripped the sides of the door with all his remaining strength. The doctor took his surgical scissors and cut away all the swollen and gangrenous flesh from around the wound. Pieces of flesh fell on a white cloth. Taking a bottle of iodine, the doctor poured it on the now open wound below the heart: the pain was excruciating! He momentarily lost consciousness.

"He cleaned and bandaged my wound and then said, 'The bullet is inside, just below the heart. In about three weeks we may be able to operate and get it out, but, with all this chaos, who knows what may happen by then. There is no immediate danger anyway.' The bandage and this assurance made my spirits rise and from then on I began to plan my escape."

This the English translation of the release form completed in German and signed by the doctor who treated S/Ldr Gnyś's wound:

Field Person No. 11 245
HVP 189
Current No. 883
Name: Wladislav Gnys
Rank: S/LDR
Born: [left blank]
ID No. P1298
Field Person No. 1298
Address of Next of Kin: [left blank]
Wounded On: 27.8.44
Time: [left blank]
Nature of Injury: Pistol shot to left side of chest
Graham, Dr. Lindemann (Physician)
Findings: Shot entered under the left breast towards the kidney
Surgery Results: Cut out … removal of flesh (around wound) … disinfected/wrapped in powdered bandage
G. Lindemann
To be forwarded by transport to another field hospital.
'Graham' [actual signature]

"As nobody was watching me, I took a chance that night, but didn't get very far." His escape plan was simple: he pretended to act delirious and staggered away from the large château doors, to convince the guards that he did not know what he was doing if stopped. But alas, he was discovered. Instantly, Władek pretended to faint and fell to the ground. As bad luck would have it, he fell directly on a rock on the left side of his chest. His nicely bandaged wound started to turn red and the resulting pain almost caused him to pass out.

A German patrol soon brought me back again and from then on I had a 'personal attendant.' I knew now that I had to have a well-thought-out plan and some knowledge of my surroundings before attempting another escape. I realized the best chance of getting this information would be during the few moments when even the Hun had to let me have some privacy, so at the slightest excuse I pretended I had to obey the call of nature and in this way was able to make my reconnaissance.

We arrived in Amiens on August 30th and the wounded, myself included, were dumped on the floor in one big room. As soon as we arrived I started off on my usual quest and walked all over the place. The house was surrounded by quite a large garden and in one corner of this, discreetly screened by some bushes, was a latrine. All around the garden was a wall and along this were stacks of firewood. One of these just hid a hole sufficiently big for a man to crawl through and outside were more bushes. I decided this was the place and the time would have to be the evening. I went back to the common room and tried to rest as much as possible. At last evening arrived. The Germans had been nervous all day and got more jumpy as the day drew to a close. They started packing again and kept shouting and gabbling to each other in very excited voices.

They carried out their wounded and loaded them into ambulances and other vehicles.

I waited until they were practically ready and then went for a walk. My "nurse" followed me but was more concerned with what was going on inside the house than with me. I walked slowly toward the latrine, but my luck was out. It was a two-seater affair and both places were occupied by enemy troops. I waited patiently and watched nurse standing on the steps of the house and getting

After pretending to go to the outhouse and while his guard was distracted, Gnyś crawled between two piles of logs and made his way to the bushes at the end where he hid and fell asleep. Next morning, he was discovered by a startled Maquis who almost shot him. "Vive la France!" shouted Władek.

impatient. Suddenly a sharp order was yelled from the house. The two occupants jumped up and ran towards the house, holding their trousers in their hands. They passed between me and my personal attendant, thus hiding me from his view for a moment. I used this brief moment to vanish behind my chosen stack of firewood and then through the hole under the bushes.

The next moment pandemonium broke loose. Nurse missed me at once and search parties were looking for me all over the place. Some rifle shots, which rang out at this moment, saved the situation. The Germans simply scrammed. The rifle shots came nearer the house, passed it and then all was quiet again. I stayed in my hiding place [and blacked out] until I heard shouts of "*Vive la France*" [next morning].

After a careful look around I crawled out. Just then, a startled Maquis soldier with a cigarette hanging from his lips thrust his rifle at me and I quickly shouted "*Vive la France! Vive la France!*" Fortunately, that stopped him from shooting and I saw French Resistance who were on the heels of the retreating Germans, carrying all sorts of arms and shouting and yelling, nearly mad with joy over their regained freedom.

The Frenchman helped him up and took him into the house to join other wounded French patriots and Canadian troops. Short of medical supplies, a French doctor cut off Władek's stained bandage and boldly disinfected the wound causing him to almost pass out. After he was cleaned up, bandaged and given fluids, he was driven to a Canadian Army field hospital.

"They escorted me to some of our troops, who sent me on here." That is, No. 77 Military Field Hospital in Plumetot, Normandy, not far from the English Channel. The ambulance from just-liberated Amiens to the field hospital, took the better part of two days as it had to make its way over battled terrain. After X-rays were taken, it was discovered that the bullet was lodged in his liver. It was from here that S/Ldr Gnyś phoned Wing Commander Gabszewicz who was stunned that Władek was alive. Very quickly afterwards, his hospital room became the scene of celebration by his colleagues who were stationed nearby. The next morning he was flown to the RAF Hospital in Wroughton, near Swindon England.

Following are two relevant reports, translated from Polish:

Missing pilot report to HQ London, August 27th, 1944
No. 317 Wileński Fighter Squadron
27.8.1944, (Document) L.dz. 148-P.2/44.
AIR FORCES COMMANDING OFFICER—London
Under the provisions stated in Article 10 of 'Property Deposit Instructions', I hereby report a pilot missing during an operational flight over the enemy's territory.

Identification Number/English/: P.1298
Rank: Polish and English: Captain, A/S/LDR
Specialty: Pilot
Name and Surname: GNYŚ, Władysław
Date and Place of the Incident: On August 27th 1944 at about 6 p.m. while carrying out a fighter flight over the enemy's territory in the south-west direction from Mailleraye, the pilot went missing. Members of the Pilot's Family and Exact Address: England, Coppathorne, Poundstock, Bude, Cornwall. Wife—B. Gnyś.

Adviser for No. 317 Fighter Squadron
Signed: KRZEMIŃSKI, E. por. pil. (Flying Officer)
Attention: Liaison Officer at HQ 84 Group, Inheritance-Deposit Committee

Good news report to HQ London, September 4th, 1944
No. 317 Wileński Fighter Squadron
4.9.1944
(Document) L.dz. 148-P.2/44.
AIR FORCES COMMANDING OFFICER London

With reference to the document L.dz. 148-P.2/44 dated August 27th 1944 concerning the incident in which a pilot, squadron leader capt. pil. S/LDR. P.1298 GNYŚ, Władysław went missing, I hereby report that capt. Gnyś reported his return from the enemy's captivity on September 3rd 1944 and is currently undergoing treatment in hospital B. 14.

Adviser for No. 317 Wilenski Fighter Squadron
Signed: CHELMECKI, M. kpt pil. (F/Lt)
Attention: Liaison Officer at HQ 84 Group Inheritance-Deposit Committee

The joyous clamor among Władek's comrades when they heard the news of his miraculous escape, bears repeating:[6]

> The third of September started very quietly with two uneventful Fighter Sweeps carried out by the "Krakow" (308) and "Wilno" (317) squadrons.
>
> Around mid-day, a telephone message came from 84 Group saying that S/Ldr. Gnyś, O.C. of the "Wilno" Squadron, who was shot down by flak South of Rouen on the 27th August, was in enemy hands and wounded. Most of us had given up all hope, as pilots who saw him crash-land, did not think it possible for anyone to come out of that wreck alive. We were all very glad and delighted to hear that he was alive at any rate. At about 1900 hours our Ops. telephone rang again and was answered by the duty Ops. Officer with the usual non-committal "131 Ops." and then things happened. At the other end a voice just said; "S/Ldr. Gnyś speaking." The next moment the whole place was in an uproar. Everyone immediately wanted to know everything and consequently nobody heard anything. We learned eventually that S/Ldr. Gnyś was at No. 77 M.F.H. expecting a visit from us. A remarkable coincidence was the fact that F/Lt. Wandzilak, a member of the "Krakow" Sqdn who had just returned to us after also having been shot down, was the Officer who took this call. A party, loaded with everything they could think of, went off to the Hospital. There they found S/Ldr. Gnyś, rather quiet and very careful when walking but still smiling and the "Old Soldier" as usual. The welcome was very affectionate (we Poles just have to kiss each other on such occasions) and then S/Ldr. Gnyś told us the story of his being taken prisoner and subsequent escape.

Almost immediately, in fact three days after he was shot down, recognizing the fact that he had accomplished his mission and was initially reported missing in action, an Application (#12/970) for Decoration with Class 5 Virtuti Military Cross was issued in France by Polish Command within the RAF on August 30th, 1944. It is one of the oldest military decorations in the world still in use. The following are excerpts from the application:

> Rank and Military Status: Captain Pilot [Polish Rank], Permanent Active Duty.
> Posting and Function at Time of Deed: S/Ldr 317 Wileński Fighter Sqn C/O.
> [Previously] Awarded Decorations: Cross of Merit, Cross of Valor—twice, Croix de Guerre—French.
> Detailed Description of Deed Qualified for Decoration including Time, Place and Combat Circumstances: In the afternoon time of August 27th, 1944, Captain Pilot W. Gnyś was assigned to serve as a commanding officer of a section which was to identify target directly before bombing. The target was a German military unit in retreat crossing the river Seine outside MAILLERAYE sur SEINE. After identifying the target, Cpt. Gnyś was supposed to report over the radio the exact spots which were to be bombed. Having accomplished the task, Cpt. Pil. Gnyś was shot down by the enemy's anti-aircraft artillery. The target [barges loaded with troops, military equipment, various vehicles and supplies] was destroyed—the crossing was withheld for a long period of time which was confirmed by 35 Reconnaissance Wing with an aerial photograph. 131 Wing was congratulated in person by the 84th Group commanding officer. The enemy put up about 100 cannons of anti-aircraft artillery in order to protect the target.
> Number of Flights and Combat Hours since Last Application for Polish Decorations: According to O.Ł.A.D.G.B. Gnyś carried out 10 combat flights lasting 18 hours 05 minutes.
> No. of Combat Flights and Combat Hours: 50 flights during 83 hours, 35 minutes.
> Wounded or Killed: missing … wounded.

Suggested Type of Decoration: Class 5 VIRTUTI MILITARI CROSS.
Opinion of Superiors: Outstanding officer … Very good fighter pilot … Deserves decoration with tremendous support.

Stamp: Class 5 Silver Virtuti Military Cross to be awarded upon order dated February 2nd, 1945 [he received it on June 1st, 1945].
Signed Stamp: 131 field airport commanding officer mjr. pil. A. Gabszewicz.
Signed Stamp September 8th, 1944: I am strongly in favour of the application as Cpt. Gnyś showed courage and quick thinking not only in combat, but also while returning from captivity.
Polish Liaison Officer, Group 84, M. Mümler, Wing Commander.
In Favour: Sept 22, 1944 by Polish Liaison Officer (nn).
In Favour: Oct 22, 1944 Signed Stamp by Air Force C-in-C, M. Iżycki (Brig Gen) AVM.

While still at the Salt House Cottage in Bude, Barbara and little Haydn enjoyed the safety and tranquility of this slice of 'Cornish heaven' on the north coast of Cornwall.

She received a letter from her mother Eva in London saying that she and Barbara's pregnant sister Norah had decided to get away from the city (where buzz bombs were still falling) and come to Bude to join Barbara. Her friend Kay and son Nigel had left by now to join her mother near Wales. Kay had been great company for Barbara and the boys got on well too.

The three women spent most of the time looking after Haydn, doing normal household things, reminiscing about old times, walking along the beach and along country roads searching for wild blackberries from which they made jam.

Then one morning, Mrs. Roland from the local general store and post office came knocking at the door with a telegram. Her face was ashen as she handed it to Eva: it was for Barbara. "I'm afraid it's bad news," Mrs. Roland said.

Barbara stood motionless and then with shaking hands tore into the telegram. It read: "REGRET TO INFORM YOU THAT SQUADRON LEADER WŁADYSŁAW GNYŚ P1298 FAILED TO RETURN FROM AN OPERATION ON AUGUST 27, 1944. FURTHER INFORMATION FOLLOWS BY LETTER. THIS SHOULD NOT BE DISCUSSED TO THE PRESS FOR THE TIME BEING … AIR OFFICE, COMMANDER IN CHIEF RAF."

Barbara later said, "I don't remember how long I stood there as if frozen to the floor, my brain rejecting the words I had just read. My mother and sister were silent and then Mother took the telegram from me, read it, and passed it to my sister. Then she turned to me, her face full of concern, told me in a quiet voice to come and sit down. I looked at her without expression and said, 'It's not true, there's been a mistake! I don't believe it … I won't believe it … no, no, no!'"

Barbara decided to go to Nottingham to see the Chałupas, Staszek and wife Stefa. In June 1944, Staszek had been posted to RAF Newton east of Nottingham to 16 Service Flying Training School as an instructor for Polish airmen RAF. Staszek had flown with Władek and had been his closest friend since before the war. She knew that if anyone could get relevant information from Władek's squadron, he could. Unfortunately, there was no additional news other than he had been shot down and was missing.

Three days later, Barbara returned to Salt House. Her mother, sister and son were all very happy to see her. However, she had no news about Władek's condition or whereabouts. The days dragged until September 8th when somebody came banging loudly on the door. It was Mrs. Roland again from the post office. "He's alive, he's alive!" she shouted, waving a telegram, "he's wounded but he's alive … it just came through!"

It read: "Arrived in UK. Slightly wounded shoulder, don't worry, writing address soon. Władek." All at once, they went crazy, hugging, crying and laughing with joy.

For an official debriefing, Gnyś was flown to the PAF Depot Blackpool, on September 5th and immediately after was transferred to the RAF Hospital in Wroughton, not far from Swindon in southwest England. Despite the wound, he was able to walk slowly while under medical care, but did not overexert himself as his body was healing. Being in fine physical shape with a strong heart before he was shot, really contributed to his survival. Of course, there were other external factors such as his life being saved by the enemy and of course, luck.

The "good news" telegram (8 SP 44) from Władek had been sent on his behalf from Trowbridge, Wiltshire, about an hour away from the hospital. Once Barbara discovered his whereabouts, she was on a train within an hour, bound for Swindon, a distance of 137 miles. Once in Swindon, she took a bus to the hospital. With trepidation she walked through the entrance to reception where she asked about her husband: he was at mass (a faithful churchgoer) and would be back to his room shortly. This was good news about his mobility, but her heart was really thumping with anticipation. Then, down the long corridor, she saw a man slowly walking towards her. Barbara couldn't wait any longer and started in his direction. Was it him? Yes, it was! She ran forward with a cry and threw her arms around him. His folded left arm protected his wounded chest. Emotion ran high as they kissed and held each other. The nightmare was over.

The doctor who treated S/Ldr Gnyś told Barbara that the bullet was in his liver and had entered the body just below the heart on a sharp angle as he was crouched over at the time. It was amazing that it missed his heart, lodging itself in the liver on the lower right side of the body. On the way, however, it pierced his diaphragm, breaking some ribs and puncturing his lungs. If there was no discomfort, the bullet could stay in that organ for the rest of his life: an operation to remove it was too risky. Fortunately, the liver was able to heal itself around the projectile and make a home for it. In fact, it remained there for 56 years.

Władek and Barbara stayed in Swindon until he was discharged on September 17th from RAF Hospital Wroughton into the care of his wife. With a new lease on life, they both returned to the Salt House: for the moment, recuperation and a little R&R was in order with Barbara and their two-year-old son.

CHAPTER 9

Canada

"How hard it must have been given that he was a military man, distinguished in one field, and suddenly he couldn't do it anymore, but still had to make a living."

AGNIESZKA GNYŚ

Whenever Władek commented about something serious, he would always say, "It's no joke!" It was one of his favorite English expressions.

In September 1944, due to his wound, his career as a fighter pilot came to an abrupt end. Gnyś was now in unchartered waters, a most unpleasant predicament. For the first time since 1931 when he signed up with the Polish Armed Forces, his future was unknown, and he felt very insecure at the age of 34. Not only that, but how would he provide for his wife and son? What other work was he capable of doing? It was no joke!

Fortunately, the RAF/PAF were not going to abandon him or other pilots who had risked their lives and had been injured or maimed in the line of duty. Related placements other than being a pilot, were available but re-training/re-education was necessary.

After a period of convalescence at Salt House in Cornwall, they returned to London at the end of September to live at home with Barbara's mother in Pinner. Even though the Germans were in retreat, they were still sending flying bombs to London. V-2 rockets with their long-range capability were devastating. It was still risky business to return.

On October 2nd 1944, Gnyś was assigned to HQ Fighter Command ADGB (Air Defence of Great Britain) in Stanmore as a liaison officer—at least for now. This worked out really well as their home was only minutes away. The last thing he and Barbara wanted was to be separated again.

Two weeks later, on the 16th, Władek reported to the Polish Air Force Depot in Blackpool for administrative and reassessment purposes. Special courses had been started at the PAF Staff College (Aviation Academy, a higher aviation school for staff officers) in Weston-super-Mare, a seaside town on the Bristol Channel coast, 18 miles southwest of Bristol. So on November 22nd, he decided to sit the entrance exam and if successful, he would take the courses in the New Year. He passed and was accepted into the six-month program.

While there, to their good fortune, he found an apartment on the promenade which overlooked the sea: such a reprieve from war. Three days later he reported back to the PAF Depot in Blackpool.

In December, they received a very special Christmas present: Barbara was pregnant again.

The PAF Staff College (Wyższa Szkoła Lotnicza, W.S.L.) exposed the student officers to a variety of future opportunities for them to consider. This upgrading was most welcomed. Lectures were given by experienced Polish airmen and high-ranking RAF and army officers. The college was also open to non-air force officers from the army and navy. However, the bulk of the candidates were Polish Air Force officers.

January 2nd, 1945 was the beginning of a new chapter in Władek's life. He began his studies with anticipation. This was the sixth graduate course offered by the college since its inception before the war.

Being an enthusiastic learner, he whizzed through the course like a sponge, soaking up everything that was presented. He particularly enjoyed the Polish Engineering and Armored Training course, but found that working in a limited capacity, with No. 300 "Land of Masovia" Polish Bomber Squadron was closer to his heart.

Gnyś was given a good evaluation overall which was validated by the Commandant of W.S.L. For successfully completing the course, he proudly received an Aviation Academy badge, no. 139, on December 18th, 1945.

However, while Władek was still enrolled in the program, an announcement of massive proportion occurred: On May 7th, 1945, Germany officially surrendered to the Allies, bringing an end to the European conflict. This historic moment made newspaper headlines around the world. People danced in the streets with uncontrollable joy and relief.

At 11 p.m. on August 11th, 1945, Barbara gave birth to a baby boy whom they named Stefan Władysław Chester. They were now a family of four and with the war in Europe over, life was going to be different.

While still pondering his future, he assumed the position of liaison officer at Fighter Command HQ in Stanmore, West London, on September 17th, 1945. Later on, Władek enrolled in a two-year course in commerce and economics at the London Polytechnic with the thought that it could be beneficial in the future. Taking evening classes made sense as then he could work during the day as Ops Controller at Fighter Command.

In terms of his competence with English as a second language, on February 15th, 1946, he was given an English degree which was recorded on his Qualification Card.

Unable to have a "proper" wedding during the war, they got married once more in a Polish Catholic church in London on May 18th, 1946. Close friends, family on Barbara's side were there and of course two little boys all cheered them on.

As with most of the men who were either still in the armed forces or those who had been demobilized, the question of civilian occupations was foremost in their minds. Happy that he might be working for the RAF for a couple of years, the question of what he could do afterwards in his mid- to late 30s worried him.

On February 20th, 1947, he was transferred for a short time to 5PRU (Photographic Reconnaissance Unit) to check out future prospects. The PRU was a flying unit of the RAF, first formed in 1940. It had previously been owned by a private company that was hired by British intelligence to take clandestine photos over Europe.

A week later, Władek enlisted and was granted a temporary commission in the General Duties Branch of the Polish Resettlement Corps (PRC) with the rank of flight lieutenant for the maximum period of two years as of February 28th, 1947. The PRC was an organization formed by the British government in 1946 as a holding unit for members of the Polish armed forces who had been serving with the British armed forces and did not wish to return to a communist Poland after the war. It was designed to ease their transition from military to civilian life, keeping them under military control until they were fully adjusted to British life.

Despite this welcomed two-year paid commission, he still knew that a scheduled visit to the Aircrew Allocation Center (A.C.A.C.) to be interviewed by qualified staff might be useful in finding a suitable and sustainable job in which he felt confident and secure going forward. With this thought in mind, he would soon travel up to the center in Yorkshire in April. There were literally thousands of airmen wanting work and wishing to feel useful. One function of the allocation center was to interview aircrew, extract information, create profiles and make employment recommendations.

The following A.C.A.C. report on Gnyś was completed over a two-day period, April 17th and 18th, 1947 and the interviewer was W/Cdr A. James. Relevant extracts are:

Special Qualifications including Service Jobs other than Aircrew: Operational Controllers' Course … employed as Ops. Controller for 1 year.

Future Wishes/Service including Ground Jobs: Desirous of being employed as an Ops. Controller. Failing that he wishes to be employed on flying control duties. Does not wish to remain in the RAF. [Recent] Education: 1 year Commerce & Economics at London Polytechnic."

Post War Job Search Activity: Is uncertain but is awaiting to hear from two offers to go into business one of which would entail immigration to S. Africa.

Education Officer Notes: Discussed possibilities of further study at London Polytechnic if offers [of employment] are delayed or fail to materialize. Advised to contact Education Officer of Unit re-entrance [to Poly] when he decides.

Board's General Observations:
1. F/Lt Gnyś is a very smart, presentable and intelligent officer who converses freely in English.
2. He has seen continuous air force service since 1931 and has undoubtedly developed a sound sense of responsibility. He is however not desirous of remaining in the RAF because of the present uncertainty of an offer being made. He is now anxiously awaiting the results of two projects in business life and has a marked preference for the S. African venture which he considers offers the better prospect. He is fully aware of financial aid for studying which he intends to examine with a view to continuing his studies in Commerce and Economics at the London Poly.
3. Although his first choice is Operations Controller in view of his previous experience, his second choice is Air Traffic Control in which he should be quite useful after a period of supervision. The Board pointed out that there was possible scope in this latter field in civil aviation and recommended to him that he investigate this as a possible career.

Recommendations:
1. Available: Operations Controller … Short period of supervision … Recommended in view of his previous experience.
2. Air Traffic Control: Under supervision … Aircrew experience useful.
3. Link Trainer Instructor: Under supervision … Aircrew experience useful.

There were many restless Polish and Allied air force veterans seeking to emigrate overcrowded England for either their country of origin or to countries such as Australia, South Africa, the United States or to Canada in search of a new start. By the end of the war, over 19,000 Poles were serving in the PAF and the RAF in Great Britain.

Władek and Barbara seriously contemplated the idea of emigration, but she was very concerned about her mother, sister Norah and leaving friends and the security of their home in Pinner, with two small children to make a new life in an unknown country. They decided to sleep on the idea, but kept the "emigration door" partially open.

Several fellow officers were immigrating to Canada and buying farms, mostly in the province of Ontario. Władek again approached Barbara, curious for her reaction to such an idea. As before, her main concern was leaving her family.

Generally, employment in England was hard to find and there were rumors of directed labor. Canada seemed to hold new hope and letters from friends already there were encouraging. A government scheme paid first-class passage for officers and their families plus a small subsidy for immigrants agreeing to farm. Mortgages were offered at low interest rates.

At the end of September 1947, they came to a decision about leaving England. They discussed the very real possibility of Barbara's mother, sister and her child coming over to Ontario and staying with them for extended periods of time once they were settled on a farm. This thought made Barbara more relaxed about leaving the comfort and security of her English family and home. Besides that, Władek was getting impatient trying to find long-term employment despite all the courses and professional help given to him. He knew that there was no future with the RAF and came to the conclusion that as much as he respected them, he no longer wanted to remain in the force. With their minds made up to leave Britain, Barbara and Władek applied for passports and visas to travel to perhaps their pot of gold: Canada.

Friends, Muriel and Aubrey Atkinson, a former pilot, had already immigrated to America and were living in a nice home in Huntington, Long Island, New York. They had kept up correspondence and upon learning of the impending trip to Canada, Muriel and Aubrey suggested that Barbara and the two boys (plus Sasha, their German shepherd) come and stay with them while Władek searched for a suitable farm to purchase in Ontario. March 1948 was the designated month of departure.

Eva spent countless hours in February at her sewing machine making suitable apparel and warm coats for the boys in anticipation of the low temperatures in Ontario that time of year. Keeping busy helped her not to think about how badly she would miss them and how much she worried about how they would manage in a strange country without a home, little money and how they would take care of two small children and a dog.

By the middle of March, twenty-one pieces of luggage were assembled plus a pram filled with toys and other bits and pieces. The date of sailing was March 16th on the RMS *Aquitania*. From Waterloo Station in London, they took the boat train to Southampton where the old troop ship was docked, waiting to take her human cargo to Halifax, Nova Scotia, Canada.

It was agreed that when the train from Pinner reached Waterloo, final goodbyes were to be said there and not at Southampton as Eva couldn't bear to see them on board the ship sailing out of her life. Barbara's sister Norah and her daughter Cherrie were equally sad. The boat train platform at Waterloo was very crowded with similar families saying farewell to loved ones who were also on their way to the docks at Southampton.

Władek found an empty compartment for them and he put the hand luggage inside; the main cases were being transferred over to the Southampton train. After long hugs, kisses and tears, the Gnyś family boarded the train. Barbara promised to write her mother every week and said optimistically that it wouldn't be long before they would be reunited once settled in Canada. The hiss of the engine and squeaking wheels drowned out the goodbyes as the train moved along the platform and was gone.

Launched in April 1913 in Scotland, the RMS *Aquitania* made her maiden voyage to New York in May 1914. She was the third in Cunard's line of the "grand trio" of ships, preceded by the *Mauretania* and the *Lusitania*. She was the last surviving four-funneled liner. By the end of 1919, the *Aquitania* was converted from coal to fuel oil. This luxurious "transatlantic queen" earned the honor of being called the "Ship Beautiful". She survived both World Wars mainly as a troop carrier, but was returned to passenger service after each conflict. In 1950, after 36 years of transatlantic service, she was taken out of commission and scrapped.[1]

Once on board, the Gnyś family was given their cabin number in the first-class section (compliments of the Canadian government to officers and their families) and then directed to the ship's kennels on a lower deck with their dog Sasha.

As the tugs towed the large ship out to sea, Władek and family went up on the main deck; the English coastline become more and more distant. They wondered how many years would pass before setting foot again on British soil. They were filled with anxiety, but also anticipation for what Canada might have in store for them.

By late afternoon on Tuesday, March 16th, the "Ship Beautiful" was well out to sea with its 1,685 passengers. The weather was damp and cold as she cut through the mist over the rough and choppy waves of the Atlantic. Many of the passengers were showing signs of seasickness especially after a stormy first night, so some decided to stay wrapped up with blankets and sat in deck chairs despite the frigid conditions. If they had to vomit, at least they were able to conveniently do so overboard.

The Gnyś cabin was roomy enough and consisted of two lower and two upper berths, a table and two chairs and an adjoining bathroom. It was very comfortable and the boys found the new accommodation quite curious.

Normally when the gong sounded for supper, passengers would make their way along the deck to the broad staircase that led to a large luxurious dining room where waiters would show them to their tables. However, the first morning at sea produced an almost empty dining room for most of the day. Barbara and Haydn were among those who were feeling out of sorts. When Władek and little Stefan appeared hand in hand at the top of the staircase eager to have breakfast, the waiters gave them a round of applause: they were the only ones there at the time.

Entertainment on board was limited to a library. So for most of the voyage, they read and walked Sasha and kept her company. The boys always enjoyed being with her and she loved the fuss they made of her. Władek took pleasure being at the ship's bow with the pitch and spray and thinking about his father, brother Antoni, his six sisters and his uncle Toni and family. He wondered if they had survived the German and Russian invasions and, if they had, what was life like now living under Soviet rule and a repressive communist government.

Approaching five days at sea, one could sense the excitement among the passengers especially during the last night on board. Barbara and her husband discussed in detail what they had to do once the ship docked at Pier 21 in Halifax, Nova Scotia and put their tentative settlement plan in motion. For example, train schedules had to be confirmed for Barbara and the boys to travel to Long Island, N.Y., to stay with Muriel and Aubrey and for Władek to travel to southern Ontario to search for available farm real estate.

All persons in the armed forces were demobilized upon reaching Canada. F/Lt W. Gnyś formally relinquished his commission in the Polish Resettlement Corps on immigration to Canada on March 20th, 1948. He was now honorably discharged and officially unemployed. He was content with this new status as he knew that he couldn't have stayed with the RAF forever. He did know, however, that a great deal of hard work lay ahead.

Above left: This is an actual photo of Gnyś's Spitfire shortly after the crash. The three young people are standing on the intrados (underside) of the starboard wing. Notice the white "invasion stripe" and two metal stakes that ripped the wings off the plane. This rare photo was provided by Laurent Viton.

Above right: Historian and aviation archaeologist Laurent Viton made an amazing discovery in 1999. He found the 6.5-feet engine cowling to Gnyś's Spitfire IX c JH-A (NH 365). It was located in the town of La Mailleraye-sur-Seine, at a house belonging to a woman who, as a girl (with her sister), witnessed Gnyś's capture. The cowling was being used to cover firewood.

Fighter-bomber RAF Hawker Typhoon Mk 1B, 1943. The identification markings were adopted as it was frequently mistaken for the German Focke-Wulf (Fw) 190. With its 20mm cannons, rockets and bombs, it became well known for its ground-attack role. German tanks, armored vehicles and trains feared it.

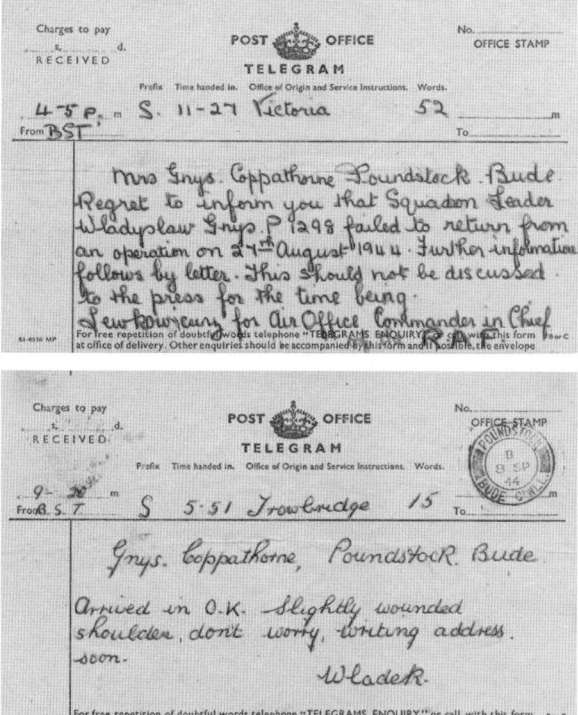

No. 131 Wing Commander Aleksander Gabszewicz wrote in his diary two diametrically opposite comments (a week apart) about Gnyś being shot down over France. Top: "On 27.8.1944 during a combat flight, kapitan pilot Gnyś was killed while doing a reconnaissance of the target for the bombardment." Bottom: "Hurrah! Władzio Gnyś is okay, he is in hospital in England!"

Plumetot, France, September 3rd, 1944. S/Ldr W. Gnyś is surrounded by colleagues from No. 317 Squadron. From left: nn, nn, Stanisław Zych, Zygmunt Wodecki, Edmund Sienkiewicz (intelligence officer), Marian Cholewka, Marian Chełmecki, nn, Jerzy Zbrożek and Jarosław Giejsztowt *(PISM)*

Top: The telegram that was delivered to Barbara Gnyś while in Poundstock, Bude from the Air Office Commander-in-Chief. Shocked and in disbelief, she refused to accept that he "failed to return from an operation" over France on August 27th, 1944. This was the moment she had always dreaded.

Above: September 8th, 1944: A telegram from S/Ldr Gnyś to his wife Barbara living temporarily with their son in the safety of Bude, Cornwall. He trivializes his wound as being just a "slightly wounded shoulder." The bullet was actually lodged in his liver.

The Virtuti Military is Poland's highest award and one of the oldest (1792) military decorations in the world still in use. It is given for heroism and courage in the face of the enemy. S/Ldr Gnyś was awarded this medal for his reconnaissance mission over the Seine on August 27th, 1944 when he was shot down.

Squadron Leader Gnyś, lucky to have survived the war, is ready to face a new world of employment.
With a lovely wife and child, he is optimistic, looking forward to the challenges ahead.

"Germany Surrenders." Newspaper headlines, Toronto, Canada, May 7, 1945. William "Lefty" Thomas (37) next to his stacks of papers is selling them briskly to a jubilant crowd. It was a happy and memorable day for Europe and the free world. (Sharyn Thomas-Counce via Ray Ravoi)

March 1948: F/Lt Gnyś in his RAF coat, Stefan in his blue Harris tweed coat and hat with Sasha on "dogs' deck"

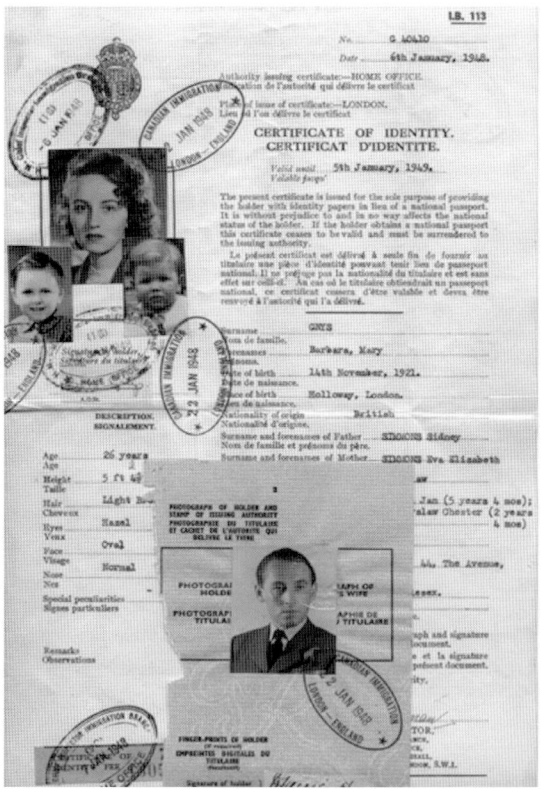

The family's immigration papers.

Barbara Simmons-Gnyś, January 1948, two months before departure.

A 100-acre mixed farm was purchased in Vinemount, just east of Hamilton, Ontario in 1948.

"Former Polish Squadron Leader who Shot Down First German Plane in World War II is now Farmer at Vinemount." These were the front page headlines of the (then) *Toronto Daily Star* (now *Toronto Star*) on Saturday, April 15, 1950. The March paid circulation at this time was 408,256 copies per day. *(Toronto Daily Star)*

As of April 15th, 1950, Stefan was (4), Barbara (28), Władek (39) and Haydn (7). Władek's darkened front tooth was caused by getting kicked in the mouth by a frisky heifer; eventually, he lost the tooth. He has aged somewhat after two hard years working their rustic farm.

Stefan (6) and Haydn (9) were delighted to have a sister, Sydney, born May 8th, 1951. She is about four months here.

This magnificent house in Grimsby, Ontario was built circa 1900. The family's second home in Canada was just down the road from Lake Ontario.

From left: Cousin Cherrie Cutler, Sydney and Stefan Gnyś and grandma Ninna (Eva Simmons) with spaniel puppies in front of Grimsby home, 1954.

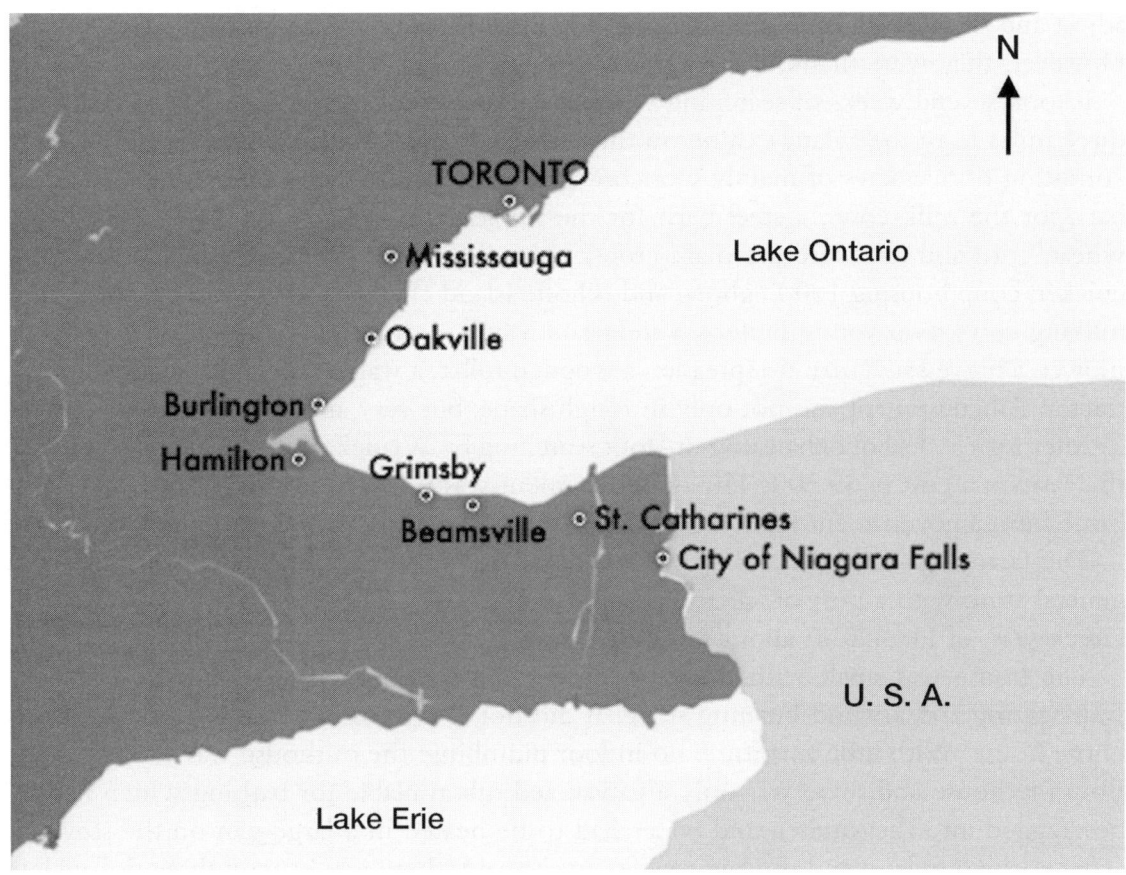

Locations around Lake Ontario, Canada.

Fortunately, Władek was offered accommodation with three Polish officers who had already purchased farms in southern Ontario. After a month in New York, the plan was for Barbara and the boys to join him in Smithville, Ontario, at the home of the Sałattas. On March 5th 1948, prior to leaving England, he gave air force officials a contact name and a permanent address regarding his whereabouts:

> c/o Jerzy Orzechowski [Battle of Britain pilot with Gnyś]
> Maple Tree Farm, R.R.8,
> Dunnville, Ontario, [Smithville is just north of Dunnville—north shore of Lake Erie]
> Canada

After staying overnight in Halifax, Nova Scotia, they made their way to the train station with their 21 pieces of luggage and caught the train to Montreal. From there, they temporarily went their separate ways: Barbara with Haydn, Stefan and their dog Sasha to Long Island, and Władek to southern Ontario.

After a month they were all reunited and given accommodation with a Polish couple, the Sałattas, who had migrated to Ontario in the twenties. It took some doing to adjust and fit a family of four with a big dog into the spare bedroom of the farmhouse. However, they were thankful for a place to stay.

It took several weeks of searching without the use of a car, but eventually a farm just three miles from the Sałatta's came on the market. It was in fact a mixed farm 100 acres consisting of five acres of mainly Concord grapes and some pink dessert grapes, a main barn for the milk cows, a steel barn for the implements, a barn for the granary (oats, wheat, corn and hay were the main crops), a small barn for the garage and tool shed, a chicken coup housing 100 Leghorn and Rhode Island chickens, three work horses, nine milking cows, two young heifers, a steer and a bull, a disk, a plow, a set of harrows, a mower, a harvester, a manure spreader, a wooden roller, a wagon and a hay loader, but no tractor. All equipment was not only in rough shape, but very antiquated, even primitive.

After a great deal of exhausting on-foot searching by Władek, they decided to settle for this farm at a cost of $9,500. The down payment was $4,000 and the balance of $5,500 came from a government loan. They closed the deal and moved in on June 23rd, 1948.

The farm was on Hyland Road, three miles from Vinemount which consisted of a general store with a post office and a handful of houses. The nearest town was Stoney Creek (east of Hamilton) about ten miles away.

The house was small with three bedrooms, a small kitchen, a sink with a broken water pump and a wood burning stove. It did not seem possible that it could heat the entire house. With little furniture, no indoor plumbing: the outhouse was about 40 feet from the house and there was only a galvanized tub available for bathing which had to be dragged into the kitchen and water had to be heated in a large pan on the stove.

After the purchase and the lawyer's fees were paid, there was exactly three dollars left to exist on for a month until the local cheese factory paid for their daily can of milk. Fortunately, there was nothing essential to buy for the house as they already had blankets, linen, dishes, pots, pans and cutlery.

How they got through the first month was nothing short of miraculous. Their diet consisted mainly of eggs prepared in every which way imaginable. There was no bread, but there were potatoes, onions and a few carrots left in the cellar from last year's harvest which were used in making vegetable soup. Later, they were able to sell a few dozen eggs to the grading station which helped, until the $25 cheque for the milk arrived from the dairy.

Farming was hard work: they would get up at sunrise to milk the cows by hand and spend the rest of the day trying to cultivate the vineyard. The weeds were almost as high as the vines themselves. The farm had been neglected for years but Władek was resolved to get it back into shape. With only a grape hoe and King, one of the large work horses, he attempted to break through the hard ground. The spring of 1948 had been very dry and the soil was like concrete. Barbara watched as he walked behind the horse, the reins round his shoulders as he pressed down on the handles of the hoe causing his hands and fingers to blister and bleed. Not having a tractor was brutally difficult and there was no way they could afford one.

For three weeks the struggle continued. Along with caring for the animals and the two boys, Barbara tried to help break the hard baked earth around the grape vines with a hoe but it was a losing battle. The never ending work was frustrating and the constant worry about putting food on the table weighed heavily on their minds. In addition, they both lost a lot of weight, especially Władek who toiled up to 18 hours a day with a bullet still in his liver.

The work was all new and they both had been used to a comfortable home in England. The RAF of course, could not have prepared Władek for this incredibly hard life. However, he seemed to know instinctively when the hay was ready to be cut and brought to the barn. As each load was stored, he would insist on collecting just one more until Barbara begged for mercy. There were still cows to milk, supper to make and even after supper they returned for more hay until it was too dark to see. Rain was always the enemy during harvest time hence the urgency to bring in the hay which was the main staple for the livestock.

Harvesting the oats and wheat and the straw was an even harder task. The mechanical harvester called for three horses, but unfortunately the young black mare Black Beauty

There were no tractors on the Gnyś farm in Vinemount, Ontario, just beautiful horses. It was pioneer farming in the twentieth century. Black Beauty was skittish at the best of times and one day, spooked by a wasp, she bolted, causing Dapple to do the same while Władek was adjusting a strap in between them. The consequence was almost fatal.

would panic when harnessed. King and Dapple were no problem and were amazingly easygoing and reliable. This author vividly remembers his father tossing him up onto the monstrous backs of these two lovely creatures for a ride. Beauty on the other hand, couldn't be trusted and didn't like being a beast of burden and would only calm down after a while in the presence of the other two horses. At times she was dangerous to be around as she was very skittish. Several times, she nearly kicked Władek's head in and almost cut him to bits with the field disc machine as he was standing in between the two harnessed horses and the disc blades. A hornet had spooked her and she bolted. Władek had to jump straight up in the air as the apparatus flew under him. They knew that they would have to replace her, but could not bear the thought of putting her down.

The grapes were the final crop of the season. Every morning they would rise early, milk the cows and then go into the vineyard. They cut and transported the crop back to the yard to be collected by, as it turned out, an unscrupulous dealer. The $500—a fortune at the time—he owed at the end of the season was never paid as the man disappeared without a trace. Their hopes of installing electricity and a milking machine were now out of the question.

Before they knew it, their first winter was upon them. The temperatures were sub-zero and the ice-cold winds blew open the barn doors and sometimes the front door of their uninsulated house. The walls were paper thin and the only heat was from the stove in the kitchen. Several times a night, Władek would get up and make sure that the stove had plenty of wood in it otherwise they would have frozen. The doors to the bedrooms were left open so that the heat could freely penetrate them. Barbara made sure that the boys were well covered and each had a hot water bottle in their beds. The wind whistled and wailed around the old house during the dark winter nights. Every morning upon waking, everyone would head to the kitchen and warm their backs against the stove before doing anything else. They had never known such cold and heavy snow. It was a real shock to them. And so, winter, for the most part, was kept at arms' length during their first Canadian winter. However, February 1949 proved to be particularly harsh and almost cost the life of young Haydn.

It was snowing heavily one morning when Władek drove Haydn to the one-room school in Tapleytown. His mother had packed the six-and-a-half-year-old a lunch and a warm drink and said that his daddy would bring him home after school was done. She pulled the red tuque over his ears and tied the scarf around his neck. After hugging his mother, he climbed into the truck next to his father and waved goodbye.

The weather got worse after lunch and Władek decided to leave earlier than usual to fetch Haydn. However, the truck would not start so he decided to go on foot to get him. The wind was cruel as it lashed against his face and the snow was thigh deep making it extremely difficult to walk. Finally he arrived at the school and pushed open the door; no one was there except for the janitor.

"Where are the children?" he asked frantically.

The janitor said that they were sent home earlier.

"How long ago?" Władek screamed.

"About half an hour. Some were driven home and some walked."

Wasting no more time he headed back the way he came, but Haydn had not arrived home. Barbara went mad. Like a wild bull he charged down the road, flashlight in hand and disappeared round the corner. Strong winds blew huge snowdrifts across the road, burying fences bordering the fields. The roads were hidden but he was able to follow the tree line which kept him on course. His legs felt like rubber as he waded through the almost waist-deep snow. His squinting eyes and frozen ears searched for any movement or sound that could be from his son.

Suddenly, something caught his eye: a bright red splash of color peaked above the snow. It was near a large tree behind a snowdrift. Władek struggled towards it. "Haydie! Haydie!" he frantically called over and over again. As he got nearer, he saw that it was indeed a bright red tuque. He reached the tree and found a small figure completely covered with snow. Quickly brushing the snow away, a little body moved and two big eyes looked up at him! "Daddy! Daddy!" Haydn cried out as he lifted his arms and tried to stand up. Instantly, Władek picked him up and held him close, brushed off the snow from his shivering little body and assured him that everything was okay. Another hour or so and their son would have been totally covered up and not visible at all: he would have frozen to death.

It had been a terrifying experience for everyone. It was decided that in the spring, Haydn would be transferred to St. Francis Xavier Catholic School in Stoney Creek which had buses available to transport the children, although there was a mile to walk to the bus stop and the same coming home. When Stefan was six, he too went to the same school with his big brother who looked after him as they walked to and fro when the weather was fine.

Barbara of course had pangs of homesickness. She really missed her mother, sister Norah and young niece Cherrie and wrote every week to them describing their life on an old farm in Canada. Her mum was most concerned about how hard her daughter and husband had to work and worried about them constantly.

During the first Canadian Christmas, Barbara received the best present she could have hoped for: a letter from her mother saying that they had booked passage on the Empress of Canada and would sail from Liverpool for Halifax on March 30th, 1949, arriving on April 5th. Barbara was ecstatic. From there, they would take a train to Hamilton, not far from the farm in Vinemount, where they would be met.

When March came around, she spent every spare minute in preparation for her family's arrival. She painted and decorated the extra bedroom and spruced up the rest of the house making it more inviting. The day of arrival found the Gnyś family waiting

At the last minute, Władek spots his small son's red tuque. He was sitting under a large tree trying to hide from the raging storm. It wouldn't have taken much longer before the snow had totally concealed him.

on the platform as the train pulled into the station. The reunion was full of happy tears and unforgettable joy.

For the first few days they never stopped talking. So many things had happened in that year of separation. During their seven-month stay, Eva and Norah did what they could to help around the farm which included looking after Haydn and Stefan and of course their almost-six-year-old Cherrie.

★

"FORMER POLISH SQUADRON LEADER WHO SHOT DOWN FIRST GERMAN PLANE IN WORLD WAR II IS NOW FARMER AT VINEMOUNT"

These were the front page headlines of the *Toronto Daily Star* on Saturday, April 15th, 1950. The March paid circulation at this time was 408,256 copies a day. Several years after taking possession of their farms, word spread about a group of former Polish pilots who left England after the war and were in the Niagara region trying to make a living as farmers. The front page is condensed here,[2] Polish accents omitted:

POLE FLIER NOW FARMS HERE
by Lloyd Lockhart
Toronto Daily Star Staff Correspondent
Star Photos by Lloyd Lockhart
Vinemount, Saturday, April 15th, 1950

Trying to make a go of it here in Vinemount, like any other Canadian farmer, is Wladek Gnys, the Polish pilot who shot down the first German plane of World War II.

The former Sqdn.-Ldr. is one of several Polish airmen who till the soil in the Niagara area. One blast from the whistle could rouse enough fliers to man a squadron. Wearing overalls in this group and spitting on their hands when necessary, are two former wing commanders, two group captains and other high-ranking officers.

"Before we came to Canada, few of us had milked a cow," said Gnys. "I didn't know how to plow or do anything. We had to learn farming from the ground up."

Gnys had been in the Polish air force nine years when Germany invaded his homeland. At dawn, Sep. 1, 1939, he was in the air as a fighter pilot.

"Our squadron intercepted two German bombers and immediately our leader was shot down," recalled Gnys. "I took after the Germans and sent both their planes down in flames. Later, in London, I was gratified to learn I scored the first official air victory over the enemy."

But not the last, Gnys was still in action long after D-Day. He crashed four times as a Spitfire pilot. He was shot by storm troopers and the bullet still lies lodged in his kidney [sic]. He was taken prisoner and given up for dead even by his captors. Three days later he escaped.

"That's past," shrugged Gnys. "Other fellows in our group had experiences just as bad. We forget the war to concentrate on egg production, cream separation and other problems which concern every farmer."

As a rural landholder, Gnys has no immediate use for his air force tunic. This glittering garment holds three tiers of ribbons, including the highest Polish decoration. But it hangs in the closet collecting dust. His peak cap is there too and once in a while, the two Gnys children try it for size.

Mrs. Gnys, an English war bride, raises German shepherd dogs to help the family income.

"We bought this 100-acre farm for $9,500," said the Polish veteran. "We had enough money to make a down payment. We also managed to buy some chickens and a few cows. But when my wife and I and Haydn and Stefan moved to the land we had exactly $3 in cash. And we had no prospect for making any more."

For one month the Gnys family lived on that $3. "We ate eggs and milk and milk and eggs until a cheque arrived from the dairy," said Mrs. Gnys.

The Gnys family owns nine cows, 10 heifers, three horses, four pigs, 130 chickens. They raise grain and grapes. Mrs. Gnys helps harvest the crops.

For some time, they had discussed a desire to have another child. In October 1950, the doctor confirmed that Barbara was pregnant and was due in May. They were so happy to hear this news. However, the doctor detected a heart murmur which was apparently caused by a mild case of rheumatic fever when Barbara was a child. Fortunately, she had a good pregnancy, but as she became more cumbersome, Władek insisted she refrain from working in the fields. She still continued to milk the cows (they now had electric milkers) and care for the young animals and chickens. In fact, she worked right up to when she went to the Henderson Hospital in Hamilton.

On May 8th, 1951, a little girl they called Sydney, was born.

In a series of long hot summers, Władek and Barbara felt like slaves chained to the earth, prisoners to a process of plowing, discing, fertilizing the land with manure, seeding, harvesting and storage. On top of this the cows still had to be milked, livestock fed, including her many dogs, and stalls cleaned. Looking after the boys and doing household chores were also ongoing. It was very helpful having Barbara's mum and sister helping out for six months, but once they left, Barbara was on her own again.

During the five days Władek had been alone on the farm while his wife was in hospital, he had plowed the fields with the horses (Black Beauty had been removed) using the primitive plough, and cut the fields of hay but 10 acres of hay still needed gathering. The forecast predicted rain on May 12th. There was no one else to help and despite Władek's objection, Barbara convinced him she could work. The hay was a vital food source for the animals over the winter. So it was settled. The next morning, just after getting home with Sydney, a net was secured over the pram and the boys guarded her while they watched their parents labor for four days as they collected the hay. Fortunately, it did not rain. The field was cleared and the animals' winter rations were stored securely in the large dry loft of the big barn. But the work never stopped and Barbara never stopped either.

During the following exhausting three weeks she noticed that her heart was beating irregularly, plus she felt poorly all over and was not sleeping well. She assumed it was because she was overworked and overtired. Because Barbara loved animals, she also got stressed when an animal like a pig had to go to market: she was too soft and knew farming was not for her. To add fuel to the fire, she took codeine to help her sleep at the same time she was on painkillers for an abscessed tooth.

One late night during a thunderstorm, Barbara woke up with a start as a lightning flash lit up the room. Her heart started to pound rapidly, beating with extreme intensity and irregularity. Was she having a heart attack? The doctor was called and came immediately along with their priest. After an injection and a thorough examination, the doctor concluded that she had experienced a severe attack of tachycardia on her rheumatic heart which had reacted violently to an overdose of a combination of pain pills and codeine.

Over the next week or more, while Barbara stayed in bed, the two boys helped to prepare meals and cared for their new baby sister. All this time, Władek worked tirelessly keeping the farm afloat. Little by little, Barbara's health improved to the point of taking an active part again caring for her family and helping to work the farm: milking the cows twice a day and selling the milk to a local dairy was, after all, their major source of income.

In March 1952, Eva came over from England again but this time alone. She was very concerned about her daughter's health and wanted to help out and of course see her three grandchildren. Sydney was about ten months old at the time.

It was shortly after Sydney's first birthday in May 1952 that an accident happened. Both boys attended St. Francis Xavier Catholic School in Stoney Creek. Stefan was in grade one. While watching a baseball game at recess, the batter hit the ball but let the bat fly which struck Stefan (who was a spectator) in the face, breaking his nose and causing eye damage. The staff did nothing to help this bloodied little boy who was semiconscious afterwards with his head down on his desk. They did not even call a doctor or his parents. At the end of the day and without older brother Haydn's help, Stefan would not have made it home once the bus dropped them off a mile from the farm. Władek, Barbara and Eva were shocked to see his swollen and unrecognizable face: they rushed him to the hospital emergency ward immediately. The doctors were afraid of him getting meningitis—a life-threatening condition. The priest even came and administered last rites. During his stay in hospital, his parents were there almost constantly, but had to rise very early each day to begin the endless chores and stay up late completing them when they got home from the hospital. Fortunately, the doctors pulled him through and after several weeks, the swelling started to abate. Needless to say, Władek and Barbara lambasted the school officials for their total incompetence and pulled Stefan and Haydn out of the school permanently.

Shortly after Stefan returned home from the hospital, and to make matters worse, Władek came down with a severe attack of tonsillitis, running a high fever. The doctor prescribed antibiotics and a week in bed. To feed, shovel manure for 26 cows and heifers, three sows and 12 piglets, two horses, 150 hens, 16 kittens, five cats, and four dogs, there was no way he could afford to be in bed. Stubbornly, he ignored his weakened state and tackled all these things head on, but this made things worse. He had no choice but to retreat to his bed. Between Barbara taking over the tasks and Eva looking after the children, the farm work got done. Within a week Władek seemed to recover. However, he reflected on his present life and at times wished he had never left the Royal Air Force and the comforts of England.

By the end of the summer, Eva had to return to England, but before she left she said to Władek, "Why don't you sell the farm? You are both killing yourselves … enough is enough! Try and get an easier job and buy a house and live a 'normal' life."

Władek mildly protested and said that for the first time the farm was showing a profit, but would consider her forceful suggestion.

They did indeed consider moving: in fact, the property was put up for sale and within three weeks it was sold. They found an ideal, older home on a big lot in the town of Grimsby not far away. It was just before Christmas 1953 when they sadly and reluctantly said a tearful goodbye to their dear horses and herding dog Poochie who stayed behind. Poochie would continue to roam the vast farm property which he loved to do for days at a time.

★

The picturesque town of Grimsby is nestled in between Lake Ontario and the Niagara Escarpment which runs east–west from New York State, through Ontario, Michigan,

Wisconsin and Illinois. Its highest elevation is about 1,625 feet. The Niagara River plunges over the escarpment at Niagara Falls. This protected landform is mainly a forested ridge of fossil-rich sedimentary rock.

Moving from a paper-thin old farmhouse in December 1953, to a white-frame two-story home in nearby Grimsby was quite a change in lifestyle. It was situated on about an acre of well-landscaped grounds with several large trees including one extremely large weeping willow which, at the time, was the largest in Grimsby. Lake Ontario and a beautiful beach were literally at the end of the street i.e.: 104 Maple Avenue. Grimsby Central Public School, at the other end of town on Livingston Avenue, was about a mile away and the boys could walk there quite easily. Due to the bad experience with the Catholic School in Stoney Creek, their parents refused to send them to another Catholic institution.

The large and stately home (circa 1900) had an air of elegance to it and was in good condition. The previous owners had planted shrubs and a variety of bulbs. The beds contained masses of hollyhocks, lily-of-the-valley, tulips, daffodils, crocuses, bluebells, lilac, wisteria, laburnum bushes and there were a number of mature fruit trees—cherry, apple and damson. An extensive manicured peach orchard abutted the back of the property.

Wide entrance steps led to glass front doors and an open verandah wrapped around the front. Parquet flooring in the entrance introduced a majestic oak staircase and off to the right side was a huge living room with a high ceiling, many windows and a large fireplace. Glass doors joined the family room which led to a modern kitchen and dining area. The back staircase was off the laundry room and a screened-in sun room was at the rear of the house. Upstairs were five spacious bedrooms and two full bathrooms. Household items could be stored in the generous attic. Medium-sized boulders mortared together formed the walls of a large dirt-floor basement (later paved) which contained a coal storage room with chute and a coal-burning furnace.

Now that Władek was no longer a farmer, the big question at the time was what will he do to make a living to support his family? A number of former Polish officers who had settled in this area had found employment in local factories such as International Harvester, Stelco, Ford and Studebaker. His pilot friend Staszek Chałupa was able to get a job at the Studebaker car plant in Hamilton working on the assembly line and suggested Władek do the same. He took the advice and got the job. The pay was low, but at least it paid for food basics.

Two chicken houses were purchased and moved to the end of the property and converted into dog kennels. One thing was sure and that was Barbara would expand her dog business and help provide extra income. Gnyś built a sturdy fence around the perimeter to keep their roaming dogs confined.

Working at the Studebaker assembly plant was strenuous and demanding as the moving line of cars was nonstop. One of the tasks Władek performed was to hand-sand with wet sandpaper the car tops before they were primed and painted. At the end of each day, his arms and shoulders ached and stiffened up. Some men opposite him from time-to-time suffered so much pain and anguish from this work that they literally gave up and cried. Władek in his 40s was quite fit from farm work, showed compassion, finished his job and completed their half of the sanding while they rested. They were so grateful as they could have been fired for slacking off. On those days, he would come home more exhausted than usual and would soak his sore muscles in a hot tub.

Slaving away on a farm or straining his muscles on an assembly line for the rest of his days was not what he had in mind. He told his wife that a long lay-off was expected by Studebaker and was concerned that his earnings would only be $35 per week. It would be difficult to feed themselves and pay the bills. Their bank account was flat after selling the farm and paying back the existing mortgage and lawyer's fees. Now they had another mortgage on their new home to be concerned about.

Władek, Staszek Chałupa and three other men who worked at Studebaker picked up extra money painting the exteriors of stores in Hamilton, but the low wage was barely enough to get by on. Bills mounted.

To make ends meet, Barbara started to really focus on selling her animals. Their lovely German shepherd Sasha had had a litter of pups while on the farm and one of them, Spoona, had given birth to six puppies. At the same time, Barbara was given four pure white Persian kittens by a local fruit farmer. Within three days, she sold them for $20 each. The money paid off their telephone bill and the line reconnection. By the time the six puppies were nine weeks old, Barbara was able to sell all of them within two weeks except for one large male which they kept. They named him Asik after Władek's dog that he had as a boy in Sarnów.

Barbara made an announcement that she was expecting another baby. Sydney would be three years old by then and would have a sibling brother or sister close to her age. On August 4th, 1954, Ashley Richard joined the family. He was a healthy baby boy, brother and future playmate for Sydney.

During the layoff from Studebaker, Władek added several sturdy wired runways for the dogs near the kennels) and fenced off the whole foot of the property for the protection of the children and to prevent strangers from entering that area. All fence post holes here and around the property perimeter he dug in the sandy soil by hand using an auger.

Finally, Władek was called back to Studebaker which was a relief. However, wages were still low and making ends meet was still a challenge. In addition, the physical exertion demanded by this job started to take its toll on his body, so he told his wife that he wanted to look for other work.

After leaving the Studebaker plant, he managed to get a job as a salesman selling a food mixer called a Kenwood Chef. After a brief training period he tried his hand door-to-door canvassing. The first day he knocking on over 60 doors with no success.

He felt humiliated and discouraged. However, Barbara with her gift of the gab and using a personal approach, helped her husband develop a whole new sales technique and, as a result, he started to sell the mixers at a reasonable rate. However, this did not last indefinitely. Fuel costs for their station wagon, for example, became an issue as this line of work required him to be constantly on the move.

Since Gnyś's command of English was good, he decided to take a real estate course and get his license which allowed him to sell properties. A large, well-known company, Todd Real Estate in Hamilton, took him on to see what he could do. After all, there was a relatively large Polish population in the area, so being bilingual was a big asset. But again, like the previous job, his income was based on commission. So, he gave it a serious try and for a while was Todd's top salesperson. He proudly showed his family his name at the top of the blackboard list of sales. Selling real estate was rewarding providing he got listings and potential buyers, an ongoing challenge. Fuel and advertising costs were always major expenses. In terms of honesty, he did not like being stabbed in the back by ruthless buyers and sellers negotiating behind his back and cutting him out of a deal. Hours were long especially since he rose early to prepare food for their ever-growing canine population. Haydn and Stefan had chores too: they were up early cleaning and watering the animals. They then got washed and changed and walked to school.

Barbara and Władek were quite the team and worked very well together. They worked out a system of sharing the everyday demands of family and animal care so that each could pursue their own passion. Władek concentrated on his real estate job while Barbara bred and raised her purebred dogs. Her sales were brisk as her puppies were in demand. As she gained confidence in her sales abilities, she started to think about other possible enterprises. Using her limited knowledge and skills of hairdressing, she decided to open a beauty parlor on the north side of Grimsby where competition was nil.

With Władek's carpentry skills, over several weekends, he erected walls inside the vacant store they rented which was in a small outside strip mall. He installed all necessary items such as wash basins, mirrors, styling stations and dryers. Once completed, they hired two hairdressers. It was an attractive shop: they called it Sydney-Lynn's. After a shaky start, business boomed and they had to hire additional hairdressers. At long last, money was regularly deposited into their account.

Running two enterprises at the same time was a challenge, but this was just the tip of the iceberg. Barbara was indeed an entrepreneur. Władek couldn't have been happier.

From 1957 onward, the purebred dog population grew at a steady rate. Three large kennels were needed to house well over 50 animals at a given time. German shepherds and Welsh corgis were the main breeds, but they also raised other popular breeds such as miniature poodles. There was a great deal of work involved caring for so many animals, but each member of the family pitched in and got it done.

With so many dogs concentrated in a small area, the noise factor became a real problem for the neighborhood. Complaints were common, but it was difficult and impossible to keep the dogs from barking. The situation reached a climax when about eight dogs were poisoned by meat laced with strychnine tossed into the yard and individual pens. Władek's second dog named Asik was one of the casualties.

It was imperative that the dogs be moved to a safe location with lots of land. Beamsville, a rural community not far away, was the answer. They still owned Sydney-Lynn's and would continue to operate it for two successful years. After giving the real estate agent their specifications for the perfect property for their animals, the search began. It didn't take long before they were introduced to a lovely piece of land tucked right under the Niagara Escarpment in Beamsville, only 20 minutes away from the Grimsby house. The property was approximately 38 acres with a 700-foot frontage. It was gorgeous. Once a thriving peach orchard, it sat neglected and most of the trees had either died or were producing undersized, poor-quality fruit. However, they were not interested in being fruit farmers. The deal was closed and they had two months to get ready for the immense job of moving all their household possessions and the countless dogs. They wasted no time hiring a contractor who built a multi-run kennel that could house scores of animals. They also moved a smaller kennel building from the Grimsby property to the new site and purchased a prefabricated model home which they moved and converted into a split-level dwelling. All buildings were well back on the property. From the top floor of the house, one could see Lake Ontario in the distance and the manicured property through which the lane ran and connected with the main north–south artery—Mountain View Road. Władek built a fenced parking lot for customers.

In the early 1960s, the Gnyś family planted hundreds of pine tree seedlings which, as they matured, became a protective sanctuary for such wildlife as deer, pheasants and rabbits. On the far right of the property was a large pond which was stocked with fish by Haydn. Also, when the fields got too overgrown, he cut them using their tractor-mower.

In Beamsville, by the end of 1962, the main kennel and house were almost completed. The smaller kennel moved there from Grimsby was used for newborn puppies and purebred cats. Haydn had secured a full-time job in the region, Ashley and Sydney went to the local public school while Stefan attended Beamsville Secondary School.

Władek had aspirations of becoming a real estate broker and opening his own office in Hamilton. A decision was made. Barbara sold her hair salon business and joined her husband part time in his new office. In 1964, Dick W. Gnys Real Estate was in operation. Because Władek was difficult to pronounce for the English population, he changed it to Dick as it rhymed closely to his first name. Shortly afterwards, for the same reason, Gnys became Guys, as in Dick W. Guys Real Estate. These name changes worked out well for the English-speaking clientele.

Once the kennels were finished, the dog business just took off. Not only did they have their own dogs and cats for sale, but they advertised their boarding facility.

Later in 1964, he closed the Hamilton real estate office and rented a house on busy Geneva Street in St. Catharines east of Beamsville. The house was converted into a real estate office. They worked together for several months until Władek got the new business up and running. Barbara opened a pet shop right next door and, although small, the shop did well and proved successful.

Being an entrepreneur, Barbara went into the production of pet-coats of her own design. They sold like hot cakes in her store so much so that she had to hire over 15 more sewers to keep up with demand. She approached several large department stores such as K-Mart, Simpson-Sears, Eaton's, The Bay and Hartz Mountain (pet supply company) who were eager to carry her products. Her dog coats even made it into the Sears catalogue and were sold coast-to-coast. In hot pursuit came the dog beds which in terms of distribution and sales, followed in the footsteps of her dog coats. The pet shop eventually moved to a larger nearby store on St. Paul Street and became The Puppy in the Window. It became a huge success, but the work involved was monumental.

The kennels had increased to an average of 100 dogs, puppies and purebred kittens. Included in this total were boarders and several dozen unwanted dogs and cats destined to be destroyed. In terms of competition, their kennel operation was likely the largest in Canada.

In 2000, after Barbara had passed, and just before Władek's passing, the property was sold and was later transformed into a productive winery.

CHAPTER 10

Return to Poland

After the Germans surrendered unconditionally, Stalin set in motion the annexation of Poland by creating a pro-communist Polish government, a Soviet puppet state. He had already cut relations with General Sikorski and the Polish government-in-exile in London in 1943, but since Roosevelt and Churchill were still in the picture, he agreed at Yalta that a coalition government would be formed. However, as the new government unfolded, the communists held a majority of the key positions and soon gained total control through the rigging of elections.

Shortly after the war was officially over, a number of Polish pilots returned to their homeland, mainly to be reunited with loved ones. However, rumors abounded that returning servicemen faced arrest or worse.

Władek believed very seriously that the communists in Poland were not to be trusted and as much as he yearned to go back to Sarnów to see his family, he resisted the temptation. He warned his pilot friends not to go back to Poland just yet, but wait until it was safe to do so. However, many did not listen to common sense and were also fooled by false communist promises of good will. A number of high-ranking pilots were harassed, arrested and jailed and some were executed after phony "spy trials" were held. Two pilots who Władek knew personally suffered under the hands of the communist regime. Colonel Józef Jungrav was a kind and patriotic man, who returned to Poland in the early 1950s. He was subsequently arrested, convicted of being a spy and executed in 1952. Brig Gen Stanisław Skalski returned to Poland in 1947 and joined the Air Force of the Polish Army. But in 1948, he was arrested and falsely charged with espionage and sentenced to death. He was on death row for three years, but later his sentence was changed to life imprisonment in the notorious Wronki Prison, northwest of Poznań. After Stalin's death in 1953, his successor Nikita Khrushchev rejected Stalin's harsh policies and Skalski was released in 1956. Thus, this Polish ace spent eight unnecessary years of his life incarcerated and suffered extreme anguish because he went back to Poland too soon.

Even though the communist regime was still in control, it was safe enough for Władek to return to Poland to visit his family in 1965. However, he was followed by regime agents wherever he went, but was never interrogated or arrested.

His only brother Toni met him at the airport in Warsaw and they went straight up to Nowy Dwór Gdański, southeast of Gdańsk, to be with Toni's family. They then travelled together around neighboring cities like Gdynia, Gdańsk and Sopot after which they went to the village of Sarnów, their birthplace. Here they spent quality time with their Uncle Antoni (Toni), Aunt Franciszka and family. The war and its effects were discussed at length.

Toni told his brother that during the war, most non-Jewish Polish households were resettled to undesirable locations with substandard accommodation. Poles had to work for *bauern*—German farmers occupying Polish farms. Toni, who had finished agricultural college and his matriculation just before the war, had to work on such farms. His wife Lodzia, who never had a chance to finish business college, worked in the fields. They got married quickly after the war broke out, because in the case of relocation, married couples could go together. They were fortunate in that many others were sent to Germany, Siberia or concentration camps. The youngest sister Jadzia went to live with Uncle Antoni and Aunt Franciszka in Sarnów who still ran the grist mill and the carp farm.

On the outskirts of Sarnów, the car stopped at the site of the large wooden cross that Władek vowed to come back to if he survived the war—a promise he made 26 years earlier: "Jesus, if you allow me to survive the war, I will come here again, bow down and kiss your feet." The cross was still there, but had a slight lean to it. He got out, put his arms around the base and kissed it. He thanked God for allowing him to see Poland and his birthplace again. The people who lived around there were curious to know his story. Ever since then, there is still talk about the pilot who remembered his wartime promise to come back and kiss the cross. This wasn't the last time Władek would return to the cross as the pilgrimage was repeated in 1976, 1996 and 1998.

The old mill and property in Sarnów had changed physically. The huge ponds which were once full of carp had all dried up. One reason was that the canopy of trees had been cut down by the Germans which allowed increased evaporation. Mainly though, the stream that fed the reservoir which worked the grinding wheel was a mere trickle due to overuse and diversions upstream. Their family home which once stood on the edge of the old mill property was no longer there, as it had been destroyed by fire.

All his sisters and Uncle Toni and family had miraculously survived the war (Władek's father had passed away in 1962: he was notified while living in Beamsville). Władek significantly upgraded his parents' grave marker in Łążyn near Kawęczyn. Meanwhile, his sisters had settled down with their own families: Anna in Zawada, Helena, Stanisława and Marysia in Kawęczyn, Bronka in Radom, and Jadwiga in Kolbudy.

Władysław Molenda (the groom and farmhand) at the age of 67 was alive but ailing. Their reunion was very emotional: Molenda broke down at the sight of Władek for he had loved him as a son. They reminisced for days and brought each other up to date. One tragic event that Molenda related concerned the small, predominantly Jewish town of Gniewoszów about three miles northeast of Sarnów. On the eve of World War II, a total of 1,580 Jews lived in the town. Gniewoszów was overrun by the Nazis in mid-September 1939. Jews were ordered to wear a Star of David and forced into slave labor. In the spring of 1942, Jews from surrounding towns and villages were forced to move into a formal ghetto at Gniewoszów and by August the population had swelled to about 6,580. Of those, approximately 5,600 were moved elsewhere and the remaining 1,000 were exterminated at Treblinka. By the end of November, there were no Jews left in Gniewoszów.[1] One reason Molenda spoke of this atrocity was that Władek and his family in Sarnów became friends with a number of Jewish families in Gniewoszów when he was growing up. One boy in particular, Zoref, a tailor's son, had become his good friend. Molenda was convinced that only one member of the family of eight survived and it wasn't Zoref.

In 1971, six years after Gnyś's visit, his father figure, Władysław Molenda or "Serce"—"The Heart" or "Władziu Serce" passed away at the age of 73; he is buried in the Oleksów Cemetery not far from Gniewoszów and Sarnów.

Aunt Franciszka and Uncle Antoni told Władek that the German military didn't move into the area of Sarnów until around 1943. From every household along the way, they took young men and boys to work as slave labor either in Poland, Germany or elsewhere. This was a major concern for the Gnyś family so they devised several ways in which to hide vulnerable family members and neighbors.

In the living quarters of the mill were a number of bedrooms and a fairly large kitchen/dining area with a corner stove. In the adjacent bedroom, on the other side of the wall, was a tall tiled heating unit. Beside it were several deep horizontal compartments, one of which was a bread oven. Above it was a similar space that was used like a closet for the storage of old clothes. On one occasion, Antoni, Franciszka, his cousins Władziu (16) and Gienia (22) and her husband Stanisław Deska (27) were in the mill. When the Germans approached Franciszka and her daughter Gienia in a panic decided to hide Władziu and Stanisław in the hot, dark space above the bread oven and cover them up with old clothes. After a thorough search outside and in the barns, the soldiers came inside to continue looking, but did not find the young men. Gienia[2] and Franciszka were interrogated for several hours, but did not give up their secret. Suffering from excessive heat, dehydration and suffocating conditions, Władziu and Stanisław kept perfectly still except for one time: the interrogating German heard a noise and became suspicious. Being quick on her feet, Gienia said that it was a goose outside the door and changed the subject. The young men were hidden many times in this space and the hiding place was never discovered.

In the old mill, Antoni used a container, such as a large rectangular bin or barrel, with a covered false bottom into which a person could fit and hide. Then "groats"—hulled or crushed grain-like oats—were poured on the top simulating a full container of freshly ground grain. This container was located in the dark basement or cellar below the floor accessible by a ladder. The entrance had a trapdoor which was covered, and thus hidden by an object like a piece of machinery or a tarp. If the Germans found the trapdoor, they would still be hard pressed to find anyone inside the container unless they smashed or fired on it. Like the oven, the container was never discovered. The village was constantly on the lookout for enemy troops and as soon as they were spotted, the 'hide-and-seek' process began in earnest using both hiding places.

Before the Germans dismantled the mill's inner structure and carried off the large wooden beams, Antoni and Franciszka saved family members and many local young men and women from the hands of the Nazis and the Red Army. They were very brave and put their lives at risk every time the Germans came into Sarnów.

The question of female abuse and rape by invading forces is a very real one. In Sarnów anyway, Franciszka said, "The German soldiers were strict and disciplined, but Russian soldiers were 'wild pigs' and inhumane." She said that the Germans were only on the lookout for young men to be used as slave labor, but the Russians were out for rape, death and destruction.

The following by Kasia Terech (née Kowalska) is a true story passed down by the family in Sarnów. It involves Władek's Aunt Franciszka and his youngest sister, Jadwiga (Jadzia).

> Jadzia, for a long time, was living in Sarnów because of the war. It was a sunny day. My great grandmother Franciszka and Jadzia were doing laundry in the river near the mill. Suddenly, two Russian soldiers came. Jadzia was a young and very attractive woman, so they wanted her to go with them. Franciszka told them that Jadzia will go with them when she finishes doing the laundry. After a while, they agreed. When the soldiers went away Franciszka sent Jadzia to hide in a neighbor's barn. When the soldiers came back Jadzia was already gone. Franciszka was alone and the soldiers put a gun to her head. They told her that they will kill her if she doesn't tell them where Jadzia is. Frania (Franciszka) told them that Jadzia was just a girl from the village who was helping with the laundry. The soldiers were drunk and very aggressive. They were arguing with her for a long time, but Franciszka didn't tell them where Jadzia was. It was a miracle that they didn't kill her. When the soldiers went away, Franciszka went for Jadzia and brought her home.

Brave Franciszka lied more than once about the whereabouts of Jadzia and others. Franciszka was known to have said, "I would rather be shot in the face than give information to the Germans or Russians!"

Around the dinner table in the living quarters of the old mill, Reginka Gnyś (wife of Władziu, son of Antoni and Franciszka) told a story about a dogfight she witnessed in early September 1939. She was seven at the time and lived in a place called Zdunków four miles from Sarnów on the west side of the Vistula. Reginka was minding cows in a field close to home when suddenly she saw two planes approaching, one chasing the other. They were flying low and bullets were striking the ground around her. Fearing for her safety, she fell face down and tried to make herself as small as she could next to an unplowed ridge. When she got up, Reginka saw them fly in the direction of Gniewoszów and then towards Dęblin Air Force Base on the other side of the Vistula—Władek was stationed there at the time. When he heard her eyewitness account, he shrieked! "That was me chasing a German plane! I shot him down on the other side of the river!" Everyone was astonished! He told them that this was part of the region that he patrolled on the lookout for enemy aircraft. However, it's unlikely that any official record of this kill survived, as the buildings at the Dęblin base were almost totally destroyed by the Luftwaffe.

The Germans made many non-Jewish families leave their own homes and go elsewhere. Homes were confiscated for their own uses. Władziu Gnyś told Władek that they first went to live in Czarnolas with an aunt from the Popis family. However, one of the aunt's daughters did not like the fact that the house was suddenly overcrowded so she complained to the Germans who made the Gnyś family move again. They were forced to live with strangers in a village called Wilczowola which is about nine miles from Sarnów. They stayed there for five months. Of course this was not ideal, but at least they had a roof over their heads.

Once the Germans moved into an area, they cut down trees and took lumber from existing homes and barns; this was commonplace and used, for example, in the construction of defensive bunkers. Unfortunately, the mill was not spared. Eventually, it was stripped of its good-quality timber, leaving only the outer shell of stone walls. Władziu said he and his father Antoni came back on foot to check on the mill. His dad was heartbroken and collapsed to the ground and wept; he just sat there for some time while Władziu consoled him. They then went back to their relocation site, hitched up a horse and carriage and returned to the mill to see what they could salvage. Later, when the Germans had gone, they ripped apart the bunkers and took back their lumber. After a stove-fitter was found, they started to arrange the kitchen. Slowly, step by step, they managed to rebuild the mill, but it took years.

★

After the first trip back to his homeland, Władek wanted to show off his country to Barbara who had never ventured into Eastern Europe. He was 66 and she was 55 years old. They arrived in Warsaw in the summer of 1976. The journey would take them to his familiar haunts such as Nowy Dwór Gdański to see his brother Toni, wife Lodzia and their son Zbyszek.

After that they went to see his sisters who were scattered around the northern half of Poland with their families. Sarnów was a hit for Barbara because she had heard so much about his birthplace. She loved the rural setting and the family was so warm and friendly. In fact, all the families they went to and stayed with were amazing and couldn't do enough to make them feel welcome—Barbara loved them all. Barbara later admitted back in Canada that she found it frustrating not understanding the language as her husband would always forget to translate. She loved the food but found it rich, and the accessibility to public washrooms limiting.

★

By 1970, the pet shop and kennels were well established and successful businesses. Their excellent reputation for boarding animals and selling purebred dogs and cats was well known across the country. Many animal owners were repeat customers from across Ontario and their loyalty was greatly appreciated.

The business was so robust that Władek decided to discontinue his real estate business to devote all his time to their canine and feline endeavors. Barbara could not have been happier to now have her husband working with her shoulder-to-shoulder.

A well-earned vacation to Florida in 1970 ignited the desire to live there during the Canadian winter. They purchased several acres of beautiful land in Bradenton on Florida's west coast on the Braden River with about 600 feet of shoreline. It was a picturesque setting on which they built a pretty bungalow among the pine trees; large palms were later added along with orange and grapefruit trees. While they were away, Haydn and his wife Christine kindly looked after the dog and cat business back home in Beamsville.

So for some 23 years, they happily wintered in sunny Florida. During this time, they invited their grown children and grandchildren to visit, plus other relatives and friends from England, Poland, Canada and the U.S. They loved the company and enjoyed people staying with them. Sadly, the property was sold after Barbara discovered that she had terminal cancer before passing away in 1995. Their love and devotion for each other during all those years was unparalleled since they first met in 1940 in England.

CHAPTER 11

Reconciliation

"It is high time that we forget about war and instead make friends and build towards ongoing peace and understanding."

WŁADYSŁAW GNYŚ, AUGUST 30TH, 1989

"Today we are good friends who do not want war, but friendship between countries."

FRANK NEUBERT, AUGUST 30TH, 1989

Mike Dobrzelecki recalls:

In 1988 I met with Lawrence Sowinski, Exhibit Director of the Intrepid Sea, Air & Space Museum, to discuss future plans for projects at the Essex Class aircraft carrier-turned museum ship berthed at Pier 86 on the Hudson River in New York City.[1] Since the opening of the museum in 1982, I had worked on several other exhibits providing research, writing text for the display panels, as well as, building museum models and supervising the work of other modelers. This exhibit was shaping up to be quite a leap forward. Larry outlined an ambitious and exciting program, namely a series of exhibits commemorating the 50th Anniversary of World War II. The first of which was the "Poland Invaded" Exhibit, marking the opening phase of the war. The exhibit's opening day would be, appropriately enough, September 1st, 1989. When Larry related that the Intrepid would also be receiving tremendous support from the Muzeum Wojske Polskiego (Polish Army Museum) in Warsaw, Poland, which would lend the Intrepid significant artifacts of the September Campaign from its main collection, "Poland Invaded" was shaping up to be the most significant exhibit attempted by the museum to date. It also began the minor conspiracy I had going with Larry, a fellow Polish-American, to include the contribution of Polish veterans in as many of these exhibits as possible over the next five years.

Being a firm believer in the maxim that historical events should be related on both a broad overview basis and fleshed out with personal accounts of those who participated, I set about searching for just the right stories to accomplish that goal. One of the reference books I would rely heavily on was Jerzy Cynk's book, *History of the Polish Air Force 1918–1968*, Osprey Publishing, London, 1972. That book included a short account of the first aerial combat between a Polish pilot, ppor Władek Gnyś and a Luftwaffe pilot, Lt Frank Neubert, in the early morning hours of September 1st, 1939. Another was *The Luftwaffe War Diaries*, by Cajus Bekker (Doubleday Garden

City 1968), which was the translation of his original 1964 German language *Angriffshohe 4000* (Gergard Stalling, Hamburg), which included an account of the Neubert/Gnyś encounter on that first day of the war, based on original research by Polish military historian, Janusz Piekałkiewicz.[2] My main source, however, became Władek Gnyś's book, *First Kill, A Fighter Pilot's Autobiography* (W. Kimber, London, 1981), which I acquired earlier in 1988. Clearly, the *First Kill* story would be a great addition to the Intrepid's "Poland Invaded" exhibit.

Initially my intent was to just build models of aircraft involved along with the basic story, but I mused over the possibility of tracking down Gnyś and getting some additional information and inviting him to the opening. Larry Sowinski thought this was a great idea.

Through my local contacts with the Polish Air Force Veterans' Association and with the assistance of Jerzy Cynk, Polish Air Force historian, I managed to obtain Gnyś's contact information and sent him an introductory letter. Gnyś called me soon after receiving my letter and was very enthusiastic about the exhibit offering to support the effort. During our conversation, Władek and I both agreed that it would be great if we could track down Frank Neubert and arrange a reunion, but neither one of us was very hopeful about being able to make this happen.

A couple of weeks after of our initial conversation Władek telephoned me again: "We found him! I just received a letter from Frank Neubert. Can you believe it!"

Apparently, by some quirk of fate, Frank Neubert, having read the same account in Bekker's original German language book, was trying to find Gnyś to extend his hand in friendship, hopefully burying any animosity built up over the previous 50 years between opposite combatants. Frank had obtained Gnyś's address from the previously mentioned Polish aviation historian, Janusz Piekałkiewicz and sent him the letter, despite his reservations on how his offer would be received by Gnyś.

Now that I had Neubert's address, the long-shot possibility of arranging a "reunion" between the two had a real chance of becoming a reality.

Right after I hung up with Władek, I contacted Larry Sowinski and told him that we found Neubert. I quickly outlined my proposal to have the Intrepid Museum fly Neubert and his wife over from Germany and coordinate a reunion with Gnyś. He did not hesitate a second in approving the project, appointing me as the coordinator. Originally, we wanted to have it aboard the Intrepid Museum, but Władek's health issues prevented him from traveling, so we agreed to have it at the Gnyś home in Beamsville, Ontario, Canada. The Intrepid Museum would provide a translator, Ellen Goldstein, to travel with the Neuberts to Canada and arrange for a film crew to meet us in Beamsville.

The rest, as the saying goes, is history. Looking back, it's fascinating to consider the unique series of events leading up to their reunion. Here we had two pilots, both aging warriors and former adversaries, driven by some impulse, known only to them, to meet 50 years after they faced each other in the skies over Poland, a combat which resulted in the death of Gnyś's commanding officer, M. Medwecki, who was shot down by Neubert. On that basis alone, one can understand Neubert's trepidation on how his peace offering would be received by Gnyś. Time and tide over the intervening 50 years had mellowed both men. They found common ground in both surviving the war and the warmth of forgiveness, serving as the foundation for a friendship that would last them the rest of their lives.

In early 1989 while wintering in Florida, a letter addressed to Władek arrived from Germany. Upon opening it, he was astounded to learn that it was from Frank Neubert, the Stuka pilot with the Luftwaffe who, during the early hours of September 1st, 1939 had shot down Squadron Leader Medwecki when he and S-Lt Gnyś took off together to intercept German aircraft that had just bombed Kraków. It was apparently the only plane the German pilot ever shot down, because he was strictly a dive-bomber specialist who, by the end of the war, had rained down terror and caused great damage to Allied forces throughout all of Europe.

April 4th, 1989

Mr. Gnys

I have Your name and adress [sic] from Mr. Janusz Piekalkiewicz.

    50 years is a long time and nearly 50 years ago we had the order to be enemy. And so we had the fight in the air near Krakau on the 1. Sept 1939. I am the pilot of the Stuka Ju 87. It was war and now we have peace. Therefore I mean we could now have a friendship.

    If you think so, please give me an answer.

    I greet you

[Signature] Frank Neubert

As scheduled, at ten in the morning on August 30th, 1989, Lawrence Sowinski's representative and coordinator Michael Dobrzelecki drove up the long Beamsville driveway. With Michael was Frank Neubert, a man of stature about 6 feet 2 inches tall and 235 pounds. He was slightly tanned, wore glasses and had a friendly smile. With him was his wife Sigrid who was rather petite with a kind face and greying hair and also wearing glasses. Frank was 74 at the time, five years younger than Władek.

Barbara being friendly and hospitable, walked down to the car and greeted them. She took Sigrid by the hand and led her and the others to where Władek and the rest of the family were anxiously waiting. The press were jockeying for position, cameras clicked and the film rolled; this historic meeting was to be preserved forever.

Fifty years, almost to the day, had passed since they met in the skies over Poland. They shook hands and embraced warmly. Even though Frank could speak and write in broken English, the Intrepid Museum had secured a translator, Ellen Goldstein from New York, to accompany the Neuberts with Dobrzelecki to Canada. The following dialogue is quoted almost word for word and appeared in Barbara's manuscript *First Encounter*, translated into Polish as *Pierwsze Spotkanie* in 1996:

"Welcome to Canada," Władek said.

"It's a pleasure to meet you," replied Frank.

"Tell me please," Władek asked, "how did you find me?"

"I read about you in this book *Luftkrieg 1939–1945*, please accept it as a gift from me," replied Frank.

"Thank you very much. It will be a nice souvenir." Władek examined the contents. Turning, he asked, "Were you in operations over France?"

"I was. I also flew over Greece, the Balkans and of course England."

"What part of England?"

Frank Neubert   W-Germany   Gütersloh,27.4.1989
                             D 4830   Welplagestraße 2

Herrn
Wladyslaw Gnys
1900-54 Str.E.
Bradenton

33508 Florida USA

Mr. Gnys! Sehr geehrter Herr Gnys!

Ihre Anschrift erhielt ich über den Schriftsteller Janusz
Piekalkiewicz. Sie werden sich wundern,daß ich Ihnen schreibe.
50 Jahre sind eine lange Zeit.Und vor nun fast 50 Jahren sind wir
uns auf Befehl als Feinde in der Luft begegnet und zwar am 1.Sept
1939. Ihr in dem Buch Luftkrieg von Herrn Piekalkiewicz veröffent-
lichter Bericht besagt dies. Ich bin der Pilot des Stuka Ju 87
und wie erwähnt der befohlene Gegner in dem Luftkampf im Westen von
Krakau. Es war Krieg, heute haben wir Frieden.
Deshalb meine ich, wer früher auf Befehl Feind sein mußte, könnte
heute Bekannter oder besser Freund sein. Falls Sie auch dieser
Meinung sind oder sein können,dann bitte ich um eine Antwort.
Sie finden hierzu anbei einen internationalen Antwortschein.

Es grüßt Sie,

[signature: Frank Neubert]

I have Your name and adress from Mr.Janusz Piekalkiewicz.
50 years are a long time and nearly 50 years ago we had the order
to be enemy.And so we had the fight in the air near Krakau on
the 1.Sept 1939.I am the pilot of the Stuka Ju 87.It was war and
now we have peace. Therefore I mean we could now have a friendship.
If You think so,please giv me an answer.
I greet You

"Mostly the south … Heston-Tangmere."

"Tangmere! That's phenomenal. I was there! You naughty chap!" Władek joked, wagging his finger at him.

"My apologies," Frank replied and they both laughed.

"Do you still have your uniform, sir?" one of the reporters asked Władek. "If it still fits, we would like a picture of you in it."

Haydn helped his father into his RAF flying jacket and Frank zipped it up, then the RAF cap went on next. Władek didn't have the jacket on for too long as it was rather warm, so it was replaced by his still smart-looking tunic.

"Slightly tight!" he chuckled. Cameras flashed the whole time.

With the aid of the interpreter, the two men conversed for a while and then settled themselves down beneath the shade of a tree, being joined by their wives.

Kelly Crowe, a reporter from CBC in Toronto, started the television interview. She turned to Władek: "Fifty years have passed since World War II. What goes on in your mind?"

"To stop blaming each other for everything and to start building peace in the world," he replied.

"And how do you view the war?"

"As completely unnecessary, very cruel and a terrible waste of millions of lovely people. I myself feel no personal hatred."

"What do you think about Frank? He fought against your country."

"It was war. He did his duty. He carried out his orders the same as I did. It is high time that we forget about war and instead make friends and build towards ongoing peace and understanding."

Kelly turned to Frank: "What would you have thought if fifty years ago someone had told you that you would be sitting here today with an old enemy?"

The interpreter translated as Neubert replied: "In 1939 we were given orders to dive-bomb Kraków, to destroy the so-called enemies of Hitler. I was a young man of twenty-four—I had many friends, but no enemies. Suddenly one day, I had many. I never felt this way, but I was a Stuka pilot in the Luftwaffe and had to obey orders. Today we are good friends who do not want war, but friendship between countries. One should be able to solve all problems in a peaceful way."

Kelly turned again to Władek: "What do you say to that?"

"I am happy to meet Frank. Reflections of war after fifty years are different. When I was shot down on August 27th, 1944, two young German soldiers, mere boys, stood in front of me. Their guns protected me from a German corporal who wanted to kill me. These soldiers were kind to me, they saved my life and I will always be grateful to them. I am also grateful to the German doctor who helped me by attending to my wound and making such a fantastic bandage that stopped the bleeding. I wish I could meet them all and shake their hands and thank them."

"But Frank was trying to shoot you!"

"That's where you are wrong. Fighter pilots do not try to shoot the pilot, but aim to shoot down the enemy aircraft."

"But he shot down your commanding officer. Your friend."

"You can't look at it from that point of view. I remember once I was involved in a dogfight with a Messerschmitt. In passing, I was so close that I could see the pilot's face—he appeared to be a very young boy. After returning to base, I thought about him—he was someone's son. He had not asked for war."

"What do you think of Frank?"

Władek smiled. "He looks like a typical Stuka pilot and a nice-looking gentleman!"

"Have you any comments?" the interviewer asked Frank.

"I am happy to have lived to this day and able to come and meet Władek, thanks to Lawrence Sowinski and Mike Dobrzelecki of the Intrepid."

"Why do you want to be friends with a former enemy?"

"Why not? I never had him personally as an enemy. I had my orders … I could never feel badly towards him," replied Frank.

"But you were shooting at him."

"No, I was shooting at an airplane, not a man."

"Exactly!" Władek agreed. "We shot at the aircraft and not at the pilot."

"What do you think of Władek?" Kelly asked Frank.

The German patted Władek's arm affectionately. "We are good friends. I am happy we both survived and that I can sit together now with my good friend Władek."

The interview with Kelly ended and was to be viewed later, nationally, on the CBC news that day. The other reporters took over and coverage continued with their respective newspapers and networks. The meeting of the two former enemies made world news that day.

At 3 p.m., Frank, Sigrid, Mike, Ellen Goldstein the translator and all the Gnyś clan sat down together to enjoy a meal at the Beacon Restaurant in nearby Jordan which overlooks beautiful Lake Ontario.

When the party finally broke up, Frank walked with Władek and Barbara to the parking lot. With tears in his eyes, he embraced them in turn and said, "Auf wiedersehen my dear, dear friends. I will never forget this wonderful day." He walked away towards Mike's waiting car but then stopped, turned and came back to their side and hugged them again with obvious emotion. "Goodbye dear friends, God bless you." He turned and walked slowly to the car and drove off.

Speechless and moved, Władek and Barbara got into theirs and just sat there.

Douglas Cockell was at the reunion:

> It was a sunny day, or perhaps we just brought our own glow to this optimistic and positive day. I was there as a friend to Stefan, Władysław Gnyś's son, but also because my own father had been a part of the Battle of Britain. A young Flight Sergeant with the RAF, my father had loaded tightly wound belts of bullets into the Spitfire's wings, doping the fabric over the gun ports to streamline it for its next flight and aligning the four Browning machine guns so they would converge at just the right distance to create their own devastating crossfire. But Władysław had been the pilot in that battle, far from home by then and still fighting for his country.
>
> And now he was standing in the driveway before us, with a supporting walker as I recall which at times he set aside for the meeting. Stefan's father had fought for his place in history in the skies above Poland while my own father was helping his Scottish squadron prepare for war.

I had grown up surrounded by books on the air war, so the German bomber Frank had flown in 1939 was vivid in my imagination and now here in front of me, stepping out of a car in the Niagara orchard country, was Frank himself, a living connection to those wartime illustrations printed in shades of grey. In my recollection Stefan and I watched from the dappled shadows as the meeting took place, wondering what must be going through the minds of these men—Frank taller and balding, Władysław thinner and with swept-back hair. Both men wore white shirts—the uniform of their generation.

Kelly Crowe was there holding a microphone and representing the CBC but, blond and attractive, she also represented the new type of telegenic celebrity that grew up after the war when genuine heroes like Władysław Gnyś were in shorter supply.

And so it was that Frank, who had taken a long journey in anticipation of this moment, walked forward up the path while Władysław waited. There was an offered hand, which quickly became an embrace, as though their former enmity was far less significant than their brotherhood as airmen. I don't suppose either man felt nostalgia for the moments of mutual, heart-pounding terror they had to have experienced high above a burning Polish landscape, but, meeting beneath the green trees, they must have shared thoughts of their unrecoverable youth stolen away by war.

One negative result for Gnyś was the feedback received from an old Polish Air Force friend living near Montreal, Quebec. He expressed contempt for Władek's willingness to reconcile with a former enemy that had caused death and destruction to the Poles and their Allies on the seas, in the air and on the ground. Władek was of course very hurt because his old air force buddy thought it was inappropriate to "fraternize with the enemy" even though the war was long over.

On the other hand, feedback from many other sources such as the media, was very positive in that Gnyś's and Neubert's behaviour was exemplary and was encouraging to others who were in a state of conflict, to "make peace not war."

From 1989 until the death of Barbara in 1995 and Władek in the year 2000, dozens of friendship letters exchanged hands to and from Germany. Independently, Stefan and Frank wrote many letters to each other until Frank passed away in 2003 at the age of 88 in Gütersloh, Germany. Over that period of 14 years, in every single letter, Frank would refer to that "wonderful day" in Beamsville.

CHAPTER 12

A Hero's Welcome

It was not until 1989—thanks to Lech Wałęsa and the Solidarity movement—that Poland started to discover, and learn about, its World War II freedom fighters. There were many.

By 1995, the Polish nation was very knowledgeable about its actual political, economic and social history, and had an excellent grasp of the events of that impacted their country so greatly. In addition, there was a working familiarity of their courageous men and women who fought so hard against oppressive rule during and after the war.

In 1996, with his sons Stefan and Ashley, 86-year-old W. Gnyś returned again, but this time as a national hero recognized by the Polish Air Force and citizens of a country who craved to see and learn more about their soldiers of freedom. Sadly, Barbara was not able to witness her husband's glorious reception as she had passed away the previous year on August 8th.

Over the course of two weeks, 14 places were visited. The 86-year-old did very well as the schedule was quite demanding. Stepping foot on Polish soil on June 18th was the beginning of an adventure for Władek, but even more so for his sons who had never been to Poland before. Some of the trip is highlighted in the following pages.

Władek was elated to revisit Dęblin where he was a student and instructor 60 years ago. Over a two day period, he was given a personalized tour of the whole facility, met with Commandant Brig Gen Ryszard Olszewski and gave an inspirational talk to a group of pilots in training.

Olkusz, the capital of Olkusz County, is a beautiful town dating back to the eleventh century with a population of over 36,000 in southern Poland about 23 miles northwest of Kraków. Its claim to fame was the mining of lead ore. When the Nazis occupied Olkusz in July, 1940, almost all the Jewish population was deported to the Auschwitz death camp, where they perished in the Holocaust.

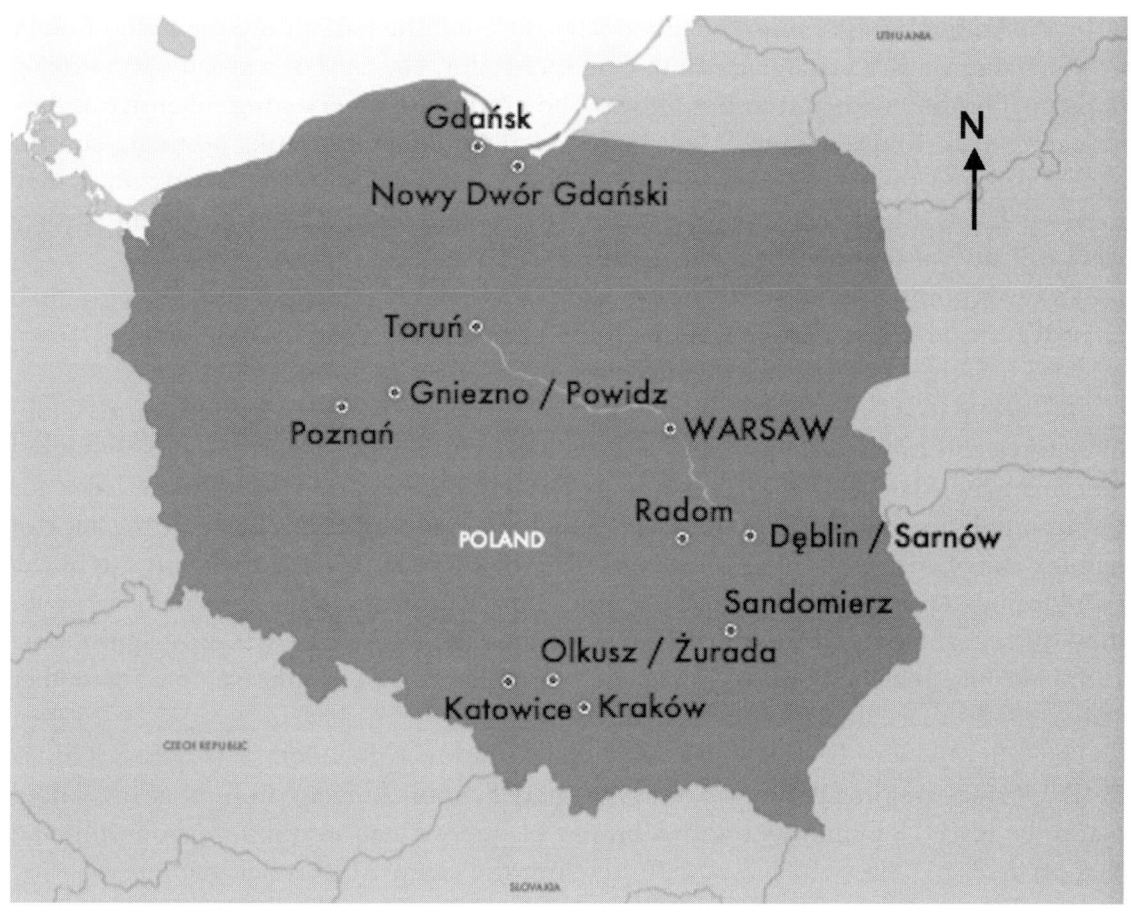

Some centers visited by Władek in 1996 and 1998.

On June 19th, Władek was greeted with incredible fanfare by government and air force officials, the press, school children (who danced for him in traditional costumes) and the general public. He and many others proceeded into a large municipal boardroom where warm greetings and heartfelt speeches took place. He was showered with gifts such as original paintings of the city. A special highlight was when he was made an Honorary Citizen of the city, the second only person in almost 700 years to receive such an honor! His impromptu thank-you speech was moving and well received.

Żurada is a village within Olkusz County in southern Poland. It is about three miles southwest of Olkusz and about 22 miles northwest of the regional capital, Kraków. It has a hotel, quaint, well-kept houses in a picturesque rural landscape, surrounded by manicured farms. But just on the outskirts, is a large, attractive two-storied rectangular building with many large windows. This is the community's primary (elementary) school. It is a hive of educational activity. The principal in 1996 was Krystyna Włodarczyk, who loved her job working with her small staff educating the village children. This is the school that was named after Gnyś in 1995.

In 1989 a book (title omitted deliberately) was published about the men who fought in the Battle of Britain and beyond. For each pilot, the author expertly worked up individual profiles with a headshot photo. The profiles were very comprehensive as they including such things as birth information, military training, rank, postings, combat experience and results e.g. victories if applicable, medals/awards received and if they survived the war and concluded by stating where the pilots settled down and if they were still alive at the time of publication.

However, sometimes mistakes or omissions can occur for various reasons. One such error was made about W. Gnyś. The profile concluded that he immigrated to Canada on March 15th, 1948 and that he died in 1983.

One group in Poland called Klub Seniorow Lotnictwa (Polish Aviation Seniors' Club) in Katowice, read this date at the time to be correct. The president of the club, retired Cpt Stanisław Majcherczyk, and members wanted to recognize and honor Władek for his accomplishments. So they put their heads together and came up with the idea of naming the primary school in Żurada after him. After all, this was the crash site of the two Dorniers that Gnyś brought down on the first day of the war. They then met with local officials and those from nearby Olkusz. It was agreed that this was most appropriate and deserving and the naming ceremony would happen posthumously on September 1st, 1995, 50 years after the war ended.

The school was to be called Szkoła Podstawowa im. Kpt. Pilota Władysława Gnysia W Żuradzie (Cpt Pilot Władysław Gnyś Primary School, Żurada). In front of the school was to be placed a monument with a bronze plaque with an inscription about him and that he died in 1983 (which was definitely not the case). All this became a reality.

Grandiose plans were made for a day of celebration at the school. Despite the deluge of rain, the whole village turned out to witness this memorable event. Also in attendance was the school principal, her staff and the children. Fortunately, the press were present and recorded the festivities for posterity. Before the speeches started, a full band played in the rain as a squad of soldiers presented arms. The speeches were many and heartfelt and were given by air force officers, municipal leaders, politicians, school administrators and clergy. Władek's name and his accomplishments were mentioned, but all in the past tense because they all believed that he had passed away in 1983.

In the latter part of 1995, a most astounding discovery was made: Cpt Pilot Władysław Gnyś was alive, living in Ontario Canada!

This author had written a song about his father which was entitled "Daddy's Uniform." It was recorded earlier in 1995 and then played on CHAM Radio in Hamilton not far from where he lived in Burlington. It was aired a half dozen times on November 11th, Remembrance Day. A radio interview took place where he talked about his father who lived locally in Beamsville and his RAF uniform which inspired the writing of the song.

One listener in Hamilton who recognized the Gnyś name was Czesław "George" Obminski, who had been a radio operator with No. 300 Polish Bomber Squadron

RAF. George called Stefan and they arranged a meeting with his father. They had a lot in common: both had been shot down and became POWs, but in George, who had most of his limbs badly broken, remained incarcerated for the remainder of the war.

George stayed in touch with Polish Air Force groups and organizations in Britain, Canada and in Poland and informed them that Władek Gnyś was very much alive and that he and his two sons (Stefan and Ashley) were planning a trip to Poland in 1996. The news was electrifying. Cpt Majcherczyk and his enthusiastic Polish Aviation Seniors' Club in Katowice couldn't have been happier. From that point on, they put the wheels in motion and organized an itinerary and reception for the Gnyś family in June, 1996. It was Majcherczyk who spearheaded the idea of the monument in front of the school.

Władek's nephew Waldemar (Waldek) Serocki accompanied his uncle, and two cousins. Lt Col Jan B. Leśniewski of the PAF provided security and a large comfortable van with a driver. This entourage stayed together from June 18th to 24th.

As they left the hotel in Olkusz, there was excitement in the air. Żurada was only a short distance away and the school was waiting for the arrival of Cpt Pilot Gnyś. As the van and police escort approached the school, a full brass band started to play, dancers wearing traditional costumes whirled about, masses of people crammed the grounds eager to see him; it was like a Hollywood movie set.

As Waldemar pushed Gnyś in his wheelchair onto the walkway leading to the school entrance, Władek was applauded and gently mobbed, people anxiously shook his hand and simply touched him. He was grinning from ear to ear affectionately acknowledging this incredibly warm reception. To think that 57 years earlier, he was fighting for his life above Żurada.

After enthusiastic speeches by such people as school principal Krystyna Włodarczyk, Lt Col Jan B. Leśniewski and various officials, schoolgirls recited an emotional poem dedicated to Władek. Then a choir sang a few familiar songs. Since June 20th was the last day of school, a brief graduation ceremony was held where a few awards were handed out.

One unexpected moment was when lifelong friend and former colleague from No. 302 Squadron, Stanisław (Staszek) Chałupa stepped out of the crowd and surprised Władek in the front row. They hadn't seen each other in many years so it was a grand emotional reunion. Staszek, who had achieved ace status, had also immigrated after the war to Stoney Creek, Ontario, not far from the Gnyś's homes in Grimsby and Beamsville. He was like an uncle to Haydn, Stefan, Ashley and sister Sydney. He did not have any children of his own. After his second wife passed away, Staszek moved back to Kraków to be with his sister and other relatives. He joined the touring entourage on several other occasions to take part in the festivities and be with his old friend.

One really big surprise for Stefan occurred when girls, Dorota Stachowicz and Anna Koryczan, performed his song "Daddy's Uniform" in Polish—"Mundur Taty."

Unknown to most, the local population had kept several remnants of the destroyed Dornier 17e bombers from 1939. One such piece was brought to the surprised attention of Władek and his sons. It was a large fragment that had distinct bullet holes in it.

To finish off, Cpt Majcherczyk and his group thought it would be memorable for Gnyś to plant a tree in front of the school to commemorate his visit. They had acquired a young healthy cedar and prepared a plot for it in the front of the school behind the monument. When it was securely in the ground the Mayor of Olkusz, Janusz Dudkiewicz, made sure that it was well watered.

The following is the English translation of the plaque:

> At dawn on September 1st, 1939, two Nazi bombers were shot down over Żurada in a solitary combat by S-Lt Władysław Gnyś. It was the first victory of the Polish pilot who continued to fight the invader over France and England. A Knight of the Order of Virtuti Militari, Captain xxxxxxxxxx [date of death, 1983, was chiseled out before his arrival].
>
> In remembrance of the homeland defenders—with gratitude, the community of Olkusz district and Aviation Seniors' Pilot Club in Katowice.
>
> Żurada, September 1st, 1995

The Polish Aviation Museum in Kraków has the only surviving PZL P.11c fighter—No. 2—from the September campaign. Other than carrying two small bombs, it has four 7.92 mm machine guns. Władek flew No. 5.

An examination (using a metric vernier caliper) of a fragment from one of the downed Dorniers revealed at least four clearly defined bullet holes having a slightly larger diameter to the ammunition on board Gnyś's PZL P.11c fighter. This slight variation was due to the bullets' angle of entry and the resulting damage from tearing. Three of the four diameters matched up within a fraction of 1 mm of the 7.92. The fourth one was just over 1 mm. This would conclude that the two Do 17s were not brought down by anti-aircraft fire, because shrapnel from an exploding shell does not leave neat holes, but rather jagged and irregular size punctures.

This discovery puts to rest any other theory or theories about the demise of the Dorniers brought down by S-Lt Gnyś in the early morning hours of September 1st, 1939 when Germany invaded Poland.

After leaving Żurada, Władek and company set off for Kraków to pay respects to the Polish pilots who died in the war. The destination was the Polish Airmen Park which proudly displays a tall monument, probably the highest in the city.

In the park are two monuments dedicated to the Polish airmen: Glory to Polish Airmen and the Eagle Monument, a bronze/aluminum structure 89 feet high with a large eagle on the top. In fact, it is a giant *gapa* (Polish Air Force wings). The three supports resemble shaggy tree trunks. The plaques at its base are inscribed with the battlefields where Polish airmen fought and died on all fronts in the years 1939–45. It was designed by Bronisław Chromy and unveiled in 1989, 50 years after the outbreak of war.

Oberleutnant Frank Neubert as a 26-year-old Luftwaffe pilot and Staffelkapitän of 2./Sturzkampfgeschwader 2 "Immelmann." On the day of the photo, June 22nd, 1941, he was awarded the Knight's Cross of the Iron Cross. The inscription reads, "To my friend Władek, Frank Neubert."

Frank Neubert (standing extreme left) was a pilot with Stuka Geschwader 1 St/G2 in occupied France, 1940. *(F. Neubert via M. Dobrzelecki)*

Oblt. Neubert, Oblt. Winschig, Oblt. Lehmann, Oblt. Kädtler, Lt. Boerst, Oblt. Brandenburg, Lt. Pekrun
Oblt. Heins, Oblt. Palm, Lt. Lang, Lt. Brausch, Lt. Freitag, Lt. d. R. Schenkel.
Oblt. Reichardt, Oblt. Lau, Oblt. Merz, Major Dinort, Hptm. Hitschhold, Oblt. Vollmer

August 30th, 1989. Frank Neubert and Władek Gnyś, who is wearing his original RAF flying jacket and cap. *(Denis Cahill, staff photographer, courtesy of St. Catharines Standard, St. Catharines, Ontario)*

A handshake says it all. Two World War II adversaries come together and bury the proverbial hatchet.

Władek and Frank, the tall former Stuka pilot, stand in front of a poster commemorating the 50th anniversary of the invasion of Poland and the opening phase of the war. Here they are comparing model aircraft. *(Photograph courtesy of The Spectator, Hamilton, Ontario)*

Former Squadron Leader Władysław Gnyś smiles at the camera. He is wearing his RAF tunic and holding his cap. On each sleeve of his tunic are two insignia bands that indicate the rank of flight lieutenant. Interpreter Ellen Goldstein is in conversation with former Luftwaffe major, Frank Neubert.

Brig Gen Hyra presented Władek with a copper depiction of him downing the Dornier bombers on September 1st, 1939. In the lower left corner of the plaque is an original fragment from one of the Dorniers explaining what transpired on the early morning of September 1st. *(J. Leśniewski)*

A gift for the PAF contingent, a print of the painting *First Kill* by Roy Grinnell. On the far left above Gnyś is nephew Waldemar Serocki and on the far right is a PTV host who did the interview.

A rough translation of the large monument at the entrance to the training facility is "To the Memory of Brave Airmen of Dęblin's Eaglets' School." In 1936, Władek took the pilot instructor course here and became a pilot instructor in the same year.

Many older Russian fighters that have seen service in the PAF are lined up on the tarmac at Dęblin.

In return for the kindness and generosity shown by Brig Gen Ryszard Olszewski Commandant and Rector of the PAF Academy in Dęblin, Władek signed and gifted a print of *First Kill* painted by Roy Grinnell ASAA.

Warm handshakes from Olkusz town officials and Dep. Mayor Dr Włodzimierz Łysoń (not visible). Cpt Stanisław Majcherczyk, President of the Aviation Seniors' Club from Katowice, and Gnyś's former mechanic (121 Sqn), Stanisław Kłakus (not visible) look on proudly.

Right: Award from the mayor of Olkusz: "TO THE DEFENDERS OF THE COUNTRY WITH GRATITUDE AND MEMORY. The Mayor, City Council and the Town of Olkusz award an honorary citizenship to Captain Pilot Władysław Gnyś, heroic Polish Air Force aviator who first achieved victory in the defense of Poland in 1939 against the German Air Force, shooting down two German bombers in the area of Olkusz and Żurada. Andrzej Ryszka, Mayor of Olkusz and Metropolitan Area, President of Local Town Authority, Legal Affairs, MGR, In the name of Wojciech Pawlikowski, Olkusz Date: June 20th, 1996."

Below: Władek was like a celebrity surrounded by fans. In this photo at the school in Żurada, he is being surprised by lifelong friend, former pilot Staszek Chałupa (barely visible) who moved back to Kraków from Canada. The well-groomed crowd try to catch a glimpse of the reunion.

1.09.1939

O ŚWICIE 2 HITLEROWSKIE BOMBOWCE
ZOSTAŁY ZESTRZELONE NAD ŻURADĄ
W SAMOTNYM POJEDYNKU PRZEZ
PPOR. WŁADYSŁAWA GNYSIA
BYŁO TO PIERWSZE ZWYCIĘSTWO
POLSKIEGO LOTNIKA. SWĄ WALKĘ
Z NAJEŹDŹCĄ KONTYNUOWAŁ ON POD
NIEBEM FRANCJI I ANGLII. KAWALER
VIRTUTI MILITARI W STOPNIU
KAPITANA

OBROŃCOM OJCZYZNY – WDZIĘCZNA PAMIĘĆ
SPOŁECZEŃSTWO GMINY OLKUSZ I KLUB SENIORÓW
LOTNICTWA W KATOWICACH · ŻURADA 1.09.1995

Above: In front of the primary school at Żurada stands a stone monument in which a bronze plaque is embedded. It outlines the first Allied victory, by Polish pilot Władysław Gnyś.

A number of fragments from the wreckage of the Dorniers in 1939 were kept by local villagers. Some contained bullet holes from Władek's PZL P.11c fighter aircraft. A metric vernier caliper was used to measure the diameters of four holes on one fragment (below): they matched up almost perfectly to the 7.92mm bullets on board Władek's plane.

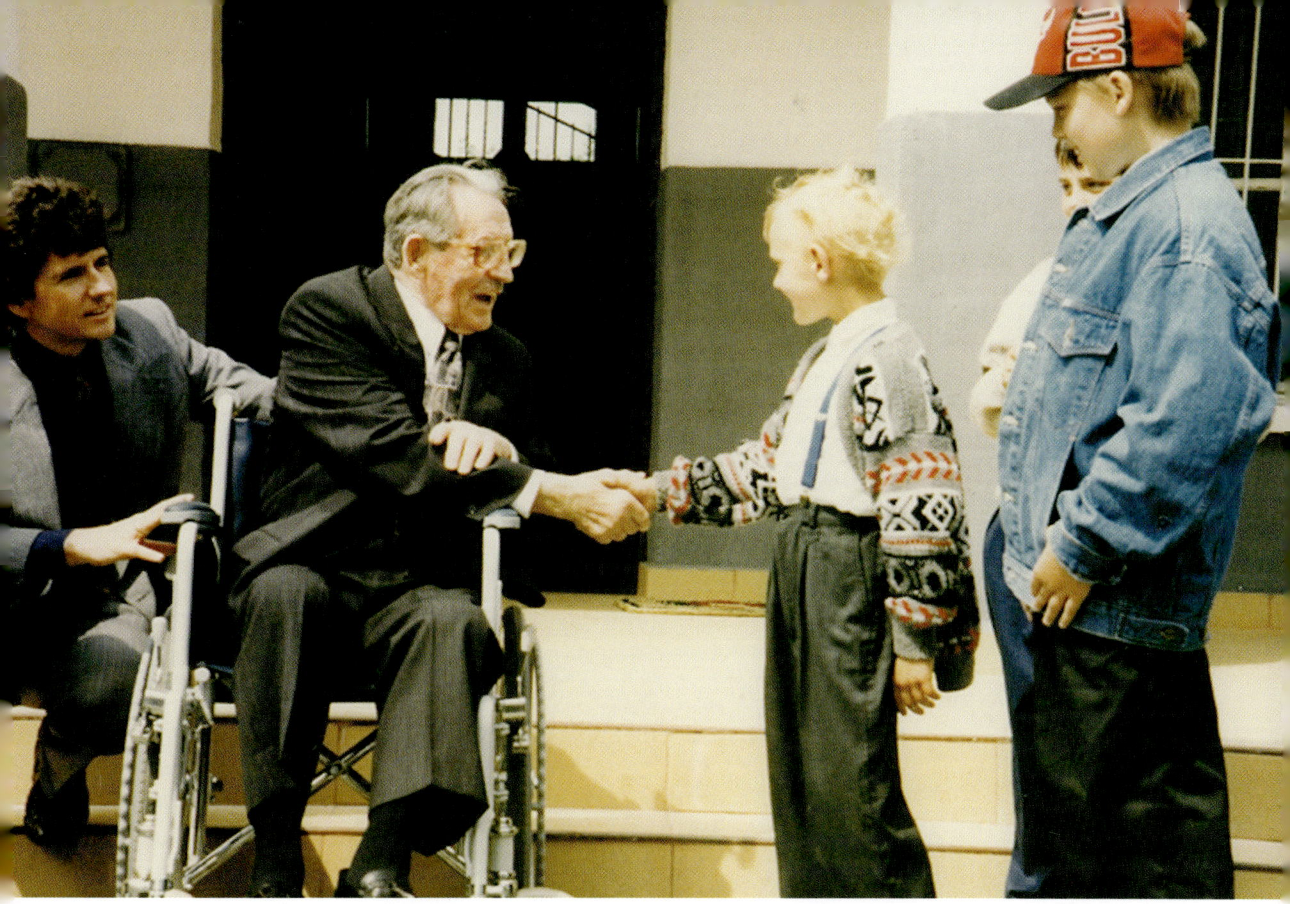

Ashley watches in admiration as three young boys shyly approach his father to say hello and goodbye at the same time, knowing that he would be leaving Żurada at any moment.

Old buddies since the 1930s, both were wounded, but survived to become aces. They stand in front of another old friend, the PZL P.11c that served them well in the Polish campaign. S. Chałupa (81) moved to Kraków from Canada in 1995.

A Katowice-Kleofas official symbolically addresses the Capt pilot as "sir" in the presence of PAF officers, Aviation Seniors' Club members and coal mining representatives. Gifts were bestowed upon him, including the sword. The Katowice-Kleofas Coal Holding Co. was very generous.

Everyone posing in front of a single-engine, two-seater trainer aircraft (SP-ADP) whose pilot is on the far right. He was disappointed that Władek (due to his leg disability) could not go up for a flight with him. On Gnyś's left stands the President of the Polish Aviation Seniors' Club, Stanisław Majcherczyk.

In 1939/40, German troops came through Stara Siekierka searching for young men to be used as forced labor. At the time, this man was about thirteen. He made a run for it, was hunted down and shot 13 times and left for dead. A Dr. Mann in Radom operated and saved his life. Before the war, he remembered pilot Gnyś flying around and waving to folks on the ground. Years later, he met the flyer and shared his story with him.

Two prints of *First Kill* by artist Roy Grinnell were presented: one for Polish President Aleksander Kwaśniewski to autograph, the other donated to the Palace for display. First Lady and lawyer, Jolanta Kwaśnieska supports the top of the print.

A group shot in the Presidential Palace grounds after which was a lavish garden party. From left: Teresa Serocka, Stefan, First Lady Jolanta Kwaśnieska, President Aleksander Kwaśniewski, Ashley, Waldemar Serocki and Władek (sitting).

Expert pilot C.O. Lt Col Leszek Cwojdziński shows the former squadron leader the cockpit of the Russian Su–22 fighter–bomber used by the PAF. Note the Road Runner holding a bomb.

Getting into the old PZL P. 11c was no easy task for the now-disabled former pilot, but it was worth it; his smile said it all. It took a number of strong men to hoist him in and out of the familiar cockpit.

Later in September 1939, S-Lt Gnyś had to escape from the Nazi invaders, but just before doing so, made a vow to Jesus on the cross that if he was allowed to survive the war, he would come back and kiss his feet. He did just that. The cross in Sarnów, which is widely known, has become a symbol of survival.

The Polish people love their flowers and they love to give them as gifts. Everywhere he went, Gnyś was given beautiful bouquets. Flanking Władek are Cpt Stanisław Majcherczyk (left) and Lt-Col Marek Zapiór. In the far right corner, the Deputy Mayor of Olkusz, Dr Włodzimierz Łysoń, looks on as Władek reads the plaque.

Out of great respect for the World War II fighter pilot, Lt Col Cwojdziński and each member of his squadron at Powidz Air Base taxied by W. Gnyś, saluted, took off, then tipped their wings in salute before landing.

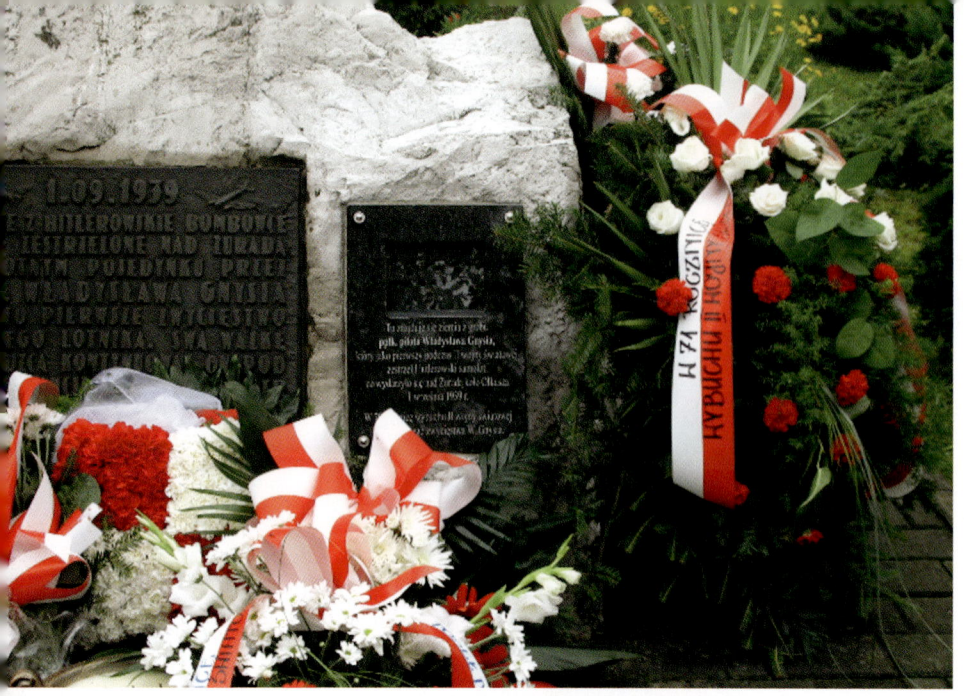

On the small plaque it says: "Here lies the soil from the grave of Col pilot Władysław Gnyś who was the first to shoot down a Nazi aircraft during World War II over Żurada near Olkusz on September 1st, 1939. To commemorate the 70th anniversary of World War II outbreak and historic victory of W. Gnyś."

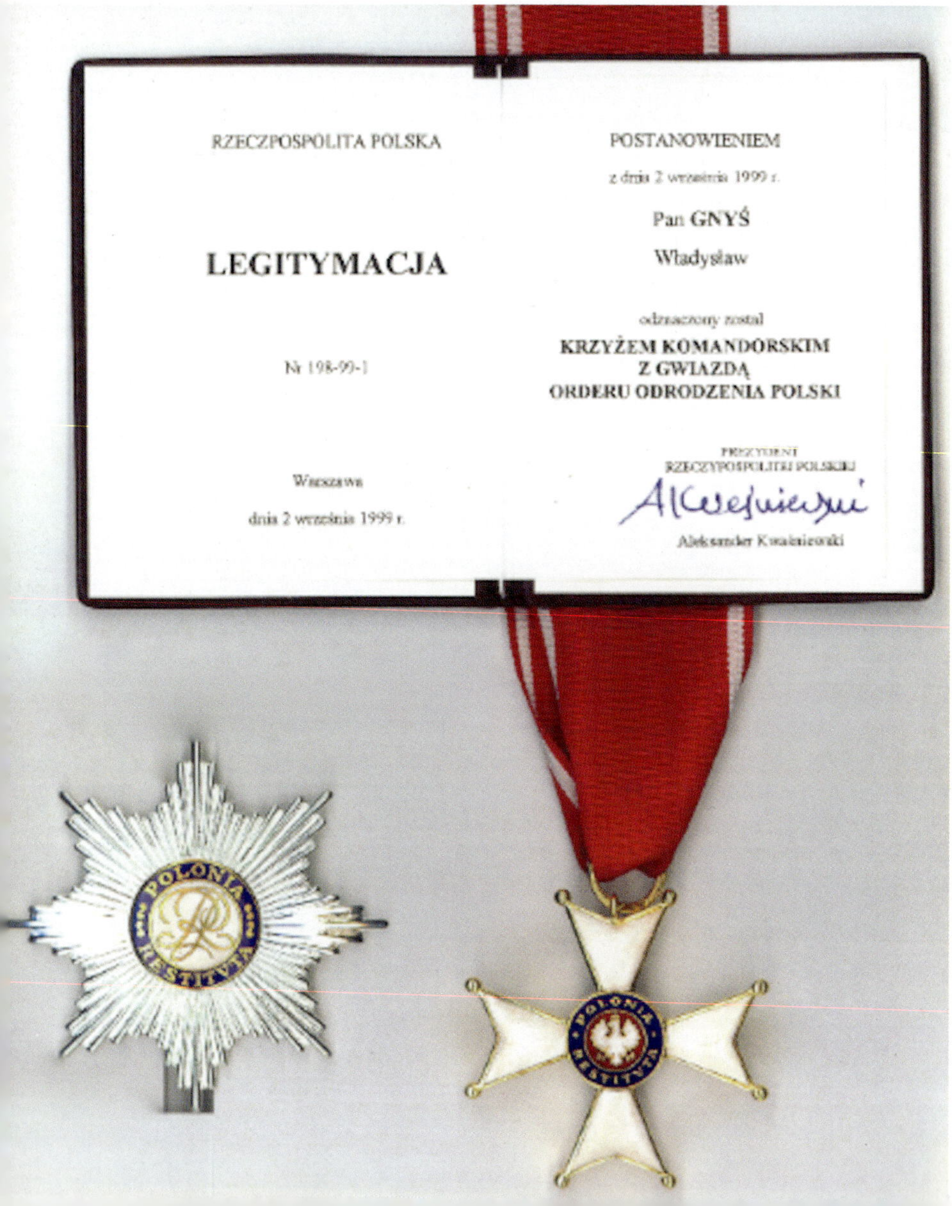
RZECZPOSPOLITA POLSKA

LEGITYMACJA

Nr 198-99-1

Warszawa

dnia 2 września 1999 r.

POSTANOWIENIEM

z dnia 2 września 1999 r.

Pan GNYŚ

Władysław

odznaczony został

KRZYŻEM KOMANDORSKIM
Z GWIAZDĄ
ORDERU ODRODZENIA POLSKI

PREZYDENT
RZECZYPOSPOLITEJ POLSKIEJ

Aleksander Kwaśniewski

The Commander's Cross with Star, Order of Rebirth of Poland (1921). It is conferred to both military personnel and civilians for extraordinary and distinguished service. Only the Polish President can award this prestigious medal. President A. Kwaśniewski's signature in the booklet is dated September 2nd, 1999.

Pierre Ben (Somme Aviation 39–45 Association, France) dug up F/Lt Gnyś's former Spitfire IX SZ-J, EN 179 of 316 Squadron, in 2005 north of Amiens. After the Spitfire had changed hands, F/O Próchnicki was shot down and killed in it in August 1943. At top right, Pierre poses alongside the plane's two excavated 20mm Hispano-Suiza Mk II cannons. Below, Rolls–Royce Merlin 61 V12 engine and nose assembly have been cleaned up and put on display. *(P. Ben)*

A love that endured for 55 years: 1940–1995.

The *First Kill* painting by American artist Roy Grinnell sits proudly in the Hall of Traditions Museum at the Dęblin Air Force Base, the PAF Academy in Poland. It was presented by S. Gnyś on September 3rd, 2010. It is a popular curiosity item for visitors.
(W. Ceglarski & Associates)

In between the laying of wreaths and flowers were speeches by PAF officers, local government officials, politicians, organizers and relatives of deceased PAF pilots.

Around the perimeter of the monument square were a few elderly veterans showing great respect for the proceedings. A few proudly wore their original military uniforms displaying wartime medals.

After leaving the Polish Airmen Park, the van arrived at the Polish Aviation Museum (Muzeum Lotnictwa Polskiego w Krakowie). This was the last stop of the day in Kraków.

The museum is quite large consisting of several unique aircraft from both wars. It has many engines on display and old aircraft frames not yet restored. It is located at the former Kraków-Rakowice-Czyżyny Airport which housed Fighter Squadrons 121, 122 and 123 of the 2nd Air Regiment prior to the war. It was the second largest PAF field in prewar Poland.

The museum opened in 1964 after the airfield closed down the year before. There were very few prewar Polish planes for visitors to see, as most were destroyed during the Nazi occupation. The only two intact examples of early Polish military aircraft that survived are a PZL P. 11c fighter and a PWS-26 trainer.

The PZL P. 11c No. 2, belonged to Wacław (Wacek) Król, a pilot trained by Gnyś at Dęblin in 1936. Władek was ecstatic to see that this plane had survived as it saw action during the invasion. The informative tour that followed was enhanced by Mr. Chałupa who joined the group. He was no stranger to this aircraft as he too flew one against the Luftwaffe.

As can be expected, much of the time was spent around the PZL P.11c aircraft. Gnyś was interviewed by Polish TV and asked many questions about his training and wartime experiences. He especially enjoyed talking about this special airplane and his association with its pilot Wacek Król.

Early on June 22nd, the van brought the group to Katowice, a large city located in southwestern Poland and the center of the Silesian metropolis and the main city in the Upper Silesian industrial region. The Silesian region is well know for its mining and processing of coal. The coal mines in Poland are commonly organized in groups and holding companies. The Kleofas Coal Mine at this time was part of the Katowice Coal Holding, a merger of a number of mines. The Katowice-Kleofas Coal Holding decided they wanted to do something special for the former squadron leader in conjunction with the Polish Aviation Seniors' Club. Their clubhouse building was next to an airfield used by small planes. While in their main building, Gnyś was given many meaningful gifts such as a personalized engraved sword. After signing their guest book, they proceeded outside for a tree planting ceremony. Then group photos were taken in front of a two-seater single-engine plane flown by a professional pilot who desperately wanted to take Władek for a flight, but unfortunately Gnyś couldn't get into the aircraft with his infirm legs. Grudgingly at first, the pilot then took Ashley and Stefan instead and gave them the "ride of their lives."

After leaving the Polish Aviation Seniors' Club, the entourage departed for a lunch reception at the headquarters of Katowice's Post Office. The host was Henryk Szafron, the Postmaster General. It was a happy occasion with gifts, great food and many toasts with fine Polish vodka. About 16 guests were present and eager to take part in the welcoming of the Gnyś family to their city. Just before the afternoon came to a close, Ashley stood up and with the help of his father who translated into Polish, made a profound announcement: "When we arrived from Canada last week, we came as a Polish father and two Canadian sons. When we leave soon to return to our home, we will be leaving as three sons of Poland!"

The group was so impressed by this young man's words that they applauded and raised a glass (or two) of Polish vodka and drank to the "Three sons of Poland."

The next few days were spent in Poznań, a very old city in west–central Poland. It was overrun by the Germans in 1939 and was severely damaged during the war. After a great deal of reconstruction, it is today a thriving center with a high standard of living and is a popular tourist destination.

Upon entering a civic building in the heart of the city, several reporters from the local press took photos and interviewed the Polish-Canadian guest. Here, the (extended) Polish version of *First Kill* (*Pierwsze Spotkanie*, First Encounter) was displayed and promoted. Władek Gnyś signed several dozen copies and shook many hands. Polish speakers at formal ceremonies are well known for their long-winded speeches: this event was no exception, in fact a professional speaker was brought in to read several passages from the book. Later, an opera singer performed a personalized song to the former pilot.

Before leaving the city, a tour was given of an air force museum housing many artifacts, models and photo exhibits of Poland's defensive war of 1939. There were wall plaques and board displays of the Polish fighter and bomber squadrons and names of ace pilots.

Over the course of the two days, June 23rd/24th, Władek and his sons traveled back and forth to Poznan from Gniezno (about 45 minutes apart) using the latter as home base. This was the home of his nephew Waldemar Serocki (son of Władek's youngest sister Jadwiga), wife Teresa, daughters Iwonka (with infant Jagoda) and Emilka. The rest of the trip was family oriented. Waldemar acted as guide; his mother Jadwiga joined the group. The new driver Kamil Kamyszek was from Gniezno. He and wife Ewa owned a restaurant there.

While in Gniezno, Mr. Gnyś attended a special mass organized just for him in the historic Royal (Gothic) Cathedral, and then was invited to the City Hall where he spent several hours with Mayor Dr. Bogdan Trepiński.

In the town of Kawęczyn they visited the house that he helped his father Jan build at age 16 in 1926. Then nearby in her summer farm was a younger sister Marysia Duklas who was 84 in 1996 and lived to be 99. The rest of the year she lived in Toruń with her family. It was a sweet reunion. While he was there, he visited his parents' grave in Łążyn Parish Cemetery.

In Nowy Dwór Gdański southeast of Gdańsk lived his only brother Toni (80), his wife Lodzia, son Zbyszek and wife Danusia with their daughters Agnieszka and Anna. Jadwiga hadn't been there for years. Her daughter Wiesia arrived to be with the family.

The next day, a tour of historic Malbork Castle was a crowd-pleaser. Before leaving Nowy Dwór, he went to the cemetery to pay respects to his departed sister Helena Mazurek (1914–1990).

Radom was another moving experience for Władek as he joined his older sister Bronka Kilyanek (88) with her daughter Basia and husband Zenek and family members. Youngest sister Jadwiga Serocka was still with the group and fondly reminisced with her sister Bronka.

At the village of Stara Siekierka he met his half-sister Anna (91), the oldest sibling who lived out in the country on a very old farm with a grist mill that was in ruins. He remembered this mill as a boy when it was in full production. Anna was bedridden and at first did not recognize her brother, but then she did and cried with happiness. She then remembered her youngest sister Jadwiga. Anna's daughter Jasia, husband Paweł and their son welcomed everyone and walked them around the property. While exploring, the group came across an elderly man fishing on the next property. In 1939–40, the Germans moved through the area looking for young men to use as forced labor. This man was 13 at the time. After he was spotted and told to halt, he made a run for it, but was pursued and shot 13 times and left for dead, but he miraculously survived!

For Władek, Sarnów was probably the most memorable part of the trip because this is where he was born, his roots were here. He and his sons just stood and stared at the old grist mill—this magnificent stone structure that was the pinnacle of the village and surrounding area. For many years it had been the life blood of the people who had their grain ground into flour and feed for their livestock. The water wheel was long gone and so was the reservoir behind the building that turned the wheel. Just a trickle of water flowed by in the small creek, but it still had its charm and intrinsic beauty.

Relatives came from miles around to see their elderly pilot and his sons. Cousin Ewa Suska (née Deska) arrived with her daughter Justyna and Ewa's mother Genowefa Deska, Władek's first cousin. For Ashley and Stefan, matching faces with names was a challenge as they did not speak Polish. However, by the end of the day, they got to know everyone on a first-name basis.

The co-owner of the property Zdziséaw Kowalski was in the construction business and had surprised everyone with the rejuvenation of the former carp ponds to their previous glory, so it was a sight for sore eyes to see the fully stocked ponds once again. Everyone enjoyed the fresh carp for dinner that evening thanks to his wife Joanna and her mother Reginka (Gnyś).

Just 100 yards from the mill was the Sarnów primary school (Szkoła Podstawowa w Sarnowie) where he attended as a young boy in 1915. Finally, on the outskirts of the village stood the old cross at which Władek prayed when he escaped Poland in September 1939. He did so again.

The last night was spent in Sarnów before departing for the airport in Warsaw the next morning. It was difficult saying goodbye because he thought that this would be the last time he would ever see his family again. However, as fortune had it, he would return again for the final time in 1998 with his two sons.

Final journey to Poland

At the age of 88, the former squadron leader was invited back to his homeland to be part of a few special happenings organized by his nephew Waldemar Serocki. Despite the fact that his troubled legs were not any better, he really wanted to return and be part of the events planned for him. But most of all, he craved to see family one last time. He would still require his walker and the help from his sons and nephew to push him around in a wheelchair. Mentally, he was still very sharp and his long-term memory was excellent ... his Polish was superb.

Waldemar was anxiously waiting at the airport in Warsaw with a van and driver, ready to whisk everyone away to the Presidential Palace to meet the Republic of Poland's most powerful man, Aleksander Kwaśniewski and the First Lady Jolanta Kwaśnieska (née Konty). A reception in the Palace Gardens was planned to honor Władek and one other man (nn) for their contribution to Polish history and culture.

Security was tight and the press area was cordoned off in the far corner of the garden against the back of the Palace. Women wore the latest fashions, the men wore dark suits, while the military looked very polished in their uniforms. Aleksander and Jolanta were dressed to perfection and were a very handsome couple indeed. Never far from their sides was Marek Dukaczewski, the Undersecretary of State, National Security Bureau.

After the couple courteously greeted Władek and company, the President got behind the microphone and introduced the two special guests and thanked them for their lasting contributions to Polish society. He was very gracious and sincere. Stefan brought forth copies of the print *First Kill*, one as a gift for the Palace and one for the President to autograph.

Waist-high circular tables were set up in the generous garden and chefs were busy cooking up delicious culinary delights. There was live music, Polish vodka, beer and wine to enjoy and the sound of glasses clinking was heard. Guests moved around the garden and intermingled with the President and First Lady. Highlights of the event were documented on film and seen across Europe that evening.

Returning to the quaint old city of Gniezno with Waldemar and family was a needed respite after a long day at the Palace, plus jet lag was ever present. His nephew's home was a haven for several days. He, Teresa, Iwonka and Emilka outdid themselves in terms of hospitality. Jagoda was now a two year old toddler.

On Sunday August 16th, another special mass in the ancient Royal Cathedral was held for the senior ex-pilot, followed by a horse-drawn carriage ride with Mayor Dr. Bogdan Trepiński around the city and to the war memorial.

Powidz Military Air Force Base is a half-hour drive southeast of Gniezno in the village of Powidz, was an air force base that housed a full squadron of 12-year-old Russian jets, Sukhoi Su-22 fighter-bombers that were commonplace in Poland during the communist occupation.

In the grounds was a small air force museum with various war artifacts and board displays and at the end of the room was a large photo mural of an Su-22 in flight. Władek, even though he was dead tired, did his best to view the contents and listen to three very enthusiastic officers who wanted to expound on all the items. Lieutenant Colonel Leszek Cwojdziński, Commander 7th Bomber Reconnaissance Aviation Regiment, presented Gnyś with gifts and an official document of his visit.

During the tour outside, the film crew making a documentary, interviewed Władek in front of a Su-22. The allure of the jet was too much for him so when the filming ended, he started to slowly climb up the ladder to the cockpit despite protests from his sons. Leszek in the cockpit explained the inner workings and complexities of the Russian jet. Władek laughed and said, "I think I will stick to my 1939 PZL P.11c aircraft if you don't mind, it's a lot less complicated."

Perhaps the most emotional moment of this 1998 trip was when Lt Col Cwojdziński and his squadron climbed into their jets, taxied past Władek in his wheelchair on the edge of the runway, saluted him in turn, took off and made a large circle in the sky tipping their wings in salute before landing. Ashley and Stefan were moved to tears.

One of the pilots within the colonel's squadron was a man by the name of Michał Erdmański who was a skilled and confident pilot, just like the others. In 2015, 17 years later, while at a function in Gniezno, Stefan and Ashley met up with him again. Over several glasses of wine, they reminisced about that day when the squadron surprised Gnyś while he sat in his wheelchair on the edge of the runway taking salutes as they took off one by one. They showed such a deep reverence for a fellow pilot who had been through so much.

Returning to Żurada again had a different focus than two years previous. Certainly, Władek wanted to see the principal Krystyna Włodarczyk, her staff and students, but this time he wanted to mingle with people of the village and talk with them about the war and if and how it affected them or their families.

The reception at the school was again very warm. The locals, including the school children, had lined up and were eager to greet him. Along with the school principal and teachers, were the Mayor of Żurada Stanisław Kasprzyk, the Deputy Mayor of Olkusz Dr. Włodzimierz Łysoń and members of the Aviation Seniors' Club (Silesian Aero Club) in Katowice, friends, Stanisław Majcherczyk, Marek Zapiór and Stanisław Kłakus.

After the previous visit, the trio felt confident about donating the RAF cap, tunic and flying boots to the school to be put on display in a secure manner. Mr. Majcherczyk and his Aero Club had constructed a large wooden cabinet with a lockable glass door into which the items would go. A mannequin was obtained and dressed in the memorabilia.

A vacant room on the upper floor was chosen for the cabinet and was decorated with military and air force items. The room was also under lock and key. On this journey, his RAF leather flying jacket was also donated to the school and was placed into the cabinet. When special guests came to the school they were invited to see the mini Cpt Pilot Exhibit.

One of the biggest surprises for Władek and group was the discovery of two gentleman from the village who, as boys, where around when the dogfight between S-Lt Gnyś and the two Dornier bombers took place. One of the boys, Tadeusz Feliksik witnessed the German planes being attacked by Gnyś and watched them descend and crash into farmyards in Żurada. Mr. Feliksik showed those who were present exactly where each of them hit the ground.

The older man, without prompting, related another story. Shortly after the invasion he and his family were harvesting potatoes when suddenly a German aircraft appeared, came down low and started shooting at them. It is not known if anyone was killed or wounded, but he became extremely angry as he told the story, in fact yelling and shaking his fist.

Another wonder: a metal fragment from one of the bombers was presented to the former pilot. It along with other pieces had been kept by the villagers as souvenirs for nearly 60 years.

On August 22nd, director Krzysztof Radwan welcomed the Gnyś family once again to his world-famous Kraków Aviation Museum established in 1964. Just prior to his greeting, two loyal PAF friends arrived: Stanisław Chałupa and Stanisław Kłakus. Just like Stanisław Majcherczyk and Marek Zapiór, they made every effort to be with their old friend on his two visits to Poland. Coincidentally, three of the men had the same first name and were warmly referred to as the three "Stans."

Other distinguished guests were Józef Zubrzycki D.F.C. a highly decorated individual who served in a number of units such as 162, 317, 301, 1586 and 300 Polish Bomber Squadrons, taking part in the bombing of Berlin in April, 1945. Over the years, he was active in the Polish Aviation Seniors' Club and the Aviation Museum in Kraków.

Dr. Jan Koniarek was born in Poland and immigrated to the U.S. and settled on a scientific career in biomedical research in New York. He was also a military history author, particularly on the role that the Polish Air Force played during the war. In the early 1990s he visited Mr. and Mrs. Gnyś in Florida.

Director Radwan had a number of exciting developments to share with the group that surfaced over the last two years, since they were last here in 1996. The first was a long-term plan regarding the construction of a modern visitor/interpretive aviation center (with emphasis on education) which opened to the public in 2010. The second was that his engineers were able to get the engine of the PZL P.11c up and running for the first time since the war, thus making it airworthy. However, since it was the most precious exhibit at the museum, they would not allow it to take off in fear of an accident. Lastly, in light of this mechanical success, the idea of building a flying replica of the PZL P.11c was on the table. A feasibility study was underway, but like any good idea, the funding for such a project was an issue.

Once Władek heard that the old PZL P.11c flown by Wacław (Wacek) Król was in running order, he immediately wanted to get in it and rev the motor. However, with his poor legs, this seemed an impossible objective, but he insisted that with help he could do it. So with Ashley and three others, he was hoisted and lifted into the cockpit. It took some doing, but there he was in the saddle of his favorite plane sitting on the tarmac raring to go.

The technicians got the motor started and the roar of the engine filled the air. The noise was almost deafening and the wind it generated was powerful enough to blow off someone's toupée. There he was, smiling like a Cheshire cat with the engine at full throttle, ready for take-off. Even though blocks had been placed under the front wheels to prevent movement, several strong men had to hold the tail down to prevent it from lifting.

Cameras clicked the whole time and film rolled capturing this rare moment. Emotions ran high and there wasn't a dry eye in the place. After 15 minutes or so, he shut the engine down not wanting to get out. Everyone came running up to congratulate this veteran pilot who still knew his way around the cockpit. Władek told his sons later that while he sat there, he thought about how many of his comrades had died flying this identical machine trying to defend Poland.

Getting out of the cockpit was no easy matter. While he pushed with his hands, others slowly but gently, lifting him up to the edge of the cockpit, swung him around and then lowered him down. It was worth the effort judging by the grin that was still on his face. August 22nd, 1998 will be remembered as the day when the "little engine that could—did."

Next was Sarnów with his sons, Waldemar and Teresa. From Kraków in the south, it was a long but scenic road trip to the rural village of Sarnów to the northeast. The household was excited and were all waiting to see him again ... his cousin Władysław Gnyś (same name) and his wife Reginka, their daughter Joanna Kowalska and her husband Zdziseaw Kowalski and children Kasia, Kamila and Ewa. Then there was their son, Tomasz Gnyś and his wife Ela with their children Piotr and Jarek.

The owners of the mill Zdziseaw and Joanna had a surprise waiting: they had totally gutted and refurbished the old mill, transforming it into a luxurious home. Construction began after the 1996 visit. Even though the outside was not yet finished, the facelift was very evident. In addition, they built a bridge-like walkway across the pond to the island and built a small gazebo there. Fishing for carp from the bridge was always fun.

Other surprises awaited. The family had planned a birthday party, Władek's 88th, on August 24th, and had invited an older sister, Bronka. On the cake was the number 100;

in Polish the expression is "Sto Lat"—live to one hundred years. The song "Sto Lat" was sung, followed by champagne and a delicious home-cooked meal followed by the cake.

After several restful days in the Polish countryside, it was time to move again, but this time to Warsaw. During the Nazi invasion and later during the Warsaw uprising of 1944, the city was reduced to rubble. But by 1998, Warsaw had risen from the ashes. The last three days were spent here before returning to Canada. Relatives from Sarnów, Nowa Dwór and Gniezno, travelled here to be with Władek and his sons to attend the culminating event.

The history of the Polish Air Force goes back to the end of World War I in 1918. Władek was exactly eight years old at the time. August 27th, 1998 marked the 80th anniversary of the Polish Air Force. Warsaw was alive with exhibits, parades, wreath laying, speeches, interviews and many other activities. Media coverage of these events was extensive. Polish squadrons with the RAF during the war such as Nos. 303 and 302 were featured.

Not to be outdone, the Canadian embassy in Warsaw had its own event planned for the 27th. The Canadian ambassador, Serge April, held a reception at his private residence to showcase former S/Ldr Gnyś and invited the Polish families, close friends and special guests. It was a black tie event with hors d'oeuvres and lots of champagne. Relatives came from Nowa Dwór Gdański, Gniezno and Sarnów. Special guests included Jerzy B. Cynk and his wife Wiesia from London; Col Allan Strynadka from the Canadian embassy; Marek Dukaczewski, Poland's Under Secretary of State, National Security Bureau; Lt Stanisław Kłakus; Cpt Stanisław Majcherczyk; principal of Żurada school Krystyna Włodarczyk; Lt Col Marek Zapiór and many others.

Prior to and after 1945, monuments had been constructed to immortalize events and participants. One such sculpture, the reconstructed 1932 Airmen Monument with a pilot holding onto a propellor blade, was a popular attraction. Many people gathered here to see it, lay wreaths and enjoy a military marching band. PAF officers in full uniform seen milling about talking with the public. Władek was introduced to an air force celebrity by the name of Brig Gen Mirosław Hermaszewski, Poland's first cosmonaut. He became the first Polish national in space when he flew aboard the Soviet Soyuz 30 spacecraft in 1978 with Russian Pyotr Klimuk.

To round off a perfect stay in Poland's capital, the Gnyś entourage was invited to attend an opera. President Aleksander Kwaśniewski and his wife Jolanta were present. Marek Dukaczewski was there to greet Gnyś's group and escorted them into the theater. He was not only an important public figure, but a genuine Polish gentleman. Another member of the audience sitting near the stage was another well-known Polish pilot from No. 303 Squadron—Stanisław Skalski.

The final leg of the journey took S/Ldr Gnyś back to Dęblin again. Two years ago in 1996, he came here expecting to see bombed-out buildings, but instead, he found a rebuilt complex with the latest pilot training methods and equipment.

So here he was on August 29th, 1998, a man in his twilight years, returning to the School of Eaglets a fourth time. A five-day event including an air show had been scheduled at Dęblin and was underway when they arrived. This put a smile on his face especially when he saw his favorite Spitfire ready to take off.

Between August 27th and 31st, Warsaw and Dęblin hosted the II Worldwide Congress of Polish Airmen. More than 600 airmen from all over the world attended plus thousands of aviation enthusiasts to take in the international air show, the culmination of the Polish Air Force 80th anniversary celebrations.[1]

Some of the special attendees included the President, Aleksander Kwaśniewski and the First Lady Jolanta Kwaśniewska. There was also Ryszard Kaczorowski, former Polish President in exile, and Gen Dr. Edward Hyra and Gen Dr. Ryszard Olszewski. In 1996, these two generals had welcomed Władek in Warsaw and Dęblin. PAF veterans and Gnyś's colleagues such as S. Skalski, T. Sawicz, F. Gabreski and F. Kornicki were also there. Very good friends of Władek's like Jerzy Obmiński, Chairman of PAF Veterans' Association Wing Council in Hamilton, Ontario, and Mr. and Mrs. Jerzy Cynk from London, all got reacquainted.

Probably the highlight of the airshow was a mock dogfight between a Messerschmitt and a Spitfire. After this amazing display of pilots and their machines, Władek and group were invited into the officers' mess for dinner. To his surprise, the Commanding Officer of the base stood up and said some very kind words of welcome and praise and presented him with gifts that carried the Dęblin name. It was very humbling, but graciously accepted. It was then time to get ready for an early start the next morning to catch a flight to Toronto. The final voyage for Mr. Gnyś was over.

CHAPTER 13

End of an Era

After his wife passed away from cancer on August 8th, 1995, Gnyś lived alone in the old house on the Beamsville property. Naturally he craved to be with family, so for many weekends henceforth, he stayed with his sons Ashley and Stefan. Ashley lived in Niagara Falls, Ontario and Stefan in Burlington, about one hour apart. Oldest son Haydn and his wife Christine (Chris) checked up on him frequently, but their house could not structurally accommodate a handicapped person. Finally, the property was put up for sale and Gnyś moved in with Ashley and his wife Valerie permanently in September 1998. Sydney, his daughter, came to visit and spent quality time with her father. Haydn and Chris also visited. Stefan would pick him up and bring him over for weekends at his home. It was a great opportunity on these occasions to scrutinize his many wartime photos.

One of the outcomes from the trips to Poland in 1996 and 1998 was the publicity Gnyś received. While his presence made an impact on his family and friends, the ripple effect on the PAF, politicians and leaders was even more profound, so much so that recommendations were made that he receive further honors due to his contribution as a pilot in the war. Such prominent figures like Polish Prime Minister Jerzy Buzek and President Aleksander Kwaśniewski put the gears in motion to do something special. In brief, two awards resulted: promotion to Colonel (retired) and the presentation of the Commander's Cross with Star to be presented in Canada.

With the assistance from the Polish embassy in Ottawa, Defense Attaché Colonel Zdzisław Przeszłowski journeyed to Niagara on August 29th, 1999 to present the papers of promotion. Family and close friends were there to witness that special moment. In front of the house with the flowers in full bloom and the sun beaming down, he was promoted to the rank of colonel. It was a proud moment for him and all those present. It was a dream come true for a young boy in rural Poland who reached for the stars and got to touch them.

After the reception for Mr. Gnyś at the Presidential Palace on August 15th, 1998, President Kwaśniewski had his office prepare one of Poland's highest medal awards and have it sent to The Embassy of Poland in Ottawa, from there, it would be presented to him. In Canada, it would be similar in status to the Order of Canada medal. The Commander's Cross with Star, the Order of Polonia Restituta (Order of Rebirth of Poland) has been around since 1921. Out of the five classes, there is only one that has the Star. It is conferred to both service personnel and civilians for extraordinary and distinguished service. Only the President of Poland can award this. It is second to Poland's highest award, the Virtuti Military, which Władek received during the war.

Since he was physically unable to travel to Ottawa, the next most logical location for the presentation was at the Royal Canadian Legion, Polish Veterans' Branch 418, St. Catharines, Ontario, next to the city of Niagara Falls. The Legion was more than happy to host this special event. So, on Saturday, September 18th, 1999, family, friends, the press and legion members filled the main room. To confer the award was Ambassador Bogdan Grzeloński, Defense Attaché Col Zdzisław Przeszłowski, the same officer who came down the previous month to bestow the rank of colonel.

In presenting the award, Ambassador Grzeloński read a letter from the Polish Prime Minister Jerzy Buzek, who stated that Mr. Gnyś had fulfilled a most sanctified duty during the Second World War and that he had done so with honor. Władek replied, "I am humbly accepting this order and I'm positive that all the people who are present around me today, would have acted in the same way I did during the war. I'm so grateful that the Polish government has not forgotten about people like us." The months of August and September 1999 were exciting ones for Władek; after all, it wasn't everyday that one gets promoted to colonel and then receives one of the highest awards by the Republic of Poland.

However, the previous winter of 1998, his health started to change. During that winter and into the spring of 1999, he was not his usual self as he slept more than usual, so Ashley took him to a local clinic and then to the Greater Niagara General Hospital for a thorough checkup.

He underwent blood tests and it was discovered that he had septicemia. He remained in the hospital for treatment for two weeks, but with further testing it was discovered that he had a form of blood cancer, multiple myeloma. It was considered treatable, but generally it is incurable. There were a number of treatments and chemotherapy was chosen. It was administered at the old St. Catharines General Hospital.

When put on low oral doses of chemo in early July, he did well for his age and became the poster boy for successful treatment. He was in great shape especially during the time he received the awards in August and September. Unfortunately, in November

1999, he was unnecessarily taken off the low oral doses of chemo which proved to be his undoing, as within no more than two to three weeks, he became very ill as the cancer raced back unchecked. He then went onto major doses of chemo which probably contributed to his death in late February 2000.

The family in Canada was shocked by his death as they were all told that he was doing really well on the chemo treatment. Of course, they did not know all the medical reasons for his rapid decline. Multiple myeloma was the cancer, but the official reason for death was congestive heart failure which is ironic considering how strong his heart was all his life. Ashley was the last one to see him alive at the St. Catharines General Hospital. In fact, he may have passed away just after Ashley left his room on the morning of February 28th, 2000.[1]

The funeral service took place on Saturday, March 4th in a quaint little Roman Catholic church called St. Helen's in Vineland, the same church for when Barbara passed away five years earlier. His coffin was draped in a Polish flag with the sword he received in Poland in 1996 laid on top. The priest, who was also a friend, spoke kindly about the fallen hero and gave his blessings. Eulogies followed from the Polish Legion and from Stefan and then Ashley, followed by the playing of "Daddy's Uniform." It was a time of grief, sadness and mourning. The pallbearers, made up of family members, then carried the coffin out of the church and down the stairs. On either side of the steps, members from the Royal Canadian Legion—Polish Veterans' Branch 418 of St. Catharines, dressed in their uniforms, stood at attention and saluted as the coffin slowly passed in front of them.

At the gravesite at Mount Osborne Cemetery in Beamsville, family, friends and members of the legion gathered. The 4th of March was an extremely cold and windy day so everyone huddled together under the temporary canopy. The words by Reverend Reid Cooke, about the son of Poland, pilot, husband, father and grandfather, brought comfort to all listening. After flowers were placed on the coffin still draped in the Polish flag, last prayers and goodbyes were whispered before the coffin was lowered into the earth, next to Barbara's.

Condolences from England, France, Germany, Poland, United States and Canada came flooding in. Words of sympathy from various individuals and organizations such as the RAF and the PAF were kind, thoughtful and respectful. Letters and phone calls from families in Poland expressed reverence and mourned his death. Letters even arrived from individuals not known to the family, but had heard of his passing. Newspapers and magazines around the country paid tribute to the Polish icon. Canada's *MacLean's* magazine for example on March 13th, 2000, wrote about him in their obituary column. The Mayor of Olkusz, Andrzej Ryszka, described Gnyś as a "fervent patriot" and "a hero of our Homeland."

On April 14th, 2000, Frank Neubert wrote on his old typewriter:

My dear friend Stefan,

I thank you very much for your letter, but I feel so sorry by your information, that one of my best friends has died. Really, for me he was more than a good friend. May I offer you and the whole family Gnys my heartfelt sympathy. Please say this to your whole family as well.

On this occasion I request you not to stop our contact.

With you and your family I am mourning for Wladek and send you once more all my deepest sympathies. And God bless you.

Your faithfully
Your good friend
Frank

Epilogue

Ashley Gnyś

Some among us pass through perilous times, beat the odds and live to tell about it. Was it great luck in the life of Władysław Gnyś, or was it great skill on his part that helped him to survive when so many others did not? Was it fate, or the hand of God? History teaches us that skill alone, even when combined with great courage often proves insufficient unless accompanied by a healthy dose of plain old luck. Heroes have a way of being in the right place at the right time.

Our father was skilled as a pilot, but it was not his superior ability that gave rise to his place in history, but happenstance. Similar to that of many heroes, he too was in the right place at the right time.

Dad was not successful because of merely what he did, but rather, because of who he was. While many of his great feats are matters of public record, more still were only known by those closest to him as he was a humble man, not prone to draw attention to himself. What each feat held in common was their source; they flowed from the nature of his character.

His rapid and early advancement through the military ranks as a young man, showed him to be exceptionally gifted at flying. He also possessed certain biological advantages that gave him an edge over many. Among them were an incredibly sharp, long-distance sight and the ability to withstand great G-forces when engaged in a dive. While these innate abilities increased the odds in his favor, they were accompanied by a keenly developed sense that told him when to boldly advance and when to hang back.

Dad represented a curious combination of being cautious yet fearless. He became adept at managing risk and that one great skill allowed him to survive while others about him perished. For the most part, he did not fear pain, nor was he ruled by his emotions. He was a logical thinker and a man of deep passion.

While he was not always right, he was always reasoned. In the big decisions of life for the most part, he was decisive. Frustrating to our mother at times, he could, in contrast, be frustratingly indecisive in the small matters of everyday life.

He willingly assumed great risk when it was demanded by circumstances, while all the while preserving a risk-adverse nature. Dad was not one to take unnecessary chances, aside perhaps from the occasion he flew his plane under a bridge, just to prove to himself it could be done. Caught in the act, had his station commander not been lenient and given him a second chance, this book would never have been written.

As kids, we sat spellbound hearing Dad retell the stories of his many dogfights, his crash landings, his near-fatal wounding, his escape and dramatic rescue as a prisoner of war and his frequent brushes with death. To us children, it sounded like a fairytale about a hero in a distant land. How could so much action and so many life and death situations be crowded into one mortal's life?

This man, who would cradle his little ones in his arms when fever gripped their bodies or who would kiss their cheeks with his tears and stroke their hair, had a gentle side which stood in stark juxtaposition to his role as a military tool of destruction. To us, he was just our Dad, not a savage killing force who had eliminated enemies in the air and on the ground.

He reached the apex in his vocational pathway in the chapter of his military career. He was a gifted servant-leader who inspired others to self-sacrifice by personal example. Sadly, once he had left the military, he never again found a fulfilling alternate career, but struggled to find his way in civilian life. His unique gift as a pilot prematurely ended due to a bullet that lodged in his liver and remained there for the rest of his life.

He was not a man rich as the world weighs wealth, but a number of times in his life, when his luck had run its course and he found himself in dire poverty in his new land of Canada, others recognized he possessed another kind of wealth—that of character. His only collateral was that of human capital which secured their faith in this young immigrant farmer (1948–53) who promised to repay their trust. They must have recognized in his character a deep sense of commitment and responsibility, that his word was his bond.

On one occasion it was a banker that lent a sizable amount of money to fund the purchase of lime to sweeten his poor soil, even though he lacked financial security for the loan. On another occasion, it was a well-to-do farmer who sold him a herd of cows with only a promise for future repayment, while turning down a much larger price offered by a competing farmer.

Dad was a larger-than-life figure, whose wartime accomplishments placed him on a short list with a handful of remarkable men, one of whom he was reunited with on August 30th, 1989, when he met Mjr Frank Neubert, formerly of the Luftwaffe, who 50 years earlier had shot down the first Allied aircraft of World War II on the first day of the war.

How would he react to this former enemy who had shot down and killed his commanding officer that fateful dawn and who had almost succeeded in killing our father? Fifty years is a long time, but not nearly long enough to forget one's former adversary. If it was fireworks and angry accusations the national media were expecting that day, they left disappointed, for Dad and Frank became good friends with their very first handshake, remaining close friends until Dad's death a decade later.

In his homeland of Poland he is given great respect as a national hero and truly he was. But to those of us who knew him simply as Dad, his greatest gift to us was in living out his fidelity, his love to our other larger-than-life parent, our mother for 54 years until the day she died at 73 in 1995.

I was privileged to be by his bedside when he passed away at the age of 89 on February 28th, 2000. With his passing, we all lost our cheerleader, friend and hero. He was gone, yes, but would never be gone from our hearts.

Dedicatory

Laurie Johnson's To The Few

Laurie R. W. Johnson MBE, is an English author, composer and bandleader who has produced and written scores for hundreds of films and themes for television series for the better part of seven decades. He has been one of the most highly regarded arrangers of instrumental pop and swing music since in the 1950s. No stranger to classical and big band music, he has recorded and sold countless albums, tapes and CDs of his compositions. Music for such television series as *The Avengers, The New Avengers* and *The Professionals* has been heard around the world.

In 1941, at the age of 14, he met P/O Gnyś. Laurie said, "When he first walked into the room, I knew that he was someone special" From that day on, they developed a lasting friendship and kept in touch over the years. Laurie had a deep respect for Władek and the Polish pilots. One of his most famous scores was *To The Few*, a 10:26-minute, three part (67-page) score which he dedicated to S/Ldr Władek Gnyś on August 28th, 1989. It took the listener through "scramble," "juke box" and "flypast." A little embarrassed, Gnyś said, "for 'gooness' sake", but graciously accepted this prestigious honor from a dear friend and musical genius.

A street in Kraków

The Polish Aviation Museum is a large museum (established in 1912) of old aircraft and aircraft engines in Kraków, Poland. It is located at the site of the no-longer functional Kraków-Rakowice-Czyżyny Airport. Regular airfield activity came to a halt in 1963 and in the following year was turned into a museum. It is regarded as one of the best aviation museums in the world.

A few years into the new millennium, plans were made to construct a new museum building (interpretive center) in the museum grounds. By 2010, its doors were open to the public. The Kraków City Council, decided to name a new street after Władek which ran in front of the new building, called Płk. Władysława Gnysia. It was a proud moment when the family discovered this street sign bearing his name.

Polish War Memorial, England

The Polish War Memorial is a stone obelisk erected to remember the contributions of airmen from Poland who helped the Allied cause during the Second World War. It is situated near RAF Northolt between Ruislip and Northolt in the County of Middlesex, in the London Borough of Hillingdon. Topped with a bronze eagle, which is the symbol of the Polish Air Force, it is a major landmark in the area. It opened in 1948. Surviving comrades realized the need for the memorial and it was PoW sculptor Mieczysław Lubelski who crafted this artistry.

It is part of a gated compound that has a shallow pond in front of it; steps lead down to a sunken half-moon walkway and inscribed on crescent panels are the names of the 2,165 Polish airmen who fell. The insignias of long-gone squadrons also adorn the walls.

Every September, hundreds gather at the memorial to pay homage and lay wreaths as part of the annual ceremony commemorating the Polish airmen. Sadly, each year participating veterans get fewer and fewer.

Capel-le-Ferne Memorial

Capel-le-Ferne is a village near Folkestone, on the coast of Kent, perched on top of the White Cliffs of Dover. Its main attraction is the Battle of Britain memorial, opened in 1993, and is dedicated to those who fought between July 10th and October 31st, 1940. The memorial is built on part of a former coastal battery overlooking the English Channel.

For P/O Gnyś and many airmen, the White Cliffs were a sight for sore eyes when returning from combat operations over the continent. Once spotted, they knew that they were home safe and sound, ready to fight another day.

The central figure is a seated airman on a large propeller-shaped base looking out across the Channel. There are replica aircraft such as the Hawker Hurricane and Supermarine Spitfire standing guard. However, the layout and design is dissimilar to the memorial in London, but both display the names of those pilots from 15 countries who took part in the Battle of Britain. At Capel-le-Ferne, there is a massive curved wall with 2,937 aircrew listed, called the Christopher Foxley-Norris Memorial Wall. On one of the many panels are the names of the 145 Polish pilots. P/O W. Gnyś's name is there sharing space with friends such as P/O S. Chałupa, F/O W. Krol, F/O A. Gabszewicz and P/O J. Żurakowski.

The Battle of Britain Monument, London

The Battle of Britain Monument in London is a bronze and granite sculpture on the Victoria Embankment overlooking the River Thames, across from the London Eye. It commemorates the British military personnel and those of 14 other nations who took part in the Battle of Britain. It was unveiled in September 2005.

The monument itself is a two-section, low-level, longish piece of work consisting of three-dimensional figures such as airmen scrambling for their planes and observers looking into the sky. It is a brilliant and complex piece of art that gives the viewer a visual account of the battle. The genius behind it is sculptor Paul Day.

On the flat surfaces are the names, by country of origin, of the 2,937 airmen and ground crew that took part. P/O Władek Gnyś's name, one of 145 Polish airmen, is embossed in bronze.

Proposed monument: The Flight of Brothers Memorial

In the very early hours on September 1st, 1939, the Blitzkrieg of Poland commenced. Once Rakowice airbase in Kraków was destroyed, the Luftwaffe turned on their heels and headed back to Germany. On the way, a Stuka formation spotted Polish fighters taking off. They attacked and pilot Frank Neubert shot and killed Cpt Mieczysław Medwecki, while S-Lt Władysław Gnyś managed to avoid the gunfire. Another flier was nearby, but not directly involved. The captain's plane crashed into a field in the little village of Chrosna near Balice, west of Kraków. He was the first air casualty of the war.

Ever since that day, various ideas of recognition for this fallen defender and hero were floated. One such idea that saw the light of day came from the Faculty of Architecture, Kraków University of Technology. Under Dr. Krzysztof Wielgus, a project team was assembled. Design entries for a memorial were submitted for appraisal in 2013. It was student Marta Gołębiewska's model that captured everyone's attention and was accepted by the committee in 2014, who then began serious talks about the construction of this memorial.

The concept was based on the pilots who defended that area of Poland in 1939, particularly Cpt Medwecki, S-Lt Gnyś and Aircraftman Tadeusz Arabski who were there above Balice.

On the monument are three silhouettes of PZL P.11c fighters. The plane in the center of the composition is that of Medwecki. This part of the monument is made of vertical elements made of curved steel. The shape of the plane is cut out in the metal beams. The figure is seen as a silhouette against the sky making the viewer feel like the plane is actually taking off. On both sides are two figures of planes devoted to Gnyś and Arabski. These sculptures are made of concrete to contrast with the steel strips. The whole monument would be ramped up next to the A4, so drivers can see the three aircraft taking off in the background sky from Cpt Medwecki's crash site.

A committee was created at the Kościuszko Foundation and discussions for acquiring the crash site property got underway. The project was a massive undertaking and was a challenge for the many eager volunteers. In 2014, at the apex of activity, there were local elections in Poland which resulted in a temporary freeze of the project. In addition to the political climate change, acquisition of the crash site, which was privately owned, ran into problems. Also, sufficient funding for this monument fell short. Then the committee ran into another problem: the owner of the A4 said that the monument would be a visual distraction and could cause traffic accidents. So, for the time being The Flight of Brothers Memorial is still grounded, but there is movement afoot for the completion of the project regardless of the obstacles. One individual who is resurrecting this initiative is Dominik Kościelny. The plan is to unveil the monument in 2018 as part of the celebration of the 100th anniversary of Polish independence and the birth of the Polish Air Force.

No. 302 Polish Squadron, RAF Leconfield

No. 302 (City of Poznań) Polish Fighter Squadron has the distinction of being the first Polish fighter unit formed on English soil under the umbrella of the RAF. Its official formation took place on July 10th, 1940 at Leconfield in northern England. 302 consisted mostly of Polish pilots who were hardened veterans from the Polish and French campaigns. They flew Hawker Hurricanes and were under No. 12 Group RAF which defended the Midlands.

P/O Gnyś joined No. 302 during the last week in August of 1940.

After the war, the original hangars and control tower still remain at Leconfield even though the function of the base has changed. One thing missing was a memorial to commemorate No. 302 Polish Squadron. Kate O'Mara from Beverley, close to Leconfield took the project on. The site chosen for the 302 memorial plaque was inside the Church of St. Catherine in Leconfield where the pilots worshipped. Another reason for this location was that there are graves of Polish pilots buried there: two from 303, one from 308 and one from 316. On November 17th, 2013 the unveiling ceremony took place. Afterwards, Kate said: "I hope that this goes a little way to say thank you to the men of 302 who defended the coast of East Yorkshire and flew so valiantly against the Axis forces."

Spitfire EN179 SZ-J "Jasia"

For 62 years buried in a lonely field in northern France, a Spitfire waited patiently to be found and brought to the surface from its cold, dark grave 13 feet down. As the excavator dug its way through the soft surface and then into the hard clay, pieces of her mutilated body started to see the light of day. The world would see her again, certainly not in her prime, but with the help of Monsieur Pierre Ben and his friends who dug her up August 21st, 2005, the pieces of EN179 would eventually find their way into his museum in Warloy-Baillon (dept. of the Somme) for all to admire and appreciate.

It all started when 25-year-old F/O Andrzej Próchnicki with No. 316 Polish Fighter Sqn RAF took off from a base in England on a Ramrod 209 mission over France. He already had several victories under his belt and was looking for a few more. But on that fateful day of August 19th, 1943, he would become the victim of a Luftwaffe Fw 190 fighter pilot.

The significance of the story is that this Spitfire Mark IX, EN179, was the aircraft of choice for F/Lt W. Gnyś with No. 316 ... it was "his" plane. According to his log book and a logged list of pilots who used it, Gnyś flew the Mark IX Spitfire SZ-J for a total of 23 times from February 26th to May 16th, 1943 (when code changed to SZ-C). Out of 23 flights, 15 were offensive combat operations mainly over occupied France.

Between March 13th and August 19th, 1943, F/O Próchnicki flew EN179 SZ-J/SZ-C a total of seven times, including the 19th, the day he was shot down and crashed near Naours about 12 miles north of Amiens (Somme). His body was found in the debris of the plane and was buried in the village before being transferred to the Polish cemetery in Normandy at Langannerie-Urville. There is an ID memorial at the scene of the crash at Naours.

A true archaeologist of the modern era, enthusiast Pierre Ben, President of the Somme Aviation 39–45 Association, was experienced in digging up crashed aircraft of the war. Cleaning and sorting the hundreds of pieces takes time, patience and dedication. Above all else, a deep affection and respect for the men who flew these amazing machines was very much apparent.

One notable excavation involved Spitfire Mk IX of P/O Piotr Kuryłłowicz of No. 315 Polish Sqn whose plane BS 410 PK-A was shot down on May 13th, 1943. He baled out and survived, but his plane burrowed itself deep into a field at Occoches north of Amiens. Piotr was captured and became a PoW in the infamous Stalag Luft III camp until liberated. Later, he went to Canada to start a new life.

Since then, Piotr's Spitfire was registered and then restored in the UK. The common practice is to take some pieces from the original plane and include them when building the new one, so the finished product is considered "historically restored" and not a brand new one even though it is. Some good news is that F/Lt Gnyś's Spitfire, EN179 has been registered and awaits construction by a private investor.

Soil from the graves

Taking soil from a person's grave, either from the excavation process or skimming it off the surface, is not a new practice. There are many reasons why this is done. For example, the use of graveyard dirt has been used in forms of folk magic and rituals of love. The significance of the soil is that it is representative of the person in the grave. It corresponds with the traits of the person buried beneath it. Soil from a famous writer's grave, for example, could be used as inspiration by those wanting to improve their writing skills. If the person is someone you cared about and who had a positive impact on your life, then earth from their grave would have much more of a personal meaning. The soil in this case would be symbolic of the relationship.

Earth from the graves of Polish airmen, no matter where they lie, represents their bravery, tenacity and love for family and country. Stefan Gnyś's cousin Waldemar Serocki was President of the Polish Soldiers' Association of Gniezno and District. He was also a standing member of the provincial board in Poznan. He and his committee discussed ways in which soil from Władek's grave and that of Frank Neubert could be used. They contacted Stefan, and Ingo Neubert and Petra Shultz, the adult children of the German pilot. Both parties complied and promptly forwarded the soil in 2006. (Permission, official supervision and certification was necessary and only small amounts were taken.)

Waldemar and his committee planned for the soil to be placed in three different locations. It took them three years, once they received the soil in 2006, to get official approval from all parties involved (religious and governmental) and work through the ranks of bureaucracy and make all the necessary logistical arrangements. The coordination of this was an immense undertaking especially when three separate ceremonies were to take place. The results were as follows: Gnyś's soil plus Neubert's in a joint urn placed into a wall inside the Garrison Church in Gniezno on April 29th, 2006, Waldemar's home city; Gnyś's soil only: into the rock monument in front of the Gnyś Elementary School, Żurada on September 16th, 2009; Gnyś's soil only: into a brass urn in the Chapel of Polish Airmen at Jaworzno on September 13th, 2009.

Waldemar and his committee decided to start their first project in Gniezno. They wanted to focus in on the event of reconciliation between Gnyś and Neubert that took place in 1989. So they put their heads together and came up with the idea of an embossed brass plaque containing the busts of the two pilots to be placed in the local Garrison Church (also known as the Church of Holy Mary Queen of Poland 1842). After getting permission from the church, they designed the plaque and had it made. It was dated Gniezno 2006. The heading read: "They Fought to be Reconciled."

It was attached on an inside wall, in its own corner not far from the entrance, visible to churchgoers and visitors alike. Shortly after, a cavity was cut into the wall beneath the plaque into which one small urn (with two compartments) containing soil from the graves of Gnyś and Neubert was placed. It was a symbolic gesture of reconciliation to complement the bronze plaque. Next on their list was Żurada and then Jaworzno.

Fixed into the rock face of the monument in front of the school in Żurada, is the large bronze plaque about S-Lt Gnyś shooting down the two bombers. A space was chiseled out of the rock face next to the plaque and a small urn containing only the soil from his grave was inserted. On 16 September 2009, a formal celebration took place.

Dariusz Rzepka, the Mayor of Olkusz (assisted by Jan Kucharzyk, City Council Chair) welcomed all the participants and inserted the urn and fitted the covering plate.

Jaworzno is located in southern Poland near Katowice and Olkusz and northwest of Kraków. It lies in the Silesian Highlands on the Przemsza River, a tributary of the Vistula. Historically, it goes back to the thirteenth century.

Jaworzno has many churches, but one in particular, the Shrine of Our Lady of Perpetual Help, houses a section of brass urns in the Chapel of Polish Airmen. Within the urns is the soil from the graves of Polish airmen whose remains lie in different cemeteries in Europe, Canada, the U.S. and elsewhere. This memorial, created in 1999, is not a museum, but rather a place for spiritual communication with those pilots who fought for the freedom of so many.

At the end of a solemn mass on September 13, 2009 before hundreds of worshippers, Col Gnyś's urn was placed on a pristine marble shelf along with those belonging to Polish heroes such as Stanisław Skalski, Mieczysław Medwecki and Czesław Główczyński.

Reconciliation Symposium, Gniezno

Waldemar and his committee came up with the concept of holding a symposium that would bring parties together from Germany, Poland and Canada in an open forum, to articulate what reconciliation meant to them. The site and date decided upon was the University of Poznań, European College, located in Gniezno, on May 5th, 2008.

When Ingo Neubert and Petra Schultz arrived in Gniezno before the event, they were welcomed by Stefan, Ashley, Waldemar and his family. This was the first time that the children of the two pilots had met. They greeted each other with warmth and enthusiasm. There was no built-up angst, but rather a curiosity and a desire to get to know each other over the next few days: after all, it was their fathers that were at war, not them.

On the first day in Gniezno, they all went to the Garrison Church where Waldemar showed Ingo and Petra the bronze plaque and the urn in the wall below it, which contained soil from their father's grave and that of pilot Gnyś. They were delighted with the craftsmanship of the two busts of the former enemies and congratulated Waldemar for bringing the project to fruition. They then laid wreaths on the floor beneath the display and bowed their heads.

Next morning, guests started to arrive at the university: Ashley and Stefan; Ingo and Petra; Renata Pogodzik, the Żurada school principal; Professor Adam Sudoł; Waldemar and family; Polish Air Force officers; university and government representatives; political history experts and university students.

During the day, speakers took their turn at the podium to expound on the pros and cons of reconciliation and Polish-German relations from their personal perspectives. In some cases, articulated questions from the audience proved to be a challenge for several of the presenters. Some speakers spoke negatively about the friendly relationship between Poland and Germany and thought that Poland was too quick to forgive and forget.

Perhaps the climax of the symposium were the presentations from Ingo, Stefan and Ashley, because they focused in on their fathers. Through translators, they were able to express their views and be understood in three languages. The following are excerpts from their speeches:

Stefan: "Our fathers met in Polish skies to kill each other and yet despite this, we, their children meet in peace today. It's quite something that they reconciled and became friends. If they could do it, then why can't other people in conflict follow their example? Anything is possible if one reaches out."

Ashley to Ingo: "I can only rejoice that your father did not kill ours, because if he had, then Stefan and I would not be standing before you today. As fate would have it, they created history."

Then in a surprise remark about his father who made the first aerial kill, Ingo said: "I do not want to view my father as a hero because victory in war always involves killing others. Reconciliation tells me that we should be ashamed of the fact that once, we ran out of mutual respect." Then he said in reference to the construction of monuments to Polish-German friendship: "I came here from Germany and no one had to show a passport. This is the best monument to reconciliation."

Petra did not speak publicly as she allowed her brother to speak on her behalf. However, they all agreed that from 1989, when Frank and Władek were brought together, each individually learned to reflect differently on world issues and how important it was for nations and people to put an end to hostilities and to compromise and negotiate a peaceful co-existence with mutual tolerance despite different ideologies or interests.

To cap the day off, Mr. Serocki showed on the large screen, a documentary of Cpt Pilot Władysław Gnyś. Follow-up newspaper reports were very positive about the symposium and paid homage to the value of such events.

By the end of several long and satisfying days, goodbyes were said to the German counterparts as they headed home. The families got to know each other on different levels and the concept of reconciliation was better understood and was no longer arcane.

Posthumous celebration of W. Gnyś's 100th birthday

It was a rainy, cold and blustery day in Żurada on September 1st, 2010. The strongest set of bright and colorful canopies that could hold up to the darkest of weather had been ordered. As it turned out, the many guests from near and far really appreciated this because it rained cats and dogs that day. This was not only the beginning of a new school year, but also the anniversary of the Invasion of Poland, 71 years ago to the day. The other unique character of this year was the inauguration of the school and community under the auspices of the large municipality of Olkusz giving Żurada certain economic, political and social advantages.

Principal Renata Pogodzik, her staff and community really wanted to do something special for their school's namesake who was there in person in 1996 and 1998. Ashley and Stefan from Canada and relatives in Poland were invited to attend the wreath-laying and other festivities along with veterans, government leaders from Żurada and Olkusz, PAF officers, firefighters and a host of others. Unfortunately Ashley was unable to go, so Stefan invited a friend and former teaching colleague, Doug Patterson, a history buff with an excellent working knowledge of World War II. He jumped at the opportunity, eager to make his first trip to Poland, a country he had heard so much about.

The sound of the rain pelting down on the shelters gave competition to Renata, the master of ceremonies. A brass band performed several inspirational numbers fitting for the occasion.

To the rapid beat of a single drum, wreaths were placed by several veterans at the base of the Gnyś stone monument. Former mayor of Olkusz Janusz Dudkiewicz and successor Mayor Dariusz Rzepka, with Jan Kucharzyk, City Council Chair, followed suit. Then Stefan, Doug, Teresa and Waldemar laid exquisite red and white flower arrangements next to the others. The very wet guard of honor on either side of the monument stood at attention the whole time. It was an impressive demonstration of respect.

Stefan was the last to speak, with the aid of a translator, even though he proudly started and ended his speech in Polish. He talked about the virtues of his father and the significance of his father's wartime contributions, and then thanked all those who had attended the celebration. He concluded by saying: "I am so very proud to be here today, thank you very very much, goodbye and 'sto lat!'"

Afterwards, everyone was invited to sample fine Polish cuisine. For dessert, Stefan cut up a large red and white checkerboard cake symbolic of the colors on Polish aircraft. Before the day ended, he was interviewed by TV Przegląd from Olkusz who integrated it with footage of the day. The coverage was broadcasted later and put on the internet.

First Kill *painting comes home to Dęblin*

Two American friends and WWII historians by the names of Jim Lansdale and Bill Wolf were aware of Gnyś's book, *First Kill*. Having read about the Polish pilot and his accomplishments, Bill made contact with Władek in 1986 asking for an autograph. This then led to phone calls by both Bill and Jim in early 1991 which resulted in an ongoing friendship with the Canadian pair. The concept of doing a painting of the first Allied victory of the war surfaced. Gnyś gave his thumbs-up and the wheels set in motion.

While wintering in their picturesque home in late 1991 on the Braden River in Bradenton, Florida, Jim and his wife Carol made their first visit. Shortly afterwards, Bill joined them and Władek was interviewed and sketches were made by Jim of the first encounter. This is when friend and talented painter of aviation, and other genres, Roy Grinnell (ASAA) entered the equation. More interviews and sketches followed and with collaborative research, Roy began the painting. Over the years he had produced dozens of original pieces of aviation art for the American Fighter Aces' Association, portraying aerial combat from both world wars and other conflicts, so he was well qualified for this project.

Once completed in early 1992, 1,000 lithographs were printed, numbered and taken to Bradenton for Władek to sign, which he did in April. They were then made available for sale and distribution to the general public.

In the late 1990s, Jim expressed the desire to keep the original painting at his home in Florida: Roy agreed. After being the custodian for almost 13 years and after discussions with Stefan in 2010, he decided to donate the painting to the Gnyś family and for them to find an appropriate resting place for it. Roy and Bill were fully behind the idea.

The painting was crated and sent to Stefan in Canada. It was decided that the best place for it to be on permanent display was in the museum at the Dęblin Air Force Base in Poland. It was a natural fit since Władek was a student there in the 1930s, and then an instructor just like his uncle who even taught young Władek basic flying. Plus, Dęblin was very close to Sarnów. Contact was made with the base and they were thrilled and honored to have this work of art placed in their Hall of Traditions in the museum.

Waldemar and Teresa agreed to take Stefan and Doug to the airbase to present the painting. On September 3rd, 2010 it was all smiles and handshakes from Lt Col Włodzimierz Ceglarski (PR officer) and Col Marek Bylinka (Vice-Rector for military and acting base commander for Brig Gen Pilot Jan Rajchel, Rector-Commandant). A tour of the museum and the training facilities followed the presentation. They said that it would be proudly displayed in the Hall of Traditions and that photos would follow. Then on November 9th, as promised, photos arrived in Canada with the following message from Lt Col Ceglarski: "I just want to send you a few photos currently taken in The Hall of Traditions where the painting presented by you is on exhibition. It gathers a lot of interest since it has been here and we inform all our visitors on the story of the picture and on your father's history as well." James, Bill and Roy were pleased that the picture had come to rest in such a magnificent place and agreed that Col Gnyś would have given his blessing.

Medals of reconciliation

The crowd was waving, cheering and taking pictures of the military parade making its way down the main street in Gniezno on its way from the Garrison Church to the City Hall. A military band led the way, followed by a Guard of Honor and Color Guard from the 3rd Airlift Wing in Powidz. Behind them were several dozen people of mixed professions, trying to march in unison to the beat of a drum.

The day was August 30th, 2015 and the occasion was the posthumous award of reconciliation medals to former enemies W. Gnyś and F. Neubert.

The reconciliation medal (Komandoria Missio Reconciliationis) is a distinction awarded by the National Association of Social Mission of Reconciliation. Its origin dates back to the Battle of Westerplatte of 1939 and subsequent meeting in 1993 of the families of the defenders of Westerplatte and German sailors from the battleship that attacked the Polish peninsula.[1]

The ceremony was attended by Canadian sons Stefan and his wife Janet Taylor, Ashley and his wife Valerie Gnyś. Unfortunately due to health reasons, Frank Neubert's son and daughter, Ingo and Petra Schultz from Germany, could not make the event. Adam Muszka representing the Ambassador of Germany to Poland, Assistant Honorary Council of Germany in Poznan, saved the day and stood in for Ingo and Petra. Skilled translator and teacher of English, Agnieszka Gnyś did a superb job of translating for the Canadians who were not fluent in Polish. Jagoda Kniaś took some professional photos of the proceedings for the family.

Music from the military band on the Garrison Church balcony set the mood that early morning. The holy mass was celebrated by Father Andrzej Grzelak whose homily focused on the importance of peace and reconciliation in the world. The congregation then moved to the back corner of the church where the memorial to the two pilots was located. Wreaths were laid at the base by Ashley and Stefan and many others under the watchful eye of members of the Honor Guard. Ashley gave a speech about how their Dad's life changed so dramatically when he was 29 when the war broke out. Then 50 years later, meeting with the enemy and becoming good friends. He concluded by saying, "Stefan and I are most blessed to have grown up in a peaceful nation of Canada, whose native soil has not known personal war and bloodshed for more than 200 years, and, unlike Poland, has had the good fortune of geography on its side."

It was late morning when everyone filed out of the church and into the hot sun. Once in formation again, the whole parade, led by the band and soldiers, proceeded to the Town Hall for the presentation of the medals. This was the second significant part of the day's ceremony. Speaker and master of ceremonies was Mjr Grzegorz Schmidt from the 33rd Air Base, Powidz. Other speakers were Maj Gen Bolesław Izydorczyk, Kazimierz Bałęczny, Professor Dr. Adam Sudoł, Waldemar Serocki and Stefan who focused on the two trips to Poland with his father and brother in 1996 and 1998. His theme was reflective and nostalgic. He then thanked the key participants of the day and the many others who made significant contributions.[2] Without the input of over 20 individuals, the ceremony would not have materialized. It took a great deal of planning and coordination on the part of Waldemar to pull off the event so seamlessly.

Medals of Reconciliation to pilots Gnyś and Neubert were awarded posthumously and put into the hands of Stefan and Ashley and German representative Adam Muszka. The presenter was Kazimierz Bałęczny a chapter member of the Commander's Mission of Reconciliation. Maj Gen Bolesław Izydorczyk, Col Michał Erdmański and Mjr Grzegorz Schmidt were also involved with the presentation of awards to family members.

Unexpectedly, Ashley and Stefan each received The Gold Badge of Merit 1981 (The Association of Polish Army Soldiers) and commemorative medallions from the 3rd Airlift Wing and 33rd Air Base, Powidz. In addition, Janet and Valerie each proudly accepted The XXXV Anniversary Medal ZŻWP 1981–2016 (The Association of Polish Army Soldiers).

To conclude, the author would like to quote Mr. Serocki[3] when he said: "I think I can confidently say that the task is now done. The presentation of the medals was the crowning achievement of the reconciliation efforts of two wartime enemies, but that this was also symbolic of the peaceful Polish–German relations that exist today. It is hoped that the younger generation going forward, understands this life-changing accomplishment."

Notes

Chapter 1: Rural Poland and the Old Mill

1. Information supplied by Władysław Macherzyński, Radom, Poland, August 15th, 1998.
2. Polish newspapers: *Ostrów*, Monday, July 25th & Friday, 29th, 1938 & *Daily Illustrated Kuryer*, No. 206, Thursday July 28th, 1938.

Chapter 2: Joining the Polish Air Force

1. Of the 114 pilots and 59 navigators of the 12th entry class, 60 were KIA (19 in Poland, 1 in France and 40 in UK), 4 were murdered at Katyn, 22 were killed in flying accidents (2 in France, 20 in UK): a total of 86 deaths out of 173 aviators, or 50% losses. Source: F. Kornicki, *The Struggle*, p. 190.

Chapter 3: September 1939: Blitzkrieg

1. https://en.wikipedia.org/wiki/Frank_Neubert. Retrieved February 28th, 2017.
2. Little did Władek know that in 1995, 56 years later, the school in Żurada would be named after him.
3. J. Cynk, *The Polish Air Force at War, Vol. 1*, 1998, p. 73.
4. Polish Institute and Sikorski Museum, London, England, Archive Doc Ref No LOT.A.II.14/1a/6.
5. This was probably a guess on his part as other sources say it was likely around 6 a.m. or slightly earlier. There was obvious confusion at the time and the last thing he would have done was to look at his watch: it was very early in the morning and it was still quite dark.
6. However, he did make reference—not written here—that he also fired at the other bomber.
7. Peter Sikora, aviation historian and author, England, correspondence May 4, 2017.
8. W. Gnyś, *First Kill*, 1981, pp. 199–202.
9. Polish Institute and Sikorski Museum, Archive Ref No LOT.A.II.14/1a/6.

Chapter 4: On the Run: Romania to the French Air Force

1. For a comprehensive coverage of this time and an assessment and conclusion of the air war over Poland, see J. Cynk, *The Polish Air Force at War, Vol. 1*, pp. 86–93.

2. J. Cynk, *The Polish Air Force at War, Vol. 1*, p. 103.
3. A group de chasse (GC) might include one to four *escadrilles* (squadrons) each of which comprised 10–12 aircraft, but varied between 6–16 aircraft.

Chapter 5: The Battle of France

1. There appears to be some misinformation about which pilot flew which aircraft. The three planes were marked with Roman numerals I, II and III, and piloted by the Poles. All three had the red and white Polish checker and "Winking Fox" emblems on the fuselage. It is assumed that the following markings were on their original aircraft: Roman numeral I with c/n 1031 (on the rudder) belonged to Lt Bursztyn; Roman numeral II with c/n 954, underwing code L-985 belonged to S-Lt Gnyś; Roman numeral III with c/n 948 belonged to S-Lt Chciuk. However, numeral III was on occasion identified with Gnyś but was most identified with Chciuk causing some confusion. They both could have shared it. After the bombing of Auchy-au-Bois airfield, Władek was quoted as saying that his own MS 406 fighter was one of those destroyed "right before my eyes." This perhaps explains why the Roman numeral II is not readily visible on photos taken during the Battle of France as his plane was destroyed on the first day of the invasion.
2. LOT.A.IV.2/1a/8/2, PISM.
3. Eric Dessouroux was responsible for making the rudder of S-Lt Chciuk's MS 406 fighter ('III' No. 948) public. From personal correspondence between him and this author, he described how it was found: "The rudder was discovered in the village of Anhée [SSE of Brussels in the province of Namur], Belgian in 2002 and was owned by the de Villegas family. I was living in the Namur area at this time and was busy creating the Aviation section of the Musée du Souvenir at Haut-le-Wastia. We were contacted by M. de Villegas who wanted to help with the museum's creation and he informed us that he owned a French aircraft rudder. After the first appointment, I quickly discovered that it was the rudder of Władysław Chciuk's Morane MS 406 which crash-landed at Braine-le-Comte on May 16th, 1940. The de Villegas family was living in this particular area in 1940 and the father of M. de Villegas removed the rudder from the aircraft. This 'relic' was kept in the family until 2002 when we acquired it for the museum."
4. Bartłomiej Belcarz, author of *Montpellier Fighter Squadron 1940* (published in 2008 by Stratus) presents an irrefutable line of logic in this dilemma: "French publications list four French pilots (Lt Tariel, Sgt Doublet, Sgt Durand) including Adj. Gagnaire as the victors in the combat. If, according to Chciuk's report, the victory was credited to the section of Lt Tariel, then Adj. Gagnarie who flew within the 'Polish section' should not be included. But if his share in the victory was acknowledged, then automatically S-Lt Chciuk and S-Lt Gnyś should also be credited with their share in the victory."
5. This chapter referenced these sources: B. Belcarz, *Montpellier Fighter Squadron*, 1940: pp. 3–17, 52–62, 63–64, 70, 77, 80–82, 111; J. Cynk, *The Polish Air Force at War: The Official History, 1939–1943*, Part I, Chapter II 'The Polish Air Force Reborn in France': pp. 94–145; W. Gnyś, *First Kill: A Fighter Pilot's Autobiography*: pp. 114–121; G. Śliżewski, *The Lost Hopes: Polish Fighters Over France in 1940*: pp. 31–35, 71–81.
6. Bartłomiej Belcarz of Stratus Books Publishing: information received April 6th, 2014.
7. Ibid.
8. J. Cynk, *The Polish Air Force at War, Vol. 1*, p. 122.
9. Not confirmed by the French, but Mr. B. Belcarz of Stratus Publishing who is an authority on the French campaign is convinced that this is a mistake. S-Lts Chciuk and Gnyś should have been officially credited also.

Chapter 6: The Battle of Britain

1. Personal letter from Władysław Chciuk to Bartłomiej Belcarz dated November 11th, 2003, shared with this author March 27th, 2014.
2. Bartłomiej Belcarz of Stratus Books Publishing: information received March 31st, 2014.
3. J. Cynk, *The Polish Air Force at War, Vol. 1*, p. 151.
4. Fighter squadrons were named after Polish cities, bomber squadrons after provinces.
5. https://en.wikipedia.org/wiki/No._302_Polish_Fighter_Squadron.
6. J. Cynk, *The Polish Air Force at War, Vol. 1*, p. 173.
7. PISM Archives Ref. No. A.XII 85/3/12. Awarded: February 1st, 1941.
8. No. 5 OTU was formed in 1940 as part of No. 12 Group Fighter Command at RAF Aston Down for training fighter pilots. In all, 153 operational units were eventually set up in Britain and Allied countries.
9. Beginning of the Blitz: on August 15th, 1940, the biggest air assault was launched by Hermann Göring; his objective was to put the RAF totally out of commission once and for all by bombing the RAF aerodromes around London and shooting down the fighter aircraft. That evening during a final raid, over 20 Bf 110 and Bf 109 fighter-bombers headed for RAF Kenley from the south, but lost their bearings and flew a little farther north of their intended target. They thought they had found their objective after seeing the airport at Croydon which was not far from central London. High explosives were dropped, but many of them went astray and fell on factories and housing around the airport resulting in numerous casualties. On the 24th, the first bombs fell on London proper and on the East End. The Luftwaffe were supposed to attack aircraft factories, but again had lost their bearings. This then, was the "accidental" beginning of blanket bombing of civilian populations in London, and the Allied retaliatory bombing of cities in Germany.
10. https://en.wikipedia.org/wiki/The_Blitz#Night_attacks.
11. http://avstop.com/history/aroundtheworld/poland/index1.html.
12. Cynk, op. cit., p. 183.
13. Cynk, op. cit., p. 185.
14. https://en.wikipedia.org/wiki/The_Blitz#Night_attacks.
15. www.polishsquadronsremembered.com/302/302story.html.
16. Ashley and Stefan Gnyś were invited to an historic celebration held at RAF Northolt airbase on March 14th, 2013. They represented their father by wearing his medals; others did the same and in some cases had their forebears' mess kits, so symbolic of the war. It was a proud moment for the two brothers as their father spent several years, off and on, at this airbase. He always spoke fondly about his experiences at RAF Northolt.

    It was a very special event for Polish veterans to gather in the historic dining room of the officers' mess for a Polish-themed evening commemorating the efforts of all who served with the Polish Air Force during World War II. Invitations were limited to veterans and immediate families of those who served at RAF Northolt. About 60 people attended this formal affair from around the globe. The evening commenced at the entrance to the historic building with a flypast by an original Hawker Hurricane. Drinks, introductions and nostalgic conversations filled the Bentley Priory Room before dinner. The newly acquired replica of the wartime Wilno Standard (1939 symbol of unity between the PAF in exile and its homeland) was on display throughout the meal and the Salon Orchestra of the Central Band of the RAF provided the music which resonated in the grandiose mess.

    The following PAF veterans had graced the halls of Northolt more than once: Ignacy Jankiewicz, Adam Ostrowski, Stanisław Włosok-Nawarski DFC, Jan Stangryciuk-Black, Marian Słomka, Andrzej Jeziorski, Roman Szymański and Franciszek Kornicki. Likely the most senior was Mr. Kornicki who was the keynote veteran speaker. He served with 303, 315 and 317 Polish Squadrons. For a

96-year-old, the delivery of his speech outshone a polished pro on a speaking circuit. Not only did he pique everyone's interest with reflections of Northolt during the war, but he made everyone laugh with his clever one-liners. His timing was perfect. On December 18th, 2016, he turned the magical 100—"Sto lat!" Others at the head table were his son Richard Kornicki; the Polish Defense Attaché to the UK; the RAF Northolt Station Commander Group Captain Tim O'Brien and S/Ldr Richard Willis (Media and Communications Officer) who was one of the organizers along with Peter Sikora (historian and author). Dan Stirland (Curator of Battle of Britain Bunker, RAF Uxbridge) was another major contributor.

Among the many guests were Stefan and Anton Gabszewicz whose father was at Northolt and Władek's commander. Then there was Jan Łaguna all the way from Australia whose father was Gnyś's S/Ldr of No. 302 at Northolt. Unfortunately, Piotr Łaguna was killed in 1941. While there, S/Ldr Willis took Ashley and Stefan to see the Sector Operations Building, the Chapel and the PAF Exhibition. Dan Stirland, Peter Sikora and team were largely responsible for the creation of this museum. The previous year while at the airbase, Stefan and his wife Janet donated a print of *First Kill* which was framed and put on display.

17. B. Simmons-Gnyś, *One Lovely Yesterday*, pp. 644–659.
18. This song followed them to their grave many decades later: "J'attendrai" is chiselled into their joint headstone located in the Mount Osborne Cemetery in Beamsville, Ontario, Canada.
19. http://www.polishsquadronsremembered.com/302/302story.html.
20. W. Gnyś, *First Kill*, pp. 141–142.
21. The Battle of Britain London Monument: bbm.org.uk.
22. The term 'airmen' refers not only to pilots, but to observer and gunner crewmen. Twin-engined Blenheim aircraft, for example, were used as fighters by the RAF. It would be incorrect to classify all participants as pilots, even though the majority were.
23. K. Wynn, *Men of the Battle of Britain*, p. 2.
24. Source M. Dobrzelecki.

Chapter 7: November 1940–June 1944

1. W. Gnyś, *First Kill*, p. 158.
2. Ibid. pp. 144, 147.
3. www.polishsquadronsremembered.com/302/302story.html.
4. Gnyś, op. cit., pp. 148–150.
5. R. Gretzyngier, "Hospital for RAF Officers in Torquay," *Gapa* No. 15, September 2015.
6. Author's comment: Even years after the war, our father at times exemplified the comment about being "unduly sensitive" if a tongue-in-cheek joke was made in reference to him or about Poles in general.
7. https://en.wikipedia.org/wiki/No._303_Polish_Fighter_Squadron.
8. Source P. Sikora.
9. Juliusz and Władek were good friends and both immigrated after the war to Ontario, Canada. At one point, they lived not far from one another and this author, remembers family get-togethers as a child.
10. https://en.wikipedia.org/wiki/No._316_Polish_Fighter_Squadron.
11. www.historyofwar.org/air/units/RAF/316_wwII.html.
12. QDM is the starting point, aircraft to the station and direction magnetic.
13. W. G.'s RAF pilot log book.
14. www.polishsquadronsremembered.com/309/309_story.html.
15. J. Cynk, *The Polish Air Force at War, Vol. 1*, pp. 271–272.

16. www.google.ca/search?q=Operation+Steinbock&ie=UTF-8&oe=UTF-8&gws_rd=cr&e-i=VX3FWJuVHarcjwSSiriwBQ.
17. www.defensemedianetwork.com/stories/operation-pied-piper-the-evacuation-of-english-children-during-world-war-ii/.
18. www.iwm.org.uk/history/the-evacuated-children-of-the-second-world-war.
19. https://en.wikipedia.org/wiki Evacuations_of_civilians_in_Britain_during_World_War_II.

Chapter 8: Shot Down Over France

1. https://en.wikipedia.org/wiki/RAF_Second_Tactical_Air_Force.
2. https://en.wikipedia.org/wiki/No._131_Wing_RAF.
3. Polish Institute and Sikorski Museum, Archives.
4. Ibid.
5. https://en.wikipedia.org/wiki/No._317_Polish_Fighter_Squadron.
6. As quoted from archival material from the Polish Institute and Sikorski Museum, London; no direct reference no.

Chapter 9: Canada

1. https://en.wikipedia.org/wiki/RMS_Aquitania.
2. Permission to reproduce front-page material granted courtesy of the *Toronto Star*.

Chapter 10: Return to Poland

1. https://en.wikipedia.org/wiki/Gniewoszów,_Masovian_Voivodeship.
2. Gienia, an attractive young woman, was not molested by the Germans. She and her husband Stanisław eventually had four children: Jurek was born in 1945, followed by Ewa, Roman and Andrzej.

Chapter 11: Reconciliation

1. Decommissioned in 1974, in 1982 *Intrepid* became the foundation of the Intrepid Sea, Air and Space Museum in New York City.
2. Janusz Piekałkiewicz (1925–88) was a Polish resistance fighter during the Warsaw uprising of 1944, a PoW, military historian, a world-renowned author of over 30 books, a television and cinema director and producer and a mountaineering guide.

Chapter 12: A Hero's Welcome

1. J. Zieliński, II Worldwide Congress of Polish Airmen, pp. 27–31, August 1998.

Chapter 13: End of an Era

1. Ashley remembered our brother Haydn prophesying that if their father sold the Beamsville property, it would kill him because he loved it so much. It sold in January 2000 and their father passed away the next month as Haydn predicted.

Addendum: Dedicatory

1. https://pl.wikipedia.org/wiki/Komandoria_Missio_Reconciliationis, retrieved February 20th, 2017.
2. Maj Gen Franciszek Puchała, President of the Board of the Association of Soldiers of the Polish Army, Warsaw, for the granting of awards; Mayor of Gniezno, Tomasz Budasz, for his patronage and support; Deputy Mayor of Gniezno, Michał Powałowski, for participation and support; Brig Gen pilot Mirosław Jemielniak, commander of 3rd Airlift Wing, Powidz; Col pilot Michał Erdmański, for special commitment and organizational assistance (including the Banner Units and the Kompania soldiers); and Mjr Grzegorz Schmidt from the 33rd Air Base, Powidz, master of ceremonies.
3. Waldemar Serocki, President of the Polish Soldiers' Association of Gniezno and District.

Polish Fighter Units, September 1939

Brygada Pościgowa (Pursuit Brigade)

III/I Dywizjon Myśliwski (III/I Fighter Wing)

- 111 Eskadra Myśliwska (111 Fighter Sqn)
- 112 Eskadra Myśliwska (112 Fighter Sqn)

IV/I Dywizjon Myśliwska (IV/I Fighter Wing)

- 113 Eskadra Myśliwska (113 Fighter Sqn)
- 114 Eskadra Myśliwska (114 Fighter Sqn)

Detached from III/2 Dywizjon Myśliwski (III/2 Fighter Wing)

- 123 Eskadra Myśliwska (123 Fighter Sqn) (Stanisław Chałupa)

Kraków Army Air Arm

III/2 Dywizjon Myśliwski (III/2 Fighter Wing)

- 121 Eskadra Myśliwska (121 Fighter Sqn) (Władysław Gnyś)
- 122 Eskadra Myśliwska (122 Fighter Sqn)

Poznań Army Air Arm

III/3 Dywizjon Myśliwski (III/3 Fighter Wing)

- 131 Eskadra Myśliwska (131 Fighter Sqn)
- 132 Eskadra Myśliwska (132 Fighter Sqn)

Pomorze Army Air Arm

III/4 Dywizjon Myśliwski (III/4 Fighter Wing)

- 141 Eskadra Myśliwska (141 Fighter Sqn)
- 142 Eskadra Myśliwska (142 Fighter Sqn)

Narew Army Group Air Arm

Detached from III/5 Dywizjon Myśliwski (III/5 Fighter Wing)

- 151 Eskadra Myśliwska (151 Fighter Sqn)

Modlin Army Air Arm

III/5 Dywizjon Myśliwski (III/5 Fighter Wing)

- 152 Eskadra Myśliwska (152 Fighter Sqn)

Łódź Army Air Arm

III/6 Dywizjon Myśliwski (III/6 Fighter Wing)

- 161 Eskadra Myśliwska (161 Fighter Sqn)
- 162 Eskadra Myśliwska (162 Fighter Sqn)

Service Record, 1931–39

Non-commissioned officer regular corps

Surname: Gnyś
Name: Władysław

Civilian education and knowledge of languages

- 6 grades of state secondary school in Radom
- School-leaving examination in Mathematics and Science before State Examination Committee appointed by the Pomorskie School Board in writing No. II/11894/38 dated May 7, 1938

Polish Air Force activities and advancements

- October 26, 1931: Assigned to training squadron
- December 20, 1931: Sworn in
- May 3, 1932: Promoted to Aircraftman No. 1
- July 23, 1932: Promoted to Leading Aircraftman
- May 4, 1933: Detailed to flying course at Aviation Shooting and Bombardment School in Grudziądz
- September 20, 1933: Appointed to a re-enlistment status until September 19, 1934
- September 26, 1933: Returned and assigned to training squadron
- April 17, 1934: Transferred to 42 Squadron
- August 8, 1934: Detailed to an advanced flying course at Aviation Shooting and Bombardment School in Grudziądz
- October 1, 1934: Re-enlistment status prolonged until September 30, 1935
- October 18, 1934: Returned and assigned to 42 Squadron

- October 24, 1934: Transferred to 143 Fighter Squadron
- November 1, 1934: Awarded title of 3rd class pilot
- March 25, 1935: Transferred to 142 Fighter Squadron
- October 1, 1935: Appointed regular soldier in Group 1
- March 12, 1936: Detailed to Training Center for Aviation Officers to attend 5th Flying Instructor Course
- March 12, 1936: Reported to the Training Center for Aviation Officers
- March 12, 1936: Assigned to Training Squadron No. 1
- April 7, 1936: Sent to 4th Aviation Regiment
- April 8, 1936: Returned, assigned to 142 Squadron
- April 18, 1936: Transferred to 1st Aviation Regiment in Training Center for Aviation Officers
- April 19, 1936: Reported to Training Center for Aviation Officers
- April 19, 1936: Assigned to 1st Flying Training Squadron
- September 1, 1936: Promoted to titular Corporal
- September 20, 1936: Transferred to Cadet School for Non-Commissioned Officers in Bydgoszcz
- September 20, 1936: Admitted to Cadet School for Non-Commissioned Officers in Bydgoszcz for a three-year XV course
- September 20, 1936: Inducted as Officer Cadet
- March 19, 1938: Promoted to regular Corporal
- August 5, 1938: Promoted to titular Sergeant
- October 17, 1938: Transferred to Cadet Aviation School in Dęblin
- October 17, 1938: Assigned to Student Squadron No. 5
- June 18, 1939: Transferred to traineeship to 2nd Aviation Regiment in accordance with the C.O.'s order dated June 12th, 1939

Summary of Polish military service

(rank order equivalents: PAF/Br. Army/RAF)

- Oct 29, 1931: Enters the military in Toruń, Poland
- Nov 29/31–Jan 1/32: Infantry training; 4th Air Regiment; rank of szeregowy (Private/Aircraftman 2nd Class)
- Jan 2/32–Apr 1/32: Mechanic's Assistant Training Course, 4th Air Regiment, student recruit
- Apr 2/32–Jul 1/32: NCOs School; 4th Air Regiment; rank of starszy szeregowy (Senior Private/Leading Aircraftman)
- Jul 2/32–May 1/33: Squadron training; 4th Air Regiment; Mechanic's Assistant; rank of kapral (Leading or Senior Aircraftman)
- May 2/33–Oct 20/33: Basic Flying Course as student pilot in Grudziądz

- Oct 21/33–May 1/34: Pilot in 42 Light Bomber Squadron; 4th Air Regiment
- May 2/34–Oct 1/34: Transferred, Advanced Flying Course
- Oct 2/34–Mar 1/36: Completes Fighter Pilot Course; transferred to Toruń, attached to 142nd Fighter Squadron, 4th Air Regiment as an NCO pilot
- Mar 2/36–May 1/36: Flying Instructor Course at C.W.O.L. (Aviation Officer Training Center), Dęblin
- May 2/36–June 1/36: Pilot instructor at S.P.L. (Aviation Cadet Officer Training School), Dęblin
- June 2/36–Sep 29/36: Continued as instructor; rank of plutonowy (Platoon Leader/ Corporal)
- Oct 1/36–Aug 15/38: Cadet School for Non-Commissioned Officers (2 years), Bydgoszcz; rank of plutonowy podchorąży (Platoon Commander Cadet or Corporal Cadet)
- Aug 16/38–June 1/39: Enrolled as student at S.P.L. (Aviation Cadet Officer Training School), Dęblin; rank of sierżant (Sergeant)
- Apr 1/39–June 1/39: also instructor to junior classes at Aviation Cadet Officer Training School)
- June 2/39–June 15/39: Assigned to 2nd Air Regiment, 121 Fighter Squadron
- June 16/39–Aug 25/39: Moved from Dęblin to Kraków as pilot and instructor, joined up with 121 Fighter Squadron at Rakowice (official airfield of 2nd Air Regiment)
- Aug 1/39: Promoted to rank of podporucznik (S-Lt/2nd Lt/P/O)
- Aug 20/39: 4 a/c from 121 left Rakowice for Aleksandrowice for ambush purposes
- Aug 26th–Aug 26/27th: During the night, ground crew moved to Balice to set up emergency base defenses
- Aug 31st: 16 a/c from 121 and 122 Squadrons and 10 a/c from 123 flew to Balice to wait
- Aug 31st at 4 p.m.: 123 left for Warsaw after being attached to the Pursuit Brigade to bolster defenses
- Sept 1/39: Commissioned, rank of podporucznik (S-Lt/2nd Lt/P/O); Germany invades Poland

Postings, 1940–45

1940

Proceeded to Blackpool: August 3rd
Posted from 3 (Polish) Wing to 302 Sqn: August 20th
Attached to 5 O.T.U.: September 2nd–26th
Transferred (302 Sqn) to RAF Station Northolt from Leconfield: October 11th
Transferred to Tangmere from Northolt: November 23rd

1941

Discharged R.G.1 Hospital Halton: May 12th
Admitted RAF Hospital Halton: May 21st
Discharged RAF Hospital Halton: June 14th
To Controllers Training Unit (C.T.U.): October 26th–November 15th

1942

To RAF Station Warmwell: January 11th
To Operations Room, RAF Station Exeter: January 23rd
To No. 302 Sqn: January 25th
To RAF Station, Heston: date unknown
To RAF Station Northolt: May 6th
To No. 302 Sqn: August 1st
To No. 303 Sqn (Operations Room): August 1st
To No. 302 Sqn: September 10th
To Station Northolt: September 22nd–December 22nd

1943

To 316 Sqn: February 10th
To 306 Sqn: February 23rd
To 316 Sqn: March 1st–15th
To School of Tactics (No. 6 Fighter Sqn Course): May 16th
To 316 Sqn: June 8th
To 1530 B.A.T. Flight, Wittering: July 24th
To 316 Sqn: July 30th
To 309 Sqn: August 11th
To No. 18 (Polish) Fighter Wing HQ: October 22nd

1944

To 131 Wing, HQ: July 12th
To 317 Sqn as Sqn Commander, France: August 25th
Missing in Action, France: August 27th
Wounded but Safe, Returned to Unit at Plumetot Normandy, France: September 3rd
Admitted to No. 77 Field Hospital: September 3rd
To PAF Depot (Blackpool): possibly September 5th
Transferred to RAF Hospital Wroughton, Wiltshire, nr. Swindon: September 5th–17th
To HQ ADGB (Air Defence of Great Britain): October 2nd
To PAF Depot (Blackpool): October 16th
To PAF Staff College: November 22nd
To PAF Depot (Blackpool): November 25th

1945

PAF Staff College: January 2nd
To Fighter Command (RAF Bentley Priory, Stanmore): September 17th

Rank achievement of W. GNYŚ with the RAF

Commissioned as Pilot Officer P/O (S-Lt) on March 1st, 1941
Promoted to Flying Officer F/O (Lt) on September 1st, 1941
Promoted to Flight Lieutenant F/Lt (Cpt) on March 1st, 1943
Promoted to Acting Squadron Leader S/Ldr (Mjr) on August 25th, 1944

Spitfire LF Mk IXc, S/No. NH 365

M. Dobrzelecki★

Aircraft JH-A (22-6-44) was assigned to S/Ldr W. Gnyś of 317 Polish Sqn RAF. On August 27th, 1944 it was shot down by flak over the River Seine, France. Aircraft was destroyed in crash-landing, but pilot survived. This was Gnyś's last Spitfire and aircraft flown.

Specifications

- Manufactured by Vickers Armstrong at Castle Bromwich (CB) from production block 349–390
- Vickers CB was known for high-quality finish often adding 20 mph to top speed
- Equipped with a Rolls-Royce Merlin M66
- 39MU 18-5-44, AST 6-6-44
- Merlin 66 equipped with Bendix-Stromberg injection carburetors
- Armament: two 20-mm cannons and four .303-in guns
- Narrow blisters over the cannon
- Aircraft had extended-horn elevators with rounded-top rudder. It could have had five-spoked wheels but four-spoked wheels were possible due to the intention of carrying bombs
- Camera gun in starboard wing root, no hole in port wing root
- Aircraft was painted in "day fighter" paint scheme: Ocean Grey and Dark Green top surfaces, with Medium Sea Grey underside
- Code "JH-A", fuselage band and spinner in sky
- Prop blades were black
- Possibly yellow recognition narrow leading-edge bands on outer wings

★*Fighter Squadrons of the RAF and Their Aircraft* by John D. R. Rawlings, Crecy Publishing 2nd Revised Edition, October 1992. ISBN-10 0947554246, ISBN-13 9780947554248.

- NH 365 serial number in black on rear fuselage—actual specific location high-medium-low and exact font not known
- Could possibly have retained black and white invasion stripes on lower fuselage, but other bands would have been painted out or removed by August 27, 1944

Honors & Awards

- Bronze Cross of Merit: June 18th, 1935
- French Croix de Guerre Avec Palm
- Silver Cross of Virtuti Militari 5th Class: June 1st, 1945
- Cross of Valor (KW): February 1st, 1941; 1 Bar/Clasp October 20th 1943; 2 more Bars/Clasps October 31st, 1947
- The 1939–1945 Star with Battle of Britain Bar/Clasp
- The 1939–1945 Defense Medal (George VI w/Green & Orange Ribbon)
- The Aircrew Europe Star with France & Germany Bar/Clasp
- British War Medal 1939–1945 (George VI w/Red, Blue & White Ribbon)
- The French Combatant's Medal
- The 1939–1945 French Victory Medal
- Polish Wound Ribbon
- Commander's Cross with Star of Polonia Restituta: 1999 (civilian award)
- Reconciliation Medal (Komandoria Missio Reconciliationis): August 30th, 2015 (posthumous)

Summary of Victories

Date	Location	Unit	Aircraft	Victim
Sept 1/39	Żurada	121	PZL P.11c	Do 17 destroyed
Sept 1/39	Żurada	121	PZL P.11c	Do 17 destroyed
May 12/40	Antwerp	GCIII/1	MS 406 1/3	He 111 destroyed[1]
May 12/40	Antwerp	GCIII/1	MS 406	He 111 damaged
May 16/40	Brussels/Moerbecke	GCIII/1	MS 406	1/3 Do 17 destroyed
May 25/40	Cambrai	GCIII/1	MS 406	1/3 Bf 109 destroyed

[1]The 1/3 refers to only the section of 3 Polish pilots, Lts Kazimierz Bursztyn and Władysław Chciuk with Gnyś, but 8 French pilots also participated in this fight, therefore, according to protocol, Gnyś's share is 1/11.

Note: There is a record of Gnyś's involvement in a battle on June 8th, 1940 northeast of Paris, when together with 4 French pilots and S-Lt Chciuk, he shot down a Ju 87 (1/6 share).

Note: There is also a record of an He 111 damaged (see September 3rd report, Chapter 3).

[Tally according to this author: 8]

(Source: P. Sikora, *Asy: polskiego lotnictwa*, p. 401)

Profile of Frank Neubert (1915–2003)

Compiled by M. Dobrzelecki & G. R. Morrison

- Born September 28th, 1915 in Bad Herrenalb/Scwarzwald, aka "The Black Forest."
- Served in the "Immelmann Geschwader" from 1936.
- On September 1st, 1939 he was a section leader (Rottenführer) of 1./St.G.2 Immelmann.
- On September 1st he attacked two Polish PZL P.11cs (Gnyś & Medwecki) taking off from Balice that appeared to be climbing (he said) to attack Lt Johannes Brandenberg's Ju-87b1 Stuka. (However, Władek said that they were just trying to get airborne with no immediate intention of attacking a specific Luftwaffe target at that time, plus it was still very dark.)
- Neubert and his gunner Franz Klinger returned to their airfield at Nieder-Ellguth (there have been references to other locations for Neubert's field).
- On September 1st, 1939 his Stuka was coded TG + GK (but it might have been T6 + GH)
- From July–September, 1940, he was Staffel Kapitan of 2./St.G.2.
- Between September 1941 and January 1942 he served as Gruppenkommandeur of his old 1./St.G.2.
- Between March 18th, 1942 and October 14th, 1942 (some sources say September) he was Gruppenkommandeur of II./Schl G.1.
- Between December 9th, 1942 and August 1943, he was Gruppenkommandeur of II./Schl.G.1.
- Between October 11th, 1943 and February 22nd, 1945, he was Gruppenkommandeur of II.SG 101.
- From February 1945 he served as a staff officer for the General of the Schlachtflieger.
- He flew on approximately 350 missions during the war, 230 in Stukas.

- He was wounded when his Henschel Hs 129B-2 (W.Nr. 0305, assigned to Stab.II Schl.G.1) was shot down in January 1943 by Soviet AA fire near the railway station at Skurbiy.
- He flew Henschel Hs 123 biplane dive-bombers, Ju 87 Stukas, Henschel Hs 129 twin-engine attack-bombers and Focke Wulf Fw 190 fighter-bombers.
- During the campaign in Yugoslavia and Greece in 1941, he was credited with sinking a freighter, a destroyer and a tanker.
- Neubert became a highly decorated major in the Luftwaffe and was the recipient of the Knight's Cross of the Iron Cross, awarded to recognize extreme bravery in battle or successful military leadership.
- He is credited with the first aerial combat victory of the war after shooting down Mieczysław Medwecki in his PZL P.11c in the early hours of September 1st, 1939.

Lyrics

Jesus I will kiss your feet

by Stefan Gnyś (SOCAN) © 1995
A song inspired by the old wooden cross at which his father prayed, in Sarnów, Poland

Tonight before I sleep, I'll get down on my knees,
For in my heart I know that you hold the keys
To a new promised land, filled only with love,
So please, hear my prayer, oh Lord above.

Chorus
Jesus I will kiss your feet,
A promise I intend to keep,
When you come back and say
That you will show us the way,
I will bow down and kiss your feet.

You gave the blind, another chance to see,
And you made the poor rich, with your honesty,
But those buyers and sellers, are in the temple again
Making deals with the devil, who lurks within.

So … *Chorus*

You said that the meek shall inherit the earth,
Just like your family who raised you from birth,

But the good and the kind, have long been left behind,
Now they search, for a home they cannot find.

Hear me … *Chorus*

Bridge
And if we ever needed you,
To pull us through,
Now is the time, now is the time.

So … *Chorus*

Daddy's Uniform

by Stefan Gnyś [SOCAN] © 1995
A song written about the symbolism of his father's RAF uniform

My Daddy was a hero, in the last big war.
Against all odds he tried, to even the score.
On his blue uniform, he wore a purple heart
And Momma always said that he looked so smart.

Refrain
Though proud of what he had done, still he was torn.
I was just a kid then who dreamed of wearin' Daddy's Uniform.

He said, "Come here my son, I've got some things to tell.
A hero is just flesh and blood, but who has seen hell.
So slip on this old jacket and I'll tell you like it was.
When the bullets started flyin', freedom became a cause.

Refrain
But bullets lead to dyin' and they can hit you like a storm."
I learned a lot about life that day, in Daddy's Uniform.

Chorus
He said, "Heroes are not born son, they're forged out of the fire.
I never tried to be one, I just wanted to be a survivor."

Refrain
Though proud of what he had done, still he was torn.
I learned a lot about life that day, in Daddy's Uniform.

Now that I'm a grown man, with a son of my own.
He wants to be a hero and asks me how it's done.
So I take my father's medals and his jacket from the drawer
And tell him that a hero knows, just what he's fighting for.

Refrain
"So slip on this old jacket, that was so proudly worn,
And I'll tell you the story of, my Daddy's Uniform."

Chorus
I said, "Heroes are not born son, they're forged out of the fire.
He never tried to be one, he just wanted to be a survivor."

Refrain
Though proud of what he had done, still he was torn.
I learned a lot about life that day, in Daddy's Uniform.
We learned a lot about life that day, in Daddy's Uniform.

Bibliography

Bartłomiej, Belcarz. *Montpellier Fighter Squadron*. Sandomierz: Stratus Publishing, 2008. ISBN 9788389450357

Chant, Chris. *Allied Fighters 1939–1945: The Essential Aircraft Identification Guide*. London: Amber Books Ltd., 2008. ISBN 9781905704699

Coughlin, Tom. *The Dangerous Sky: Canadian Airmen in World War II*. Toronto: The Ryerson Press, 1968. ISBN 770002412

Cynk, Jerzy B.: *The Polish Air Force At War: The Official History Vol. 1 1939–1943*. Atglen PA: Schiffer Publishing Ltd., 1998. ISBN 076430559X

Cynk, Jerzy B.: *The Polish Air Force At War: The Official History Vol. 2 1943–1945*. Atglen PA: Schiffer Publishing Ltd., 1998. ISBN 0764305603

Franks, Norman. *Aircraft versus Aircraft: The Illustrated Story of Fighter Pilot Combat since 1914*. New York: Macmillan Publishing Company, 1986. ISBN 0025406205

Gnyś, Władek. *First Kill: A Fighter Pilot's Autobiography*. London: William Kimber, 1981. ISBN 0718303970

Gretzyngier, Robert & Matusiak, Wojtek. *Polish Aces of World War 2*. London: Osprey Publishing, 1998. ISBN 1855327260

Hawks, Captain Ellison. *Britain's Wonderful Fighting Forces*. London: Odhams Press Ltd., 1940. ASIN B000L9K0GY

Jokiel, Jan. *Udział Polaków W Bitwie O Anglię* (Polish Participation in the Battle of Britain). Warszawa: Instytut Wydawniczy "Pax", 1968 & 1972

Koniarek, Dr. Jan. *Polish Air Force 1939–1945*. Texas: Squadron/Signal Publications Inc., 1994. ISBN 0897473248

Kornicki, Franciszek. *The Struggle: Biography of a Fighter Pilot*. Sandomierz: Stratus Publishing, 2008. ISBN 9788389450807

Król, Wacław. *302 Na Start*. Warszawa: Wydawnictwo Ministerstwa Obrony Narodowej, 1976. Biblioteka Żółtego Tygrysa, nr 4/76

Król, Wacław. *Zarys działań polskiego lotnictwa we Francji 1940*: Biblioteczka Skrzydlatej Polski. Warszawa: (WKŁ) Wydawnictwa Komunikacji i Łączności, 1988. ISBN 8320607833

Mason, Francis Kenneth. *Battle over Britain*. Bucks: Aston Publications Ltd., 1990. ISBN 0946627150

Pawlak, Jerzy. *Polskie Eskadry W Latach 1918–1939*. Warszawa: (WKŁ) Wydawnictwa Komunikacji i Łączności, 1989. ISBN 8320607604

Polish Air Force Association (Copyright 1949). *Destiny Can Wait: The Polish Air Force in the Second World War*. Nashville: The Battery Press, 1988. ISBN 089839113X

Price, Alfred. *Spitfire: A Complete Fighting History*. Leicester: The Promotional Reprint Co. Ltd., 1991. ISBN 1856480151

Price, Alfred. *Battle of Britain Day: 15 September 1940*. London: Sidgwick & Jackson, 1990. ISBN 0283999055

Price, Alfred. *Blitz on Britain: The Bomber Attacks on the United Kingdom, 1939–1945*. London: Ian Allan Ltd. 1977. ISBN 0711007233

Sikora, Piotr. *Asy: polskiego lotnictwa*. Warszawa: Alma Press 2014. ISBN 9788370205607

Śliżewski, Grzegorz. *The Lost Hopes: Polish Fighters over France in 1940*. Koszalin, Poland: Panda Publishing, 2000. ISBN 8391425908

Sutherland, Jon & Canwell, Diane. *Blitzkrieg Poland: Images of War*. Barnsley, S. Yorkshire: Pen & Sword Military, 2010. ISB N 978184 8843356

Warner, Carl & Woolford, Stephen. *Imperial War Museum Duxford*. London: Published by the Imperial War Museum, 2008. ISBN 9781904897729

Wikipedia: various articles/topics accessed (see individual chapter notes)

Wynn, Kenneth. *Men of The Battle of Britain*. Norwich, Norfolk: Gliddon Books Publishing, 1989. ISBN 0947893156

Zieliński, Józef. *Polish Airmen in The Battle of Britain*. Warsaw: Oficyna Wydawnicza, undated (circa 1998). ISBN 8390662043

Zieliński, Józef. *II Worldwide Congress of Polish Airmen 27–31 August 1998*. Printing: Drukarni Instytutu Technicznego Wojsk Lotniczych w Warszawie. ISBN 8390900816

Referenced documentation

MINISTRY OF DEFENCE (No. of Documents: 60)
APC Polish Enquiries/Polish Historical Disclosures
Building 60, RAF Northolt
West End Road, Ruislip
Middlesex, HA4 6NG
England

MINISTRY OF DEFENCE ARMY RECORDS CENTRE
Polish Section (Extracts)
Bourne Avenue Hayes
Middlesex, UA3 1RF
England

MINISTRY OF DEFENCE MEDAL OFFICE
Inssworth House
Imjin Barracks
Innsworth
Gloucester, GL3 1HW
England

POLISH INSTITUTE AND SIKORSKI MUSEUM
20 Princes Gate
Kensington
London SW7 1PT
England

No. of documents for each shown in brackets:
Lot. A. V PAF Index (1)
Lot. A V 1/4 xxx/9 (1)
Lot. A V 97/15/9 (12)
Lot. A V 44/11/68/17 (2)
Lot A V XII. 85/3/12 (2)
Lot A XII. 85/174/671 (3)
Lot A XII 85/3/12 (1)

Index